From Colonial to Post-Colonial Rule

Nguyen Van Bac

From Colonial to Post-Colonial Rule

The Transformation of Rule in an Important Strategic Area in South Vietnam

Bibliographic Information published by the Deutsche Nationalbibliothek
The Deutsche Nationalbibliothek lists this publication in the Deutsche Nationalbibliografie; detailed bibliographic data is available online at http://dnb.d-nb.de.

Library of Congress Cataloging-in-Publication Data
A CIP catalog record for this book has been applied for at the Library of Congress.

ISBN (978-3-631-74603-5)
E-ISBN (978-3-631-79232-2)
E-ISBN (978-3-631-79233-9)
E-ISBN (978-3-631-79234-6)
DOI 10.3726/b15731

Doctoral Thesis in the Faculty of Social Sciences and Cultural Studies, Giessen

© Peter Lang GmbH
Internationaler Verlag der Wissenschaften
Berlin 2019
All rights reserved.

Peter Lang – Berlin · Bern · Bruxelles · New York · Oxford · Warszawa · Wien

All parts of this publication are protected by copyright. Any utilisation outside the strict limits of the copyright law, without the permission of the publisher, is forbidden and liable to prosecution. This applies in particular to reproductions, translations, microfilming, and storage and processing in electronic retrieval systems.

This publication has been peer reviewed.

www.peterlang.com

Abstract

This study looks at the Central Highlands in South Vietnam (SVN) from the pre-colonial period through the French colonial era to the end of the Second Indochina War in 1975. The Central Highlands were until the twentieth century a sparsely populated and poorly developed area with limited contact with the outside world, inhabited by a multitude of most diverse ethnic groups, which lived together peacefully or less peacefully. In this "wilderness", which will be described in more detail, various actors from outside interfered or even invaded - first the Empire of Vietnam, then the French colonial power and finally the South Vietnamese State and thus the United States of America (U.S.). In this work, the author tries to apply some most common theories on legitimate domination to explain the transformation of rule in the Central Highlands. Those include Weber's opinion on three types of legitimate power; the French-adopted ideas of "divide and conquer" and "using the native people to rule the natives;" the theory of Post-colonialism; the American doctrines of Military Rollback, Containment, and Domino. Also, the national and indigenous perspectives such as ethnic policies of the First and Second Republics of South Vietnam; the particular Vietnamese modernization and legal concept framed by the North Vietnamese and the Việt Cộng (VC); as well as tribal peoples' concepts of the rule will be reviewed to understand each players' attempts in legitimizing its control over the important strategic area of Central Highlands.

The access of various actors as mentioned above to a region that was initially off the beaten track gradually intensified during the nineteenth and twentieth centuries. There are four different phases, which also underlie the structure of this work.

1. During the existence of an independent Vietnamese Empire until the mid of the nineteenth century, this state mainly tried to control or even block access to the Central Highlands. The Vietnamese emperors had little interest in this region and essentially restricted themselves to the formal subordination according to the East Asian system of inter-state relations by vassalage.

2. This changed when the French colonial power discovered the Highlands' resources and in particular understood the high strategic role of the Highlands. In the French epoch, the French established a system of largely indirect control of the Highlands. It was based on a policy of divide and conquer, and again on limiting external access, especially to the ethnic Việt. The French rule was based on military advisers, soldiers, researchers, missionaries, traders, and charitable

organizations whose impact on people and environment remained limited until the early 1950s.

3. The hitherto prevailing policy changed significantly with the formation of a State of SVN as a result of the Geneva Conference. It is true that all countries emerging from European colonies since the Second World War had the problem of internal nation building. However, this problem was particularly acute for SVN: the cultural center of Vietnam had always been the North, which was now under Communist control; the population of the South was much less uniform and consisted of numerous groups such as ethnic Việt, Chinese (the Hoa), Catholics, and Catholic refugees from the North, as well as other diverse ethnic groups. The latter became part of ethnic minorities for the first time on its own territory due to the massive policy of internal nation-state formation and Catholicization, which was operated by the Diệm clan, then ruling in SVN.

4. With the aggravation of the Second Indochina War in the early 1960s, the Central Highlands then became one of the main battlefields, among other things because the North Vietnamese Army and the VC were able to lead a guerrilla war in the jungle terrain there. The American strategists realized quickly that the war could be waged there only if one could win the support of the groups living there, who were now defined as ethnic minorities. As in the French era, military advisers, soldiers, researchers, missionaries, and charitable organizations swarmed into the Central Highlands to win the support of diverse ethnic groups through promotion of development (now in the American sense). This smarter access to the entire region (compared with the Diệm-policies) was essentially joined by the governments of SVN following the Diệm regime.

Needless to say, the Second Indochina War just like the First one did not end in the defeat of the U.S. on the battlefield, but at the conference table. The politics of both France and the U.S. in relation to the Central Highlands thus ultimately only influenced the outcome of the wars in a limited sense. What is more important is that in the development of the Highlands from the middle of nineteenth century to 1975, two major historical processes can be identified, which have so far been insufficiently investigated in relation to Indochina and Vietnam, respectively:

First, the respective "regime change" from pre-colonial over colonial to post-colonial systems of rule based on specific problems, here the control of a remote region. At the beginning, it was only in an insufficient sense part of a "Vietnamese" dominion. Since then, and also due to external factions, it was transformed into a decisive field of action for colonial and post-colonial actors - and this under the conditions of the longest war in the twentieth century.

Second, European historiography has long been concerned with the processes of nation-state formation, particularly in terms of the research on how groups became involved in the nation-state which were not interested in it. The development in the Central Highlands after 1954 is thus a good example of the much-uncontained strategy of "turning farmers into Frenchmen," for example. The same task stood out for (South) Vietnam after the Geneva Conference: Việt, Chinese, Khmer, Cham, farmers, fishermen, traders, and Highlanders should become modern Vietnamese.

The fact that these goals have been attempted with thoroughly questionable strategies and were accompanied by terrible wars makes them an even more critical object of research, which has so far been insufficiently researched. Thus, the purpose of this work is, firstly, to show the various forms of mastery of this strategically important region for the whole of Southeast Asia. The transformation of these strategies is then, secondly, interpreted in a new context, that of change from an old imperial system over colonial rule to the domination strategies under decolonization, national state formation and cold war.

Acknowledgments

Firstly, I am deeply appreciative of my first supervisor, PD. Dr. Detlef Briesen, for his initial ideas on the topic, endless guidance, assistance and encouragement during the writing of this thesis. I would also like to extend my gratefulness to Prof. Dr. Jörg Thomas Engelbert for his excellent suggestions, comments, and corrections.

Besides the supervisors, I am also indebted to Ministry of Education and Training of Vietnam (MoET) and the German Academic Exchange Service (DAAD) for the financial grants for my German language course in Vietnam and studying in Germany.

My sincere thanks also go to many scholars, whose works have been referenced in my research, without their silent contributions this thesis could never be finished. Special thanks to my friends and my colleagues for their positive encouragement and supports throughout writing this thesis.

I owe sincere gratitude to my flatmates, Anshula Revo and Omar Hussein, for their valuable comments and corrections to my English grammar.

Last but not least, I would like to express appreciation to my family, especially my beloved little daughter, Nguyễn Hải Anh, for all of her sacrifices during the entire time of my Ph.D. program.

Abbreviations

BAJARAKA	Bahnar, Jarai, Rhade, Kaho
CIA	Central Intelligence Agency
CIDG	Civilian Irregular Defense Group
DRV	Democratic Republic of Vietnam
FLHP	Front de Libération des Hauts Plateaux
FRUS	Foreign Relations of the United States
FULRO	Front Unifié pour la Libération des Races Opprimées
GVN	Government of the Republic of Vietnam
MACV	Military Assistance Command, Vietnam
MDEM	Ministry for Development of Ethnic Minorities
NLF	National Liberation Front
RMC	Revolutionary Military Council
RVN	Republic of Vietnam
RVNMF	Republic of Vietnam Military Forces
SVN	South Vietnam
UK	United Kingdom
U.S.	United States of America
VDP	Village Defense Program

List of Figures

Fig. 1: Estimates of Total Populations of Montagnards by Various Sources. Sources: Minority Rights Group - The Montagnards of South Vietnam. In: Texas Tech University, Vietnam Center, Virtual Archive (TTU, VC, VA) 24990112002. 59

Fig. 2: Distribution of Ethnic Minorities in SVN. Sources: Author. 63

Fig. 3: Estimates of Populations of Different Minority Groups. Sources: Minority Rights Group - The Montagnards of South Vietnam. P. 3-4. In: TTU, VC, VA 24990112002. 64

Fig. 4: Provinces of the Central Highlands in 1967. Sources: Author. 66

Fig. 5: Estimates of Population of the Montagnards by Provinces in 1967. Sources: Minority Rights Group - The Montagnards of South Vietnam. Pp. 24–25. In: TTU, VC, VA 24990112002; Manual, Michigan State University Viet-Nam Advisory Group - A Study of Montagnard Names in Vietnam. P. 6. In: TTU, VC, VA 21940102001. 74

Fig. 6: U.S. Technical Groups Trained Mountain Tribes in 1961. Sources: Training of Mountain Tribes, Vietnam. In: TTU, VC, VA 1780713024. 130

Fig. 7: The Expansion of the CIDG Program between December 1961 and October 1962. Sources: (Kelly 2004, 2, 5), edited by Author. 138

Fig. 8: General Concept of Strategic and Defensed Hamlets. Sources: State Department Strategic Hamlet Study. In: TTU, VC, VA 2130310003. 150

Fig. 9: The Reform of the Governmental Highland Affairs Agency. Sources: Author. 221

List of Table

Tab. 1: Names of Native Ethnic Minorities in the Central Highlands. Sources: General Statistics Office of Vietnam. (Danh mục các dân tộc Việt Nam. Ban hành theo Quyết định số 121-TCTK/PPCĐ ngày 02 tháng 3 năm 1979) (List of ethnic groups in Vietnam. Issued together with Decision No. 121-TCTK/PPCĐ of March 2, 1979). (Accessed 20th December 2017). At http://www.gso.gov.vn/default.aspx?tabid=405&idmid=5&ItemID=1851. 71

Contents

I Introduction 21

1.1 The Process of Decolonization and the U.S. Containment Policy in Vietnam 21
1.2 Purposes of Study 30
1.3 Theoretical Basis of the Study 31
1.4 Sources and Literature Review 43
    Studies conducted by international scholars 44
    Studies published in SVN before 1975 48
    Studies carried out by Vietnamese researchers during the unification era 50
1.5 Structure of the Thesis 54

II An Overview of the Central Highlands 57

2.1 Classification of Ethnic Minorities in Vietnam 57
2.2 Background Information on the Central Highlands 62
   2.2.1 A Brief Introduction to the Central Highlands 62
   2.2.2 Indigenous Peoples of the Central Highlands 67
      As for the number of groups and ethnic names 68
      Some key features of each tribal group 70
      The Mon-Khmer language family 72
      1 *The Pacoh* 72
      2 *The K'tu* 72
      3 *The Hré* 73
      4 *The Dié* 73
      5 *The Halang* 75
      6 *The Sédang* 75
      7 *The Bahnar* 75
      8 *The Mnong* 76

9	The Cill	76
10	The Kaho	77
11	The Maa (Ma)	78
12	The Chroo	78
13	The Stieng	79
14	The Cua	79

The Malayo-Polynesian language family 80

1	The Jarai	80
2	The Hroi	81
3	The Rhade	81
4	The Churu	82
5	The Roglai	82

III French Domination Strategies in the Central Highlands 85

3.1 The Ethnic Policies in Pre-colonial Times 86

3.2 French Domination Strategies in the Central Highlands 91

    3.2.1 Primal Contacts between Westerners and Ethnic Minorities 91

    3.2.2 French Surveys in the Central Highlands 94

    3.2.3 The Transformation of the French Domination Strategies from Colonization to Decolonization Era 95

        The domination strategies in early colonial times............ 95

        The colonial socio-economic policies in the Central Highlands 98

        The ethnic strategies of Pierre Marie Antoine Pasquier............ 101

        The domination strategies of Georges Thierry d'Argenlieu in the context of decolonization in Vietnam 104

    3.2.4 Struggle Movements of the Montagnard Groups against French Colonialism 109

IV The Policies of the First Republic toward Ethnic Minorities in the Central Highlands (1954–1963) 117

4.1 The U.S. and the Path to Power of Ngô Đình Diệm 117

4.2 The Formulation of the Diệm Ethnic Policies 122
4.3 Contents of the Diệm Highland Affairs Policies 126
    4.3.1 Merging the Crown Domain into National Territory 126
    4.3.2 Regarding Political and Armed Policies 129
        Concerning RVN military networks.............................. 133
        The Village Defense Program and the Civilian Irregular Defense Group Program.................. 134
        The Land Development Centers and the Agroville Program...... 141
        The Strategic Hamlet Program................ 143
    4.3.3 As for the Economic Policy 149
    4.3.4 The Policy of Assimilation and Discrimination of the Minorities 156
        Regarding the Montagnards................. 157
        As for the overseas Chinese.................. 160
        Concerning the Khmer...................... 162
4.4 Responses of the Minorities to the Highland Affairs Policies 162
    4.4.1 Non-BAJARAKA Political Struggles 163
    4.4.2 The BAJARAKA Movement 166

V The Policies of the Second Republic toward Ethnic Minorities in the Central Highlands (1964–1975) 171

5.1 The Ethnic Policies of the Military Junta 1964–1967 172
    5.1.1 Historical Background 172
    5.1.2 The Ethnic Strategies of the Military Junta 1964–1967 175
5.2 The Policies of the Second Republic toward the Minorities (1967–1975) 185
    5.2.1 The Americans and the Birth of the Second Republic 185
    5.2.2 The Ethnic Policies of the Second Republic 1967–1975 189
5.3 Achievements and Limitations of the Second Republic's Ethnic Policies 200
    5.3.1 Remarkable Results 200
        On administrative management................. 200

        As for economy 201
        On social welfare... 203
        Regarding the judiciary.. 203
        About education.. 204
    5.3.2 Some Limitations 206
5.4 The Reaction of the Minorities to the Second Republic's Ethnic Policies 207
    5.4.1 Political Struggles under the Influence of the NLF 207
    5.4.2 The FULRO Movement 208

VI Conclusion 215

Bibliography 225

I Introduction

This chapter firstly introduces the process of decolonization in Vietnam after the Second World War. The author then discusses the U.S. foreign policies towards Asia during the Cold War, notably the doctrine of Military Rollback applied in the Korean War (1950–1953) and the Containment Strategy pursued in the Vietnam War (1954–1975). The following section explains the reasons, for which I choose the transformation of domination strategies in the Central Highlands from pre-colonialism over colonialism to post-colonialism under the decolonization, cold-war politics, and process of national state formulation in Vietnam as the topic of my Ph.D. thesis. In the remaining parts of this chapter, the purposes of the study, theoretical basis of the study, the issues of sources and research methods, review of the literature, and finally the structure of the dissertation will be presented.

1.1 The Process of Decolonization and the U.S. Containment Policy in Vietnam

During the decolonization and cold-war times, there was a region located south of the 17th parallel of Vietnam, to that the French and their successors, American strategists devoted particular attention, the Central Highlands. The area was also home to the majority of ethnic minorities in South Vietnam.[1] The Central Highlands' strategic location together with profound changes in the national and international politics was the root of remarkable transformations in the domination strategies of different political regimes.

Looking back at the pre-colonial times, throughout the process of cultural contact, the Việt people referred to the areas spreading from the western Quảng Bình to the west of Bình Phước and Tây Ninh provinces as Trường Sơn - Tây Nguyên (Long Mountain - Highlands), (also Rừng Mọi, Rú Mọi - the Forests of the Savages). The central feudal courts considered the region "land of evil spirit forests and poisoned water" (Vietnamese: rừng thiêng nước độc) and, therefore, expressed very little interest in it.

---

1 Despite the process of invasion and occupation of the French from the late nineteenth century and the Americans later created new social classes as soldiers, civil servants, merchants, plantation workers, the majority of the population in the Central Highlands until the end of the Vietnam War was still indigenous peasants.

In contrast to the preconceptions of Vietnamese feudal aristocracy, since the late nineteenth century, French colonial tacticians highly appreciated the Central Highlands' position. With a central-Indochinese location and an exceptional altitude, the Central Highlands was seen as "the roof of Indochina" which played a strategic role in controlling not only Vietnam but also Laos and Cambodia[2]. In French official records, this area was referred to as the Chaine Annammitique; commonly known as Annam Cordillera or Annamite Chain. Since 1950, under the pressure of the emerging decolonization trends, also aimed to split minority regions from the Vietnamese society the French formed an autonomous zone called Domaine de la Couronne or Domaine de la Couronne du pays Montagnards du Sud-P.M.S. (Crown Domain) (Vietnamese: Hoàng Triều Cương Thổ)[3] and put it under the rule of former Emperor Bảo Đại. Being given a *statut particulier* (special status), the Crown Domain thenceforth belonged to the French Union but not a portion of the State of Vietnam (Thọ 1970, 92–95).

From 1954, in the American perspective, the Central Highlands was an area of utmost strategic importance not only for the control of entire Indochina but for staving off the development of the Communism in Southeast Asia. Learned from French and American strategists, SVN military officials also highly appreciated the defensive position of the Central Highlands[4]. As a part of the of nation-building process, soon after taking power, pro-American president of SVN, Ngô Đình Diệm enacted Decree No. 21 on March 11th, 1955, officially merged the Crown Domain into Central Part of the State of Vietnam and terminated privileges of the French and Emperor Bảo Đại there. Also since then, the Highlands were no longer entitled to autonomy as they had been before, and the Montagnards were identified the minorities in their own country (MDEM, 1972, 6–7). In the following years, the strategy of pacification was implemented

---

2   See: For example, (Hãn et al. 2000, 61) & (Luận 1982, 47) & (Colby&McCargar 1989).
3   Nominally, the Crown Domain consisted of both the northern plateaus and the Central Highlands of southern Vietnam. However, in practice, the highlands of the north were entirely under DRV control.
4   According to South Vietnamese Ministry of Armed Forces, *"This region has a strategic location, which is critical for military maneuver throughout Indochina. It is a pedal locates in the middle of the Central Highlands, SVN that links to battlefields in eastern Cambodia, Laos and North Vietnam."* See: Ministry of Armed Forces – the High Command Forces (1965), *Kế hoạch đối phó, triệt phá các căn cứ mật khu Việt Cộng ở Trung Nguyên Trung phần (The plan to respond and destroy secret grounds of Việt Cộng in the Central Highlands)*, the National Archives Center II, Ho Chi Minh City, dossier code PTTg 15234, P. 9.

extensively through various active programs to "win the hearts and minds" of the ethnic minorities and stabilize the situation in the Central Highlands. During the Republic of Vietnam (RVN)'s existence (1954–1975), the area was known in Vietnamese as Cao Nguyên (High Plateau) or Miền Thượng, Xứ Thượng[5] (Highland Region), while Americans referred to it as the Central Highlands (Trịnh, 2007a, 1)&(Giang & Ánh, 1974, 43–4)&(Hickey, 1982a, xiii)&(Salemink 2002, 1–2).

As World War II ended in August 1945, a different war began - the struggle for decolonization launched by colonies of the colonialism all over the world in which Southeast Asia was considered the hottest front. This context created the most significant features of the modern history of Southeast Asian nations: the endeavor of decolonization and process of nation-building (Goscha & Ostermann 2009, 1–2). Regarding this issue, interested readers can see more in: (Tonnesson 1991), (Goscha 2007), (Goscha & Ostermann 2009), (Gungwu et al. 2005), (Devillers 1962, 1969), (Marr 1997), (Baten 2016), and so on. For some more details, the French colonialists, under the auspices of the British, quickly re-invaded Indochina after the national governments of the peninsula's states formed and proclaimed independence in 1945. The French ambition to reestablish its colonial rule was the direct cause of the First Indochina War, which lasted nine years (1946–54). The same situation came with Indochina, just two days after the surrender of the Japanese Army, Sukarno proclaimed Indonesian independence on 17th August 1945 and was selected as the country's first President[6-7]. However, soon after its founding, the Indonesian national government continued to face the return of the Dutch, with the support of the British. Thanks to its persistent fighting spirit and skillful diplomatic policy, Indonesia was officially recognized by the Dutch as an independent state by the end of 1949 (Hùng 2007, 13)&(Gungwu 2005 et al., 69–81). In Malaysia, the British carried out efforts to unify the governance of the colonial Malaya in a kingdom called the Malayan Union 1946 that consisted of all British colonies in the Malay Peninsula, except for Singapore. Because of being strongly opposed by the Malayans those who rejected a weak and obsolete Malayan monarchy and

---

5   "Thượng" in Vietnamese refers to "Thượng du" or "Miền Thượng, Xứ Thượng," literally highlands, in comparison with lowlands or plains. This characterization covers cultural location meaning.
6   Hubertus van Mook (1949). *Indonesia*. Royal Institute of International Affairs. 25 (3): 274–285.
7   Charles Bidien (05 December 1945). *Independence the Issue*. Far Eastern Survey 14 (24): 345–348.

the granting of citizenship to the overseas Chinese, this union then was soon dissolved and replaced by the Federation of Malaya in 1948. With the Federation of Malaya, autonomy for the monarchs of the Malay states was restored under the protection of the British. After that long struggle, Malaya finally officially achieved its independence on 31st August 1957 (Baten 2016, 290) & (Gungwu et al. 2005, 91–116). Regarding the Philippines, this country was rapidly involved in the founding of the United Nations in October 1945, soon after the Allies defeated Japan. July 1946, the U.S. recognized the Philippines as an independent country through the Treaty of Manila (Molina 1961)[8]. In the following years, communist uprisings broke out in rural areas but finally were suppressed by the government of President Ramon Magsaysay. With regard to Burma, late 1944 Allied troops launched a series of attacks leading to the end of Japanese rule in the country of Burma in July 1945. There was a fact that while numerous Burmese fought for the Japanese as members of the Burma Independence Army, many others those who mainly were ethnic minorities followed the British Burma Army (Fellowes-Gordon, 1971)&(Gungwu et al. 2005, 39–68). The two National Armies of Burma and Arakan fought with the Japanese from 1942 to 1944 but turned allegiance to the Allied forces in 1945. After a long period of uncertainty and division due to a dispute between political forces, in 1948, Myanmar became an independent republic, named the Union of Burma[9].

Back to the case of Vietnam, although the Central Highlands is a secluded area of the country, it was significantly affected by international and regional political changes during the post-World War II period. Since the last phase of the hot war, the subsequent territorial division of Europe among leaders of the U.S., the United Kingdom (UK), and the Soviet Union had been tabled at the Yalta Conference[10]. The conference then resulted to the division of Europe and the world between the American-led Western Bloc and Soviet Russia-led Eastern Bloc, leading to the Cold War era. The U.S. and the UK sought to

---

8 Manuel S. Satorre Jr. *President Diosdado Macapagal set RP Independence Day on June 12*. positivenewsmedia.net. (Accessed 22nd November 2018).
9 *The Constitution of the Union of Burma*. Http://www.burmalibrary.org/docs5/Myanmar_Constitution-2008-en.pdf. (Accessed 20th November 2018).
10 The Yalta Conference was a gathering of the three chief Allied leaders of the U.S., the UK, and the Soviet Union from 4th to 11th February 1945 to plan the occupation of Nazi Germany and discuss Europe's postwar reorganization. This conference also was known as the Crimea Conference because it was held at Yalta in Crimea, the Soviet Union. See: Yalta Conference. Encyclopedia Britannica. At: Https://www.britannica.com/event/Yalta-Conference. (Accessed 20th November 2018).

establish influence by supporting the bourgeois democratic regimes in newly independent nations while the Soviet Union wanted to develop an area of power among socialist satellite states. Because the Central Highlands was believed to hold a strategic geopolitical position for controlling Indochina, even the whole of Southeast Asia, it was chosen as an outpost by both sides in the competition between East and West.

Taking advantage to the Second World War[11], Vietnamese people, under the leadership of the Việt Minh Front[12], successfully conducted the national liberation revolution and proclaimed independence on September 2nd, 1945. The triumph of the August Revolution in Vietnam is thought to have a substantial impact on the process of decolonization in Asia and Africa[13] (Devillers 1988)&(Tonnesson 1991)&(Lâm et al. 2000).

Post-colonial studies, however, extensively point out that despite achieving a proclaimed sovereignty, the influences of colonialism and its representatives were still enormously present in military, political and socio-economic lives of most ex-colonies. We can list out the appearance of the Western countries, for example, the American reoccupation of the Philippines, and the British retaking of Burma, and the French re-invasion of Vietnam, etc. (Tonnesson 2009,

---

11 Two years after the beginning of the Second World War, on 14th August 1941, the U.S. President Franklin D. Roosevelt and the United Kingdom Prime Minister Winston S. Churchill signed a joint declaration called Atlantic Charter. The third article of this Charter stated that the United Kingdom and the U.S. respected the right of all peoples to elect their leaders and structure of government. The two powers also wanted to see a form of sovereign and autonomous state of the citizens which had been forcibly deprived now was being restored. See: *Atlantic Charter 14th August 1941*, Lillian Goldman Law Library, Yale Law School. Sources: http://avalon.law.yale.edu/wwii/atlantic.asp. (Accessed 25th April 2016).

In Vietnam, according to Hồ Chí Minh, in the August Revolution, the Vietnamese people wrested independence from Japanese (not from the French) after the Japanese emperor declared unconditional surrender to the Allies. See: *The Declaration of Independence* (Minh 2000, 11).

12 The term Việt Minh was an abbreviation of an organization called Việt Nam Độc lập Đồng Minh Hội (League for the Independence of Vietnam), a political alliance founded by the Indochinese Communist Party on May 19th, 1941. The purpose of Viet Minh establishment was to "Unite all strata, revolutionary parties, patriotic public organizations to expel the Japanese and the French for a completely independent Vietnam" (Quýnh et al. 2006, 353).

13 The destruction of British rule in India in 1947 and the collapse of the Dutch in Indonesia in 1949 were also pieces of evidence for this claim.

13–16)[14]. According to the division of tasks among powers of Allied forces in Potsdam Conference[15], the UK and the Republic of China were responsible for disarming Japanese troops in Vietnam; particularly British force would enter to the South while Chinese Nationalist Party army would come to the North (Ninh 2013)&(Devillers & Lacouture 1969). However, instead of helping Vietnam to consolidate its claims for independence, the British colonialists turned to back the French to recapture southern Vietnam[16]. Regardless the international treaties[17] and determined resistance of the Vietnamese patriots, with the collusion of the British, France made its stubborn attempts to reestablish its colonial power in Indochina leading to the outbreak of the First Indochina War in late 1946[18] (Minh 2000, 1018–19)&(Asselin 2007, 88).

---

14 See also: Devillers, P. (2010). Foreword by Philippe Devillers. In Tonnesson S. (Author), Vietnam 1946: How the War Began. University of California Press. Retrieved from http://www.jstor.org/stable/10.1525/j.ctt1ppjg2.5.

15 Potsdam Conference was held at Cecilienhof, a palace of Prince Wilhelm Hohenzollern, in Potsdam, Germany from July 16th to August 2nd, 1945 with attendance of the Union of Soviet Socialist Republics (USSR), the UK and the U.S. Purposes of the meeting were to consent a solution for reorganizing Germany, to establish a new world order, and to deal with problems of peace treaties and consequences of the Second World War.

16 Only four days after Vietnam declared independence, the British military mission came to Saigon, followed by the Anglo-French coalition. While conducting the Allied command to monitor the Japanese surrender, British troops also to create advantageous conditions for the French forces re-occupying the South. In an effort to legitimize the French reoccupation, on 9th October, the UK approved the French Civil Department as the only legal agency in the southern 16th latitude of Vietnam. Moreover, on the same day, a Franco-British Agreement was signed in London identifying that the UK fully supported the French domination from the 16th parallel southward (Patti 2008, 517–18)&(Hãn et al. 2000, 10–11).

17 The Atlantic Charter affirmed the ideal aims of the war including no territorial changes performed against the desires of the people, self-determination; recovery of self-government to those deprived of it; as well as disarmament of aggressor nations. At Tehran and San Francisco conferences, the Allied countries acknowledged the principles of self-determination and equality of nations. See: *Atlantic Charter 14th August 1941; Charter of the United Nations; June 26th, 1945; Security Treaty Between the United States and Japan; September 8th, 1951*, Lillian Goldman Law Library, Yale Law School. Sources: Http://avalon.law.yale.edu/wwii/atlantic.asp; Http://avalon.law.yale.edu/20th_century/jap an001.asp#b1; Http://avalon.law.yale.edu/20th_century/unchart.asp. (Accessed 09th May 2018).

18 The First Indochina War (also known as the Anti-French Resistance) broke out on 19th December 1946 and lasted until 20th July 1954 between the Democratic Republic of Vietnam (DRV), headed by President Hồ Chí Minh and its People's Army of Vietnam

Disagreed with French and British efforts in undermining the emerging decolonization trends, the Americans gradually gave up their willingness in supporting colonial regimes[19]. What Americans actually cared about was how to extend the influence of the U.S., also to stem the development of Communism, not to ensure the interests of the old colonies. Also, the growth of the Vietnamese resistance activities made France increasingly bogged down in its re-occupying war in Indochina and depended on U.S. financial support (Pentagon Papers 1971, 53–75). Both the model of Southern autonomous government[20] and the Bảo Đại solution[21] which the French tried to establish in Vietnam quickly bankrupted.

Finally, following the massive defeat at the battlefield of Điện Biên Phủ, the French had to sign the Geneva Agreement on 20th July 1954 to restore peace in Indochina. The Geneva Accord officially brought an end to the presence of the French troops in Indochina peninsula and put down French colonial rule there. With Điện Biên Phủ triumph, the Vietnamese people proved there is an exception in conventional war theory that "victory only belongs to the stronger army." The success of the Anti-French Resistance was considered the first victory of the

---

directed by Võ Nguyên Giáp against the French Far East Expeditionary Corps, led by France with the support of Vietnamese National Army of former Emperor Bảo Đại.

19 For the French, the war they triggered in Indochina aiming at restoring a former colony rather than to prevent the Communism. In the first three years of the First Indochina War, the U.S. policy seemed to be contradictory. On the one hand, Washington supported the French to win the war against the Viet Minh - preferably under their guidance, on the contrary, they expected the French would withdraw from Indochina after gaining the final triumph in "An excellent way" (Pentagon Papers 1971, 53–75). The contradiction between the two countries was increasingly apparent when Washington officially notified that they were only willing to increase financial aid to a Non-communist Vietnamese administration, not a puppet of France (Pentagon Papers 1971, 53–75).

20 This government existed from June 1st, 1946 to May 22nd, 1949.

21 Along with the financial support and military equipment, the U.S. advised France to find a "political remedy" for Indochina. January 1949, the U.S. State Department pressed France to negotiate with the former Vietnamese Emperor, Bảo Đại, to establish the Vietnam National Government. Consequently, on 8th March 1949, France signed the Elysee Treaty with Bảo Đại granting nominal independence for the State of Vietnam under the French Union (Pentagon Papers 1971, 1–52). However, after realizing that "Bảo Đại adopted a retiring and passive role," "the power was turned over discreditable politicians," and "the army was powerless and strictly dependent on French leadership," the American stopped supporting this political solution (Pentagon Papers 1971, 53–75).

liberation movement within "the third world", leading to the collapse of imperialism around the world (Hãn et al. 2000, 129).

As recognized by the Geneva Convention, the 17th parallel along Bến Hải River, a natural boundary between Quảng Trị and Huế Provinces, became the demarcation line splitting Vietnam into two temporary regrouping areas. In the attempts of nation-building, while the socialist-oriented political model was chosen in the North, a pro-Western republic was rapidly built in the South. The "temporary demarcation" then would be maintained as the "national border" between "the two Vietnams" in the next twenty-one years. And, though it took nearly 100 years to expel the French, a really peace was not brought about in Indochina.

The World War II ended, instead of direct control, western powers developed a new strategy of interference in small countries based on the use of dependent governments and cultural encroachment. In Asia, despite the backing of Washington for the Chinese Nationalist Party, the victory of Communist Party led by Mao Zedong resulted to the establishment of the People Republic of China (PRC) on 1st October 1949. This made the U.S. increasingly concern that *"Communist force want to dominate Asia under the guise of the nation"* (The-Pentagon-Papers 1971, 53–75). After achieving limited success in pursuing the policy of Military Rollback against North Korea in the Korean War, U.S. President Eisenhower changed the U.S. global strategy by propounding Domino Theory; a new strategy aimed to prevent the expansion of the Communism in Southeast Asia. According to the American assumption, "if SVN comes under Communist control, other neighboring nations such as Laos, Cambodia, Thailand, Burma, etc., also will come under Communist control and threaten the remaining countries of 'free world' like the Philippines, Malaysia, Japan, Australia and New Zealand" (Institute 2013, 138)&(H. Jones 2003, 2). The Americans, therefore, believed that after French withdrawal from Indochina it was time to have an elite nationalist leader in SVN to weaken the attractiveness of Hồ Chí Minh. In order to chase that purpose, the U.S. pressured Chief of State of Vietnam, Bảo Đại, to sign the decision of appointment Ngô Đình Diệm as Premier of the State of Vietnam on June 16th, 1954[22]. Three weeks later Diệm officially established

---

22 The Ex-emperor, of course, realized that he was discarding the last bit of power by himself, whether that was only a nominal one. In his last effort, Bảo Đại asked Diệm to swear before a crucifix to defend Vietnam "Against the Communist and, if necessary, against the French" (Karnow, 218). On this issue, Bảo Đại wrote in his memoir named *Con rồng Việt Nam: Hồi ký chánh trị 1913–1987 (Bảo Đại the King of Vietnam)* that: *"Previously, I used to recruit Diệm. I know that he is fastidious. I also know about*

his government in Saigon with an eighteen-member cabinet (Cooney 1985, 307–314). As the ideological base for the establishment of a pioneering anti-communist outpost in Southeast Asia, the U.S. Containment Policy and Domino Theory, hence, resulted in the American War in Vietnam (also known as the Second Indochina War, the Vietnam War, or the Anti-American Resistance War) (1954–1975).

Right after Diệm came to power, the U.S. overtly declared its intervention into SVN *"to prevent the spread of the Communism in Southeast Asia"* and *"to help Diệm maintaining an active, viable state capable of resisting outside aggression"* (Ahern 2000, ix, 14). From that point on Eisenhower administration started supporting directly for the government of Ngô Đình Diệm. In May 1955, Diệm removed all economic, financial agreements which the State of Vietnam previously signed with France; requested the French to shelve the Geneva Accords and to sever diplomatic relations with Communist North Vietnam. Moreover, he withdrew representatives of the State of Vietnam from the French Union and quickly set up an authoritarian regime which we can refrain from describing as deeply corrupt in the South. Backed by the Americans, Diệm then rejected the reunification poll. On 10th May 1955 without caring about the Geneva Convention and the aspirations of national unity of the Vietnamese people he held a referendum to depose the Chief of State of Vietnam Bảo Đại, proclaimed himself as the first president of the newly formed RVN (Ahern 1998, 4)&(Tucker 2011, 95).

On 22nd March 1956, France negotiated with the SVN on withdrawing all French troops out of this country. As a result of the compromise, they then dissolved their Military Command Department in Saigon on 26th April 1956. And, not long afterward, France announced it would quickly withdraw all French Expeditionary Force in this country, avoiding implementing remaining provisions of the Geneva Agreement, including the organization of a unification election in Vietnam (Patti 2008, 744).

---

his fanaticism and believe in the Savior. But, in this situation, no one is more deserving. Indeed, over the years, the Americans have known him and admired his assertiveness. In their eyes, he is a character, who is capable of dealing with the situation, so Washington is ready to support him… We no longer can rely on the French. At the Geneva conference, only the Americans are our allies. Facing the changing situation, they want to build a new defensive system in Southeast Asia. They can help us to continue the fight against the Communism." The book was published in French by Los Alamitos, 1980 in Paris under the title "Le Dragon d'Annam," translated into Vietnamese by Nguyễn Phước Tộc, e-book, P. 516.

Nominally, the Americans committed to respecting the Geneva Accords; however, like representatives of the State of Vietnam, they had refused to sign to it. These refusals showed that the U.S. and its satellite state, the State of Vietnam, soon prepared for a plan of dividing the country permanently. Not to sign to the accords would help them avoid carrying out the duties of the stakeholders. Under a pre-preparing scenario, right after taking power, Prime Minister Ngô Đình Diệm declared the State of Vietnam had no obligation to implement the terms of the Geneva Accords (Ahern 2000, 1)&(Dung 2008, 3). Also, by delaying the unification vote, which had been designed to conduct in the whole country in 1956, Diệm wanted to have enough time to prop up a significant stable government to confront the Communist world. Besides that, the increase of migrants from the North to the South would be able to help to balance the population between "the two Vietnams," reducing the pressure of failure weighing on the State of Vietnam government.

Ultimately, although accepted the term of holding the whole general election in the next two years, in reality, only several months after the Geneva Conference, SVN self-regarded to be a national entity, an inviolable country under the "free world."[23] In a talk given during his visit to the U.S. on May 13th, 1957, Diệm even tried to display his loyalty to the Americans by declaring that U.S. boundary had been expanded to SVN: *"Indeed, today, more than ever, the defense of freedom is essentially a common task. With regard to security, the frontiers of the United States do not stop at the Atlantic and Pacific Coasts, but extend, in South East Asia, to the Ben Hai River, which partitions Viet-Nam at the 17th parallel, and forms the threatened border of the Free World."*[24]

1.2 Purposes of Study

Sought to win the allegiance of the indigenous peoples of the Central Highlands, like the French, the American paid meticulous attention to factors of the economy, politics, culture, education, etc., in mountainous regions. In other words, the matter of building intimate relations with ethnic minorities was considered one of the top priorities over the U.S. waring politics. However, because the political framework of the colonialism changed after the Second World War,

---

23 Alain Ruscio, *La mémoire du siècle, 1945–1954 La guerre francaise d'Indochine*, Editions Complexe. Quoted by Thụy Khuê in Journey of centuries: the Thirty Years War 1945–1975, available at the address: http://thuykhue.free.fr/stt/b/bamuoi.html. (Accessed 6th April 2017).

24 See details at TTU, VC, VA 2321507006.

along with inheritance, some new points in the ethnic policies of pro-American regimes were shaped.

So far, while substantial attention has been given to the pacification tactics, military campaigns, fighting took place in the hinterland battlefield during the two Indochina Wars, as well as socio-economic issues of the minority peoples in the post-Vietnam-war period, limited has been bestowed upon their role and fate in the waring times, even less has been dedicated to the domination strategies in the Central Highlands through Vietnamese recent history. For this reason, we chose the topic *"From Colonial to Post-Colonial Rule: the Transformation of Rule in an Important Strategic Area in South Vietnam"* for my Ph.D. dissertation at the Faculty of History and Cultural Studies, Justus Liebig University Giessen.

My research on the transformation of the policies of different political systems for ethnic minorities in the Central Highlands from French colonial rule to American warfare in the context of decolonization, cold-war politics, and attempts of national state formation, therefore, not only aims to interpret the fate of "the people-in-between" but also provide scientific evidence for current policymakers to avoid repeating the same mistakes and draws useful lessons in dealing with ongoing problematic issues[25] in this strategic area, expectedly. To achieve that goal, this study tries to present, analyze and interpret from minor to strategic changes in the policies of different administrations towards the Central Highlands under the influences of colonial, post-colonial, and cold-war politics.

1.3 Theoretical Basis of the Study

Multiple studies point out that every political institution adopts its own typical model of rule that shapes a particular government form (the type of regime). In other words, type of government (often expressed in the name of each country) is a term referring to the political institution that a state uses to handle power in organizing and governing its society[26]. For example, the current political institution of Germany or the U.S. is the Federal Republic; Democratic Republic institution is being applied in China or Vietnam, and so on.

Working on the transformation of domination in the Central Highlands from pre-colonial to colonial over post-colonial periods we should not use a single

---

25 For example, the matter of an autonomous state for the Highlands, ethnic and religious conflicts.
26 See Chapter 01: *What Is Comparative Politics?* In: Kopstein, J., Lichbach, M., & Hanson, S. E. (Eds.). (2014). *Comparative politics: interests, identities, and institutions in a changing global order*. Cambridge University Press.

theoretical form of authority since this region was a contested space. Over this important strategic region, several actors fought terrible battles to gain the control. For example, the competition among Vietnamese, Siam, Khmer, Laotian imperial dynasties during the medieval period; among French colonial, the Việt Minh, and Japanese before the Geneva Conference of 1954; among the U.S/Democratic Republic of Vietnam (GVN), the VC/Democratic Republic of Vietnam (DRV), and the tribal peoples themselves during the Vietnam War. Each of these political forces has tried to seek its most appropriate ways to legitimize and stabilize its power in the Highlands. The struggle in the different periods, therefore, reflected different (sometimes contradicted) concepts toward this contested space. For this reason, theoretical bases need to be implemented relevantly to interpret essential traits of the governing type in each particular historical phase. Deriving from such awareness, the thesis author try to work on some most common ideologies to explain the transformation of rule in the Central Highlands including *Weber's theory on three types of legitimate domination; the theory of Post-colonialism; the doctrines of Military Rollback, Containment, and Domino*. Besides, some of the conventional concepts about methods of controlling adopted successfully by colonialism worldwide such as *divide and conquer, using the native people to rule the natives* are also employed to clarify the main characteristics of the French rule in the Central Highlands. In addition, although basic principles in the ethnic policies of the First and Second Republics had not been fully developed with a stable and solid theoretical foundation, they will also be examined to figure out the relations between the state system and the process of decolonization and national-state formation in South Vietnam after the Geneva Conference. Last but not least a, particular Vietnamese modernization and legal concept, as well as tribal peoples' idea of the rule, which they used to legitimize their control over the Central Highlands, would also be analyzed in this work.

Let us begin with Weber's theory of domination that the thesis author considers the most appropriate for explaining the relationship between Vietnamese feudal dynasties and Highlanders' superiors. This theory was developed since the early 1920s by Max Weber, a German economist, and sociologist who pioneered a path towards explaining how domination is legitimated as a belief system. In an essay entitled "Die drei reinen Typen der legitimen Herrschaft"[27], Weber first raised a new perspective on domination that later became his well-known theory

---

27 The article was originally issued in the journal Preussische Jahrbücher 187, 1–2, 1922; it then was translated into English by Hans Gerth and republished in the journal Berkeley Publications in Society and Institutions 4(1): 1–11, 1958.

of "three types of a legitimate rule" (pure types) which are legal-rational, traditional, and charismatic, respectively (Weber 1958, 1). According to Weber, all rulers have an explanation for their superiority. They try to persuade their people to believe in the legitimacy of the current political system. The explanation is commonly accepted and directly contributes to the state system stability but can be suspected during a crisis[28]. Every type of legal rule can be distinguished from another based on the achievement of each particular form of political order. Namely:

- *Legal authority is one that is grounded in clearly defined laws. The characters that control those rules are appointed or elected by legal procedures. The obedience of populace is not based on the ability of any superior but on the legitimacy and competence that procedures and laws entrust with persons in authority. Leaders are also subject to rules that limit their powers, separate their private lives from official duties and require written documentation (Weber 1958, 2–3).*
- *Traditional domination indicates the presence of a dominant personality. People in leadership regularly enjoy it because they have inherited it. The rule seems to be legitimate because it "has always existed." The leader is someone who depends on established tradition or order. This kind of power is typical in a patrimonial regime with the bilateral relations between vassals and lords in feudal systems. The ruler is also a dominant personality; the prevailing order in society gives him the mandate to rule (Weber 1958, 3–6).*
- *Charismatic power points to an individual who possesses certain traits, for example, magical skills, prophecies, heroism, and so on, that makes a leader extraordinary. His power derives from the massive trust and almost unshakable faith people put in his unique qualities (which creates his charisma), not because of any tradition or legal rules (Weber 1958, 6–10).*

Looking back into the pre-colonial history of Central Highlands, it is evident that the relationship between the Vietnamese emperors and the highland leaders was a much typical example of the second type - traditional domination. In this relationship, Vietnamese feudal dynasties, which existed within the mid-tenth

---

    In term of terminology, Hans Gerth translated the German word "Herrschaft" as Rule; other translators such as Alexander M. Henderson and Talcott Parsons translated "Herrschaft" as "Authority"; in the meantime, Tony Waters and Dagmar Waters used the term "Dominion" in their translation version.

28 See more in: Reinhard Bendix (1977), *Max Weber: an intellectual portrait*. University of California Press. P. 294.

and mid-nineteenth centuries (except for the ten years Dai Viet[29] was dominated by the Ming, a Chinese Dynasty, from 1407 to 1427), the central court mainly tried to control but limited access to the Central Highlands. This administration, therefore, was quite loose in reality. Perhaps the main reason for this strategy is Vietnamese Emperors did not wish to lose the control over the hinterland to their neighbors, especially to Siam. If a strong neighbor like Siam gained the control of the Highlands, the territorial sovereignty of Vietnamese rulers could be directly or indirectly threatened. Historical documents (which will be later analyzed) point out that Vietnamese emperors was seldom interested in the Central Highlands and essentially restricted themselves to the formal subordination according to the East Asian system of inter-state relations by vassalage. In order to maintain the dependency of tribal leaders, along with receiving periodic tributes, Vietnamese feudal superiors often gave back honorific dignitaries and material gifts. The fact is that the prerogatives of highland leaders (Kings of Fire and Water) were usually similar to those of the Vietnamese rulers (who controlled over them) but, of course, reduced in scale.

Regarding French colonial political ideas, as masters of strategies of "divide and conquer" and "using the native people to rule the natives," along with the establishment of colonial authorities directly held by the French, the colonizers offered local chiefs and tribal military officials the mandates of power. With this method, the French not only abused a number respected local chief but also created suspicion and division among ethnic minorities.

Linking to Max Weber's theory on ideal types, the French model of governance can be considered as a blend of legal and traditional authorities. At the state level, after fundamentally annexing Vietnam by the Patenôtre Peace Treaty (also known as the Treaty of Huế or Protectorate Treaty) in June 1884, France separated this country into three regions of Tonkin (north), Annam (center), and Cochinchine (south) and set up different political regimes there[30]. The French later re-grouped Tonkin, Annam, Cochinchine, Cambodia to form the Indochinese Union (French: Union indochinoise; Vietnamese: Liên bang Đông Dương) in 1887. Laos and a Chinese territory named Guangzhouwan were added to this Federation in 1893 and 1898, respectively. Except for Cochinchine (where was governed as a province in "mother country"), in the remaining regions of

---

29 Dai Viet is the state name of Vietnam existed in two periods; between 1054 and 1400, and between 1428 and 1805.
30 The colonial regime was set in Cochinchine while protectorate and semi-protectorate were installed in Tonkin and Annam, respectively.

Vietnam, in nominal the Nguyễn imperial bureaucracy was maintained parallel with the colonial government apparatus. Vietnamese feudal law was also still applied in cases all litigants were Vietnamese.

In the Central Highlands, soon after fundamentally pacified a large and important area, the French established there a system of colonial government. As the same as the protectorate implemented in Tonkin, Annam, Laos, and Cambodia, in the hinterland, the colonialists merely took direct control of the top levels, from provincial upward. Once a new province was instituted, Governor-General of Indochina would quickly appoint a French provincial résident who was entrusted to build and lead a colonial apparatus there[31]. Besides the French provincial résident, the Huế Court also appointed a mandarin as head of a highland province (Vietnamese: Quản đạo). Of course, the position of Vietnamese officials was mainly symbolic; real power was in French hands and operated based on French laws.

At the grassroots level (villages), the power structure, however, was entirely different from the upper ones. In local communities, the colonizers maintained the model of traditional self-government of indigenous inhabitants. By giving benefit and formally offering the mandate of authority, the French converted village elders into their lowest civil servants; turning tribal chiefs to be pawns in their political strategy in the Highlands. With this method, in theoretical Montagnard people would still choose their community leaders according to traditional customary laws. However, all elections would only be considered legal after the list of candidates and the winners being approved by French provincial chief. Being elected as civil servants, local chiefs then received salaries from the colonial budget and served as intermediaries between their compatriots and the French rulers.

While examining the process of decolonization and national building which speeded up in Vietnam since the August Revolution of 1945, especially after the Geneva Conference of 1954, the thesis author applies the Postcolonial Theory to interpret the concepts of Containment and Rollback Policies during the cold war

---

31 The process of establishing up the government apparatus in the Central Highlands can be summarized as the following phases: Shortly after the French reached an agreement with the Huế Court on transferring of administrative rights in 1889, the Central Highlands was placed under the rule of the provincial résident of Quy Nhơn. Two years later, the colonial government settled an administrative center in Kontum to govern Kontum and Cheo Reo. In the years 1917 and 1923, the town of Đà Lạt and Darlac were established, respectively. Provincial résidents in Highlands were administered directly by Supérieur de l'Annam (Vietnamese: Khâm sứ Trung kỳ).

period. In Europe, from the 1950s onwards, scholars began investigating what would be later commonly known as "Postcolonial Theory." One of the main issues on which the Postcolonial Theory focuses is the situation of the ex-European colonies after being decolonized during and after the Second World War. In particular, how the new-in-power national leaders dealt with the ideological and political crisis left by the colonialism and built new national values during the course of national state formation (Lianeri 1999). In the case of SVN, the process of decolonization and the national state formation was relatively complex under the strong influence of international politics during the Cold War. The result of ideological disputes between Western and Eastern Blocks led to the formation of "the two Vietnams" after the Geneva Conference and a proxy war lasting in the following 21 years.

As afford mention, among U.S. foreign policies towards Asia during the Cold War, the Military Rollback and the Containment Strategies are the most critical. Initiated in 1946 by U.S. diplomat George F. Kennan and adopted by the President Harry S. Truman administration during the post-World War II, Containment Policy became the foreign policy of the U.S. and its allies during the Cold War. With this approach, the American aimed to cease the expansion of the Communism in Eastern Europe, Africa, and Asia during the Cold War. When being applied in Vietnam (and South East Asia), the Containment Strategy was converted into Domino Doctrine. It is generally acknowledged that Domino Doctrine was prominent from the 1950s to the 1980s, beginning with a more in-depth intervention of the U.S. into the Indochina War to stave off the development of the Communism in Asia (Tucker 2011, 303–306). According to the American assumptions, if SVN came under Communist control, other Southeast Asia countries like Laos, Cambodia, Thailand, etc., also would come under Communist control that could even threaten the remaining nations of the Free World like the Philippines, Japan, and Australia. Based on this theory, the U.S. gave itself the mission to lead the Free World against the expansion of Communism in Asia[32].

After the victory of Communist Party which led to the establishment of the PRC on 1st October 1949, Communist China began supporting the DRV in fighting against the French re-invasion. In order to deploy its new global doctrine, the U.S. started indirectly intervening in the war against the Communism in Indochina since the early 1950s. During the last phase of the First Indochina

---

32 Jerome Slater (Winter 1993/1994). The Domino Theory and International Politics: The Case of Vietnam. Security Studies. Vol. 3, No. 2. Pp. 186–224.

War, the U.S. continuously increased financial support to help France in defeating DRV's resistance war[33]. Concerning diplomacy, Washington quickly recognized the countries of the French Indochinese Federation[34].

In preparation for the construction of an anti-communist outpost, proactive blocking the advance of Communism in Southeast Asia, also from the early 1950s the U.S. chose and strongly supported Ngô Đình Diệm, a nationalist leader who possessed a robust anti-communist nature, to help him take over the power in SVN since mid-1954. Financially, from 1954 to 1960, Washington provided Saigon with 7 billion dollars, of which military aid was 1.5 billion accounting for 80 percent of Diệm regime's military budget[35]. In term of diplomacy, the U.S. gathered its satellite states to establish the Southeast Asia Treaty organization (SEATO)[36] moreover, mobilized the United Nations and many countries to recognize the existence of the GVN as a legitimate government[37] (Tiến 2015, 22, 25–27).

---

33 From 1950 to 1954, the total U.S. economic and military aid to France exceeded 3.5 billion dollars. In which, the military assistance increased from 10 million in 1950 to 1.1 billion dollars in 1954, accounting for 78 percent of the cost of the Indochina War (Pentagon Papers 1971, 53–75).

34 On February 4, 1950, U.S. President Truman immediately announced the recognition of Bảo Đại after the French Parliament declared that it had just passed the "independence of the State of Vietnam." See: *Học thuyết đôminô: cái cớ? (Domino Theory: an excuse?)*. Tuoi Tre News. Sources: Https://tuoitre.vn/hoc-thuyet-domino-cai-co-26092.htm (Accessed 2nd January 2019).

35 See more in: Robert S. McNamara (1995). *Nhìn lại quá khứ - Tấn thảm kịch và những bài học về Việt Nam (In retrospect: The tragedy and lessons of Vietnam)*, translated into Vietnamese by Hồ Chính Hạnh - Huy Bình - Thu Thuỷ - Minh Nga. Hanoi: National Political Publishing House. P. 43.

36 SEATO (also known as Southeast Asia Intergovernmental Organization) was established based on the Southeast Asian Collective Defense Treaty (Manila Treaty) signed in September 1954. Officially SEATO was created on February 19, 1955, in Bangkok, Thailand with the participation of 8 countries. Among the members, only Thailand and the Philippines were Southeast Asian countries; the remaining ones include the U.K, the U.S., New Zealand, Pakistan, France, the Philippines, Thailand, and Australia. In the Manila Treaty, articles 2, 4, 8 and an extra article on Indochina placed three countries of Vietnam, Laos, and Cambodia under the "protected area" of SEATO block. See in: Franklin, John K. (2006). *The Hollow Pact: Pacific Security and the Southeast Asia Treaty Organization*. ProQuest & Encyclopaedia Britannica (2000). *Students' Britannica India*, Volume Five. Popular Prakashan. P. 60.

37 By 1958, there were 50 countries recognized and established diplomatic relations with GVN. Washington also sponsored the Diem government to attend many international conferences to create a position for the Republic of Vietnam, for example, the

It is also evident that Edward Lansdale, a CIA (Central Intelligence Agency) expert who bustled in northern Vietnam during this period with the purpose of *"weakening the DRV and strengthening the GVN through whatever possible methods"*, conducted a propaganda program to entice civilians, especially Catholics to migrate to the South (Lansdale 1991, xi)&(Sheehan 1988, 137)[38].

Since the early 1960s, as approved by the U.S. Congress, President Kennedy promoted Domino Theory with a stronger commitment: the U.S. would shoulder the entire burden, associated with all the allies against all enemies to defend the Free World; enhance aid to SVN on all aspects including military and economic assistance, propaganda, education and training, advisers, etc. (Tiến 2015, 20–21)[39]. Domino Theory was then brought to the top by President Lyndon B. Johnson by taking American expeditionary forces into war, conducting Limited War from 1965 to 1968 (Pentagon Papers 1971, 1–39)&(FRUS 1985, 1270–71)[40]&(Hãn et al. 2000, 201)[41].

As for the doctrine of Military Rollback, theoretically, the term rollback was familiarized during the 1940s and the 1950s. In political science, rollback is

---

Asia-Africa Summit held in Bandung (Indonesia) in April 1955, Colombo Planning Conference in 1958, etc. Under the support of the U.S. and the Western Block, the SVN government applied to join the United Nations but was vetoed by the Soviet Union in the General Assembly sessions on September 10, 1957, and December 9, 1958. See *Văn kiện tổ chức Tòa đại diện Ngoại giao Việt Nam của Bộ Ngoại giao Việt Nam Cộng hòa năm 1956 (Documents to organize the Vietnam Diplomatic Representative Office of the Ministry of Foreign Affairs of the Republic of Vietnam in 1956)*, the National Archives Center II, Ho Chi Minh City, dossier code PTT- Đệ I CH 14445.

38 In the first exodus of 1954 what so-called Operation Passage to Freedom, there were over one million refugees from the North, those who were supported and affected by U.S. agitation propaganda to migrate to the South (of which, some 800,000 Catholics, accounted for two-thirds of northern Catholics) (Phương 1957, 70–71),(Frankum 2007) & (Lien 2005, 427–49).

39 Since mid-1961 some 65 million dollars for military equipment and 136 million dollars for economic aid were delivered to Saigon. By December that year, 3.200 U.S. troops were deployed in Vietnam. The U.S. Military Assistance Command, Vietnam (MACV) was formed in February 1962. There also was a dramatic rise in the number of U.S. advisors, reaching 1.346 in 1961 and 9.965 by the end of 1962) (FRUS 1988, 182–85) & (Hickey 1982a, 74).

40 Document 277. Memorandum from the Assistant Secretary of State for Far Eastern Affairs (Robertson) to the Under Secretary of State (Hoover). Washington November 22, 1955.

41 See also Currey, C. B. (2005). *Chiến thắng bằng mọi giá (Victory at Any Cost: The Genius of Viet Nam's Gen. Vo Nguyen Giap)*. World Publisher. P. 333.

the strategy of forcing a change in the primary policies of a country or a territory, usually by replacing its ruling regime. This word is generally considered in the scholarly record relating to U.S. foreign policy for communist countries during the Cold War. This method is different from the U.S. Cold War policies in Eastern Europe including strategies of "economic warfare" and "psychological warfare," as well as secret operations and military supplies for pro-Western political forces; also different from the U.S. Containment Policy in Southeast Asia (Borhi 1999). In South Vietnam, this theory is very evident in the American strategies as Washington supported the coups to "change personnel" in Saigon's leadership, most typical was the coup d'état to overthrow Ngô clan launched in early November 1963[42].

During the wartime, a general idea of modernization and nation-building was introduced by the Americans in the Central Highlands as one of the core elements of postcolonial theories. Needless to say, modernization is a process of transition from a "traditional" or pre-modern to a "modern" society. That is, of course, a process of anti-traditional and anti-charismatic. It is worth mentioning here that Walt Whitman Rostow who developed the modernization theory joined the U.S. State Department under President Kennedy and later became Lyndon Johnson's national security advisor during the Vietnam War[43]. Theoretically, with practical assistance of more developed countries, some internal factors of "traditional" nations could be brought to development. Based on this perspective, besides necessary military and diplomatic means the U.S. performed operations aiming at improving the living standards of the Highlanders including projects for economic, languages, cultural, social welfare, etc. Various groups of development experts from U.S. and Western countries as well as financial assistance were also sent to this strategically important area. As the "people in between," the Central Highlanders continued to have a clear differentiation when deciding their political future. While ready to receive aid from all sides, a part of tribal men chose to fight alongside the communists; others swore loyalty to the GVN in the struggle to protect the Free World.

---

42 Failed to break the deadlock over settling disputes with Diệm brothers, Washington backed the Revolutionary Military Council (RMC) to conduct the military coup on 1st November 1963 putting an end to the rule of Ngô clan. In the next two years, people witnessed the replacement of five other military and civilian governments in SVN (Hãn et al. 2000, 198–199).

43 At that time, President Lyndon B. Johnson was also a supporter of the modernization theory. See in: Lindo-Fuentes, Héctor (2009). *Educational Television in El Salvador and Modernisation Theory*. Journal of Latin American Studies. 41 (4): 757–792.

In short, it can be said that the relationship between SVN and the U.S. is fundamentally a dependent bond between a satellite country and a superpower. Based on specific expressions, we can determine this type of control as a combination of legal and traditional authority, according to Weber's theoretical model of political power. On the one hand, Washington tried to legitimize SVN on various aspects such as helping Saigon leaders in organizing referendums, elections and mobilized recognition (for GVN) from the international community, etc. In order to maximize U.S. interests of the Cold War in Southeast Asia, the Americans were willing to intervene deeply in arranging the personnel apparatus in Saigon. The combination of legal and traditional powers enabled the Americans to directly implement their strategies towards the minority groups living in the Central Highlands. Regarding this, the implementation of the modernization theory also played an important role in strengthening the influence of Americans there. On the other hand, Washington could also easily intervene in the enactment and adjustment of the GVN ethnic policy (These issues will be presented in detail in chapters 4 and 5 of this work).

As for the concept of authority, the VC and the DRV always identified Vietnam as a united nation; military demarcation at the 17th parallel was only temporary. Hanoi, therefore, did not recognize the legitimacy of the Saigon government and considered the struggle for national unification as their ultimate goal[44]. As the same as in remaining areas in southern Vietnam, the VC and the North Vietnamese Government attempted to legitimize their authority in the Highlands. The ethnic policies of Việt Minh (since 1960 and 1968 was of National Liberation Front - NLF and the Provisional Revolutionary Government of the Republic of South Vietnam, respectively) had a significant impact on tribal peoples. From our point of view, strategies of the VC and the North Vietnamese Government should be addressed as a particular Vietnamese modernization concept, a concept of legitimate rule. In this regard, we should not forget that President Hồ Chí Minh[45] did not come to Marxism and Leninism as a purely

---

44 This determination was expressed in a famous statement of President Hồ Chí Minh: *"Southern is the blood of Vietnamese blood, the flesh of Vietnamese flesh. The river may be shallow, the mountain may be worn, but that truth never changes"*. See: *Nhớ cùng năm tháng - Hồi ký của cán bộ Văn phòng Quốc hội (Remember the elapsed years - Memoir of staff of the National Assembly Office)*. (2000). Hanoi: National Political Publishing House. P. 27.

45 When he first read Lenin's essay on the issue of national and colonial in 1920, Hồ (at that point he took the name Nguyễn Ái Quốc, literally the Patriot Nguyễn) was purely a patriot who was searching for a way to save his country rather than finding a theory to solve theoretical problems.

philosophical doctrine but a sense of support for oppressed colonial peoples. With his special intellectual and moral qualities, since returning to Vietnam to establish the Việt Minh in May 1941, Hồ emerged as a most leading charismatic leader of patriotic and national liberation movement. His ideas of re-establishment of a unification country and developing a people-based legitimacy were consistent with Vietnamese tradition that had been building on the basis of nationalism molded throughout Vietnam's long history.

In order to make these ideas fit the Central Highlands, the VC and the DRV conducted a propagandist campaign to disseminate its theory of equality and national reconciliation that had been promising to be deployed in the reunification era. Also, their idea of advocating the establishment of autonomous zones for the ethnic minorities in SVN (as it had been carried out in the North) has won great sympathy from minority groups of which the majority was tribes in the Central Highlands. The fact is that the VC and the communist North, those who later made the unification of Vietnam in 1975, occupied the national idea as it was in reality not only a communist but a nationalist movement.

In term of diplomacy, after being upgraded from the NLF, the Provisional Revolutionary Government of the Republic of South Vietnam also increased mobilization of the international community, especially the Eastern Block to recognize its legitimacy. Six months after its founding ceremony in June 1969, the Provisional Revolutionary Government obtained the formal recognition of 25 countries[46].

The following brief review of tribal peoples' concept of rule, which they used to legitimize their control over the Central Highlands under reviewed period, will close the author's discussion on the theoretical basis of authority. It is worth noting that before Vietnam was temporarily divided into the North and the South in accordance with the provisions of the Geneva Agreement, the tribal peoples' political consciousness was still very vague. During the feudal period, tribal men had repeatedly raided Vietnamese villages in the west of the central coastal provinces and later carried out sporadic armed activities against French protectorate. However, these actions were fragmentary, mainly aimed at economic goals or opposing harsh treatment. Since the Crown Domain formed in 1950, although France officially recognized Bảo Đại's sovereignty over the Highlands, Paris continued to control this region through the role of its special delegate there.

---

46 See: List of Countries Having Recognized the Provisional Revolutionary Government of the Republic of South Viet Nam. In: TTU, VC, VA 2310605017.

Contrary to the wishes of the colonialists, as a result of the meeting of local leaders in inter-village events and young highland elite in French schools or the military units, a collective identity of being Highlanders was slowly created and grown. It is believed that this common identity and the liberal ideals of the Protestantism, which was widespread in the Central Highlands during the decolonization era, contributed to the gathering of advanced tribal men, leading to the creation of struggling organizations for the autonomy and equality of the Montagnards like BAJARAKA[47] and FULRO[48] in 1957 and 1964, respectively. Together with repeatedly sending petitions or delegations to Saigon to require GVN to respect the Montagnard traditions, customs; the right of land ownership and the right to be equally treated with the Việt people, Highlanders also made a formal request for their own flag as it had been allowed under the Crown Domain. Furthermore, in mid-1958, the BAJARAKA continued to dispatch petitions to diplomatic missions in Saigon of the United Nations and some countries such as the U.S., UK, France, India, and Laos to denounce the Diệm racist policies and to request the world powers to intervene in creating an "Autonomous Highland." As its greatest attempt, the BAJARAKA even proposed an aspiration for an independent Central Highlands within the French Union or under the direct leadership of the U.S. (Hickey 1982a, 57)&(Dharma 2012, 36).

In short, the concept of the authority of the Central Highlanders has made significant changes from the periods of pre-colonial through colonial to post-colonial. From a very vague understanding of political power, this community gradually perceived significant of rights of being equal treatment, culturally respected; and further was autonomy, even independent within the French or U.S. control. After some adjustments in its ethnic policy, GVN has passed many Highlanders' proposals, for example, appointed some minority elite as deputy province chiefs of highland provinces and upgraded the governmental agency in charge of minority affairs to the Ministry for Development of Ethnic Minorities in 1967. However, until the end of the Vietnam War, the tribes' struggle for being recognized as an indigenous instead of minority community did not yield the expected results yet; greater demands such as an own flag for the tribal peoples, autonomy or independence from SVN, of course, were not adopted also.

---

47 BAJARAKA is a combination of the first two letters in names of the four main tribal groups including Bahnar, Jarai, Rhadé, and Kaho.

48 Front Unifié pour la Libération des Races Opprimées (English: Front for the Liberation of Oppressed People). According to Po Dharma, the term FULRO is the abbreviation of Front Unifié de Lutte des Races Opprimées instead of Front Unifié pour la Libération des Races Opprimées as most documents mentioned (Dharma 2012, 13, 94).

1.4 Sources and Literature Review

The war the Americans carried out in Vietnam is one of the longest ever and the most expensive warfares in the history of the U.S. which pulled the involvement of many large and small nations (Congressional Research Service 1984, v). Because of having a far-reaching influence level and leaving severe consequences for the warring parties over decades[49], the Vietnam War has been attracting numerous historians and other writers. In addition to primary sources, secondary studies associated with various aspects of the war, therefore, also become more and more abundant. In an attempt to review the influences of the U.S. on the transformation in ethnic policies of the GVN, the following resources are exploited:

Primary documents: This study, firstly, aims to rely on several primary archival works in both U.S. and Vietnamese archives and libraries including released accounts of Foreign Relations of the United States (FRUS) on the relations between the U.S. and RVN throughout the period of 1954–1975; declassified files of the CIA; the Pentagon Papers; the announcements of Saigon administration on its domination strategies including Acts, Edicts, Decrees, Circulars, etc., stored in the National Archives Center IV in Đà Lạt, the National Archives Center II, and the Library of Social Sciences in Ho Chi Minh City; the open access archival sources

---

49 There are many different aspects to examine the representation of full effects of the Vietnam War such as socio-economic effects on Vietnam, veterans returning from the war, the anti-war movement of the progressive people over the world, etc. Statistics point out that during the war 2 million Vietnamese civilians, 1.1 million North Vietnamese troops, 200.000 South Vietnamese troops, 58.000 U.S. troops were killed; $150 billion U.S. dollars spent; Agent Orange and other defoliants led to widespread health problems and environmental damages in Vietnam; Americans increasingly distrusted their military and government; profoundly changes in the U.S. military strategy and foreign policy, and so on. See: *International Relations: Vietnam War*. At: Https://aad. archives.gov/aad/series-list.jsp?cat=WR28; US Department of Defense. (n.d.). Number of killed soldiers in U.S. wars since World War I, as of March 2018. In Statista - The Statistics Portal. Retrieved May 20, 2018, from https://www-statista-com.lc.idm.oclc. org/statistics/265977/us-wars-number-of-casualties/; Casualties - US vs NVA/VC. At: http://www.rjsmith.com/kia_tbl.html; Statistical information about casualties of the Vietnam Conflict, US National Archives. At: Https://www.archives.gov/research/vietnam-war/casualty-statistics; *What effect did the Vietnam War have on the world?*; At: Https://prezi.com/zlqmhtkvxjcq/what-effect-did-the-vietnam-war-have-on-the-world/. (Accessed 09th May 2018); Clarke, Jeffrey J. (1988), *United States Army in Vietnam: Advice and Support: The Final Years, 1965–1973*, Washington, D.C: Center of Military History, United States Army, p. 275.

of Texas University; political memoirs of American and Vietnamese officials, soldiers, civilians, or of Communist cadres as well; and other printed documents and newspapers. In addition, documentary films, videos of interviews produced by television stations also help the author a lot in the course of preparing, analyzing and comparing research data.

Secondary materials: Also, secondary sources are used as a meaningful addition to the primary ones. Books and articles of forerunner scholars not only brought a valuable source of information but also suggested techniques for dealing with research materials and expressing the findings to the thesis author.

In my study, collected materials have been classified and handled carefully before being cited. Likewise, historical facts and events have been interpreted by reliable methods of historical science such as analyzing and criticizing historical documents, interpretation of printed materials and memoirs, etc., before being presented in the form of accounts of the past.

Besides, a systematic method was applied during my research. Namely, the statistical approach was adopted in the formulation of illustrative tables; the comparative and deductive methods were used to figure out most appropriate and credible information when multiple sources related to the topic were being available; last but not least, the interdisciplinary approaching method in anthropology and political sciences was implemented to re-evaluate ethnographic accounts those would be referenced in the dissertation.

It is broadly acknowledged that among scientific works on the Central Highlands the French-conducted ethnographic studies that focus on describing regional geographic issues, socio-economic lives and cultural characteristics of the Montagnards were born earliest and held most prominent scientific value. Coming to the Central Highlands later than the French over a century, American researchers tended to go deep into the psychological characteristics, racial characteristics, economic and cultural activities. Southern Vietnamese authors, meanwhile, were more concerned with describing, illustrating, and explaining the contemporary government's ethnic policies. In addition to paying attention to the propagation of government policies for ethnic minorities, after 1975 Vietnamese scholars tend to be engaged in the economic potential and the problem of preserving traditional cultural values. In this section, I will review the literature regarding the Central Highlands according to these leading trends.

Studies conducted by international scholars

Look at the academic literature on the Central Highlands; first and foremost we should mention a significant amount of ethnographic studies carried out by French ethnologists. Since the late nineteenth and early twentieth centuries, along with the promotion activities of Christian missionaries, to serve the colonial policymakers the French began paying attention in investigating all the geographic areas over Indochina comprehensively. Because of its strategic location and ethnic diversity, the Central Highlands became one of the most attractive research sites. Whether deriving from the academic or political purpose, French researchers' studies provided abundant sources on various aspects of the highland lives.

The earliest work, *Les jungles moi*, was completed in 1912 by Henri Maitre. This monograph was a result of the second survey of Henri Maitre that started in 1909 and lasted for two years. As commented by another scholar, Maitre wrote his research like a diary, in which he told a story about an adventurous journey of an expedition. In the blocks, factors such as weather, terrain, creatures, etc., in the Central Highlands were described vividly. Characteristics and customs of the Montagnards were also skillfully noted through records of brief encounters (Maitre 2008). Since the 1980s, the best-known ethnologist Jacques Dournes praised *Les jungles moi* as the best book ever written on the Central Highlands of Vietnam.

As for Jacques Dournes, who is also known by a pseudonym, DamBo. To get in-depth researches, Dournes spent twenty-five years living in the Central Highlands; converting from Christianity to the traditional belief of the tribes. And, even in his last years, he still expressed his intention to return to live in the Central Highlands. According to the French Ancient Far East Institute in Hanoi, Jacques Dournes completed 350 researches about the minorities in southern Indochina[50]. Of those, there are ten books that have been translated

---

50 During a quarter of a century living in the Central Highlands, Jacques Dournes dedicated to studying the culture of ethnic Jarai in the provinces of Phú Bổn and Kontum after having done some works on the Kaho Sré in Di Linh County (Lâm Đồng Province). According to Condominas, the ethnographic passion of Dournes was not exclusively an apparatus for pastoral activities or missions. Came to Vietnam as a missionary in 1947, he quickly learned Kaho language and noted meticulously about various aspects of the life of Sré people in Di Linh County including settlement patterns and house type; religious beliefs and practices; economic activities; traditional village management models; kinship and marriage patterns; and way of life. In early 1955, he returned to Vietnam after repatriation to the mission of evangelization for the Jarai people in Cheo Reo (Phú Bổn). The process of long-term cultural integration in local communities and his academic experiences helped Dournes perceive the treasure of knowledge over various fields of physical life as well as the spiritual life of the Jarai people.

into Vietnamese as *Miền đất huyền ảo - Các dân tộc miền núi Nam Đông Dương (Populations montagnardes du Sud-Indochinois)* (2003); *Pötao - một lý thuyết quyền lực ở người Jörai Đông Dương (Pötao, une théorie du pouvoir chez les Jörais indochinois)* (2013); *Rừng, đàn bà, điên loạn (Forêt, femme, folie - Une traversée de l'imaginaire joraï)* (2002); *Xứ* Jarai *(Pay Jörai)* (2016), etc.

In addition, it can be listed a lot of other ethnographic studies on minorities in the hinterlands as well as in Indochina, in general, such as *Chúng tôi ăn rừng núi đá - Thần Gôo (We have eaten the forest: the story of a Montagnard village in the Central Highlands of Vietnam)* (2008) of Goerges Condominas, *Dân làng Hồ (Les Sauvages Bahnars)* (2008) of Pierre-X. Dourisbour, *Xứ Đông Dương (L'Indo-Chine francaise)* (2016) of Paul Doumer, and so on.

The American ethnographers came over Vietnam since the mid-1950s and quickly took advantage of achievements in French studies. Thus, within a few years after approaching ethnic minorities in SVN, American ethnologists published many voluminous monographs. Some of which contributed significantly to U.S. and RVN's policymakers in creating effective domination strategies in the Central Highlands. There are some notable works as follows.

First and foremost is *Minority groups in the Republic of Vietnam,* published in 1966 by the U.S. Headquarters Department of the Army. According to the authors' classification, the minorities in SVN were divided into two groups: *the tribes* and *other minorities*. In which, "other minorities" included the ethnic groups, the opposition political parties, and religious denominations. This concept, however, was different from ethnic classification viewpoint of ethnologists. With approximately 1.200 printed pages, the book consists of two portions. The first one concentrates on eighteen tribal groups living in the Central Highlands. Like in many other ethnographic works about the Montagnards, the authors came up with a list of minorities and then analyzed various aspects of the life of each ethnic group respectively. It is worth mentioning here that, readers could not find classification criteria applied in the research. In the next chapter, a thorough investigation on two politico-religious sects of Cao Đài, Hòa Hảo, one quasi-political group Bình Xuyên, and five other people residing in the plain regions including the Cham, the Chinese, the Khmer, the Indians and the Pakistanis were conducted. For each group, the study provided general information on the group's size, location, settlement pattern, historical background, language, social structure, customs, taboo, religion, economic and social organization, etc. (Schrock et al. 1966).

No sooner, in 1967, Gerald C. Hickey launched his book *The People of South Vietnam Highland: Social and economic development*. Was a renowned anthropologist and had relatively long time working in SVN (6 years), Hickey himself primarily concerned about socioeconomic issues of the ethnic communities in the Highlands. In this research, he spent a considerable amount of time examining demographic characteristics, life situation, and some of the U.S.-the GVN socio-economic programs in the Central Highlands such as the Education reform, the Establishment of the Special Committee on Highland Affairs, the Reactivation traditional law court, Land tenure, Agricultural development, and Cultivation of dry and wet rice programs. The author, in the meantime, did not forget to investigate the FULRO influences on the changes in Washington and Saigon policies towards the Central Highlands (Hickey 1967).

In 1984, the U.S. Government Printing Office published a book named *The US Government and the Vietnam War: Executive and Legislative Roles and Relationships, Part I: 1945-1961*. This was the Congressional Research Service document prepared for submission to the Committee on Foreign Relations United States Senate. Together with providing an overview of the French colonial policies in Vietnam, this works cited and analyzed countless official accounts of the U.S. related to the American engagement with the Indochina War, the course of preparing to oust French, the U.S. support to help Diệm suppressing religious sects, oppositional political groups, and to consolidate his power. Thanks to the efficient support through financial aid and advisory team, Diệm gradually pacified the traditional residence of the minority groups. In an effort to "Up democracy," Diệm implemented three tactics "Throw out the French," "Throw Bảo Đại," and "Down the Communism," modeled strategic hamlets as the backbone of his long-term plan (Congressional Research Service 1984).

In the book entitled *Lost Victory: A Firsthand Account of America's Sixteen-Year Involvement in Vietnam*, William Colby and James McCargar disclosed some confidential information about the internal affairs of SVN, the U.S. strategies, the role and activities of CIA during the Vietnam War. According to the former CIA director Colby, who served as head of the U.S. pacification program in SVN after 1968 and diplomat McCargar, American soon considered the Central Highlands as a strategic area, so they speedily built up plans to stop influences of the Communism, meanwhile enticing, seducing and arming ethnic minorities against the Communists. In a little more detail, the Village Defense Program, which was piloted in Rhade villages and then, widely deployed from 1961 to 1962. Those plans, nonetheless, would not yield the expected results due to the Americans had not held a high enough role. Consequently, those programs caused severe disruptions and significant impacts on the lives of the indigenous people in many aspects (Colby & McCargar 1989).

In recent years, some of the international academics are passionately interested in issues of ethnic and religious politics in Vietnam. As a result, some scholarly works have been published such as Thomas Engelbert (2015), *Ethnic and Religious Politics in Vietnam*; Thomas Engelbert (2014), *Vom Chaos zum Inferno. Die Übergangszeit von der Ersten zur Zweiten Republik Vietnam (1963-1967)*; Oscar Salemink (1999). *Beyond complicity and naiveté: contextualizing the ethnography of Vietnam's Central Highlanders, 1850-1990*; Oscar Salemink (2002). *Vietnam: indigenous minority groups in the central highlands*, etc. In these publications, various matters related to ethnic minorities in the Central Highlands have been reviewed and resolved.

In addition to the above-stated studies, there are a lot of works, theses and political memoirs such as *Anatomy of a war: Vietnam, the United States and the modern historical experience* of Kolko, Gabriel (1985); *A soldier reports* of William C. Westmoreland (1989); *In retrospect: The tragedy and lessons of Vietnam* of McNamara Robert S. and Brian Van De Mark (1996); *The Americans and South Vietnamese Pacification Efforts During the Vietnam War* of Matthew D. Pinard (2002); *Death of a Generation: how the assassinations of Diem and JFK prolonged the Vietnam War* of Jones, Howard (2003); *America's Longest War* of George. C. Herring (Herring 2004); and so on. These publications were presented relatively systematic and also provided numerous believable documents relating to the American involvement in the Indochina Wars; the ambition as well as the maximum effort of the U.S.; the causes of the failure of American Expeditionary Forces and their military allies in Vietnam; the U.S. strategies during the wartime; the changes in the international relationships relating to the American War in Vietnam; and the battlefield and type of "people's war" of People's Army of Vietnam.

Studies published in SVN before 1975

The earliest studies regarding the GVN's ethnic policies for the Highlanders were conducted mainly by the authors living in the South; most were government civil servants. First and foremost is *Sơ lược về chính sách Thượng vụ trong lịch sử (Summary on Highland affairs policies in history)* of Paul Nưr[51] published in Saigon. In the book, Paul Nưr firstly presented an overview of the GVN's strategy from 1954 to 1966 for the minorities in mountainous areas of SVN. The assessments were relatively brief, but the author later initially propounded his comments on both outcomes and limitations of the ethnic policies made by

---

51 Paul Nưr was a Jarai intellectual, who had been one of the earliest leaders of the BAJARAKA Movement and then became the Minister of Ministry for Development of Ethnic Minorities in the GVN during 1966-1969.

the Saigon administration. According to Nứr, Diệm's "short-sighted" policies towards minority compatriots had been promulgated with some fatal mistakes those were the root causes of revolts in the Central Highlands. Some indigenous intellectuals (including Nứr) grouped against Diệm regime to regain their autonomy, and require having well-defined representatives in the agencies of law enforcement and judiciary in the central government. Although mentioned about the measures announced by the GVN for solving the ethnic crisis, Paul Nứr then did not discuss the implementation and effectiveness of those solutions (Nứr 1966).

In 1968 Nguyễn Trắc Dĩ launched his work entitled *Tìm hiểu Phong trào tranh đấu F.U.L.R.O (Understanding the F.U.L.R.O movement)*. Dĩ's research was published by the SVN Ministry for Development of Ethnic Minorities (MDEM), aiming at two specific purposes. In the first part, the author attempted to trace the mistakes in the domination strategies under Ngô Đình Diệm and Lieutenant General Nguyễn Khánh regimes; those were the direct causes leading to the outbreak of the BAJARAKA movement in 1958 and the uprising of the FULRO in 1964. In the rest portion of the book, Dĩ praised the success of the ethnic policies that were being made by Nguyễn Văn Thiệu and Nguyễn Cao Kỳ government (Dĩ 1968).

Two years later, in 1970, the MDEM continued introducing the book *Hội đồng các sắc tộc - Một tân định chế dân chủ của nền đệ nhị Cộng hòa Việt Nam (Ethnic Minorities Council - A new democratic institution of the Second Republic of Vietnam)* of Nguyễn Trắc Dĩ. In this study, Dĩ prioritized introduction the role and position of the Ethnic Minorities Council; some features of socioeconomic characteristics of ethnic minority groups in Vietnam, and in the Central Highlands in particular. Thereby, the author spent a significant proportion of his work on explaining why after Diệm era, the GVN concentrated on constructing policies of supporting ethnic minorities in the South (Dĩ 1970).

Followed the studies of Paul Nứr and Nguyễn Trắc Dĩ, in 1972, the MDEM continued publishing a fascicule named *Chính sách phát triển sắc tộc của chính phủ Việt Nam Cộng hòa (The development policies for ethnic minorities of the government of Republic of Vietnam)*. The editorial purpose of this document, undoubtedly, was to propagate and promote the Saigon's ethnic strategies. The publication, firstly overviews of the policies for ethnic minority groups under the French colony, the Crown Domain of the Southern Highlander Country (French: Domaine de la Couronne du pays Montagnards du Sud-PMS), the Communist authority, the First RVN and SVN administration after 1963. The second part then addresses briefly on the BAJARAKA Movement (1957–1958) and FULRO revolt (1964–1969). In the rest chapter, the authors suggested shortly about all measures to enforce the ethnic policies of the current administration (MDEM 1972).

Another study relating to the ethnic policies of the GVN is *Miền thượng Cao nguyên (The Central Highlands)* written in 1974 by Cửu Long Giang and Toan Ánh. Although most reviewers consider the book ethnographic research on customs and culture of the minorities in SVN, it also mentions briefly about ethnic policies of the Ngô Đình Diệm government as well as Decree 033/67 of the Second Republic (Giang & Ánh 1974).

Studies carried out by Vietnamese researchers during the unification era

After the reunification of Vietnam of 1975, especially since the Innovation Era (Vietnamese: Thời kỳ Đổi mới), starting in 1986, ethnic minority groups in the southern part of the country have been capturing the considerable domestic scholars' attention. Nevertheless, the majority of studies have been dispersed throughout surveying various aspects of socio-economic and cultural lives of the minorities living in the Central Highland, the Southern Central Lowland areas and Mekong River Delta. There have a large number of publications, for example, *Người Chăm ở Thuận Hải (The Cham in Thuận Hải)* (Biên, Xuân, An, & Dốp 1989); *Giữ gìn và phát huy bản sắc văn hoá Tây Nguyên (Preserving and promoting cultural identity of the Highland ethnic groups)* of Nguyễn Hồng Sơn and Trương Minh Dục (1996), etc. Besides, there are also some monographs on each specific particular geographical area or ethnic group, such as *Đại cương về các dân tộc Ê-đê, M'-nông ở Đắk Lắk (Outline of Ede and Mnong ethnic groups in Đắk Lắk[52] Province)* (Đẳng 1981), *Vấn đề dân tộc ở Lâm Đồng (Ethnic issues in Lâm Đồng Province)* (Đường 1983), and so on. Those either are extensive researches on many ethnic groups living in a large area or monographs on one group living in a remote village, also more or less mention the highland affairs policies of the GVN from 1954 to 1975.

As the Vietnam War has been receding into the past, together with professional researchers, each warring side has sufficient time to look back. Derived

---

52 On the name of this province, there are several ways of spellings such as Đắk Lắk, Darlac, Đăk Lăk or Đắc Lắc. In current administrative documents, the provincial name is written as Đắk Lắk. However, records composed by the U.S. before 1975 all referred to Darlac. In the Mnong language, "dak" means "water" or "lake," "Dak Lak" means "Lak Lake," a beautiful lake located in the provincial center (Dak Lak. People's Committee. Provincial Party Committee 2015).

from the purpose of reviewing the resistance war against the Americans, the Vietnamese Politburo and the Vietnam Ministry of Defense have published some documents, for example, *Tổng kết cuộc kháng chiến chống Mỹ, cứu nước thắng lợi và bài học (Summary of the Resistance War against the American invasion and lessons)* (Steering Committee for War Summarizing-Vietnam Politburo 1995); *Lịch sử kháng chiến chống Mỹ, cứu nước (1954-1975) (History of anti-US resistance War for national salvation (1954-1975)* (Institute 2013), etc. Together with giving an overview of the stages of the war; the cause of Vietnam's victory and experience lessons, the authors also analyzed the policies of each warring party, including the strategies of the U.S. and the GVN in the Central Highlands. Of those, some were seen as disastrous mistakes, which substantially contributed to the final loss of Washington and Saigon alliance.

Along with general studies in the early reunification time, recently, there have several researches relating to the ownership and utilization of land in the Central Highlands; the socio-economic transformation in ethnic minority regions; and reviews on the domination strategies of the GVN for the ethnic minority groups in the Central Highlands. We can list a couple of important studies, for instance, *Sở hữu và sử dụng đất đai ở các tỉnh Tây Nguyên (Land tenure and utilization of land in provinces of the Central Highlands)* of Vũ Đình Lợi, Bùi Minh Đạo, and Vũ Thị Hồng. In the second section of Chapter II, the researchers attempted to clarify the changes of land ownership and land using in the Highlands under the era of French colonialism and the GVN. According to the authors, Ngô Đình Diệm administration issued some guidelines and decrees to take the land of indigenous people. For example, promulgated edicts on abolishing land tenure of traditional communities, applying of state land law to the Central Highlands; used the tariff policy to force French plantation owners to sell their estates in low price; issued Decree 513 a/DT/CCRĐ to require all land transfers must be allowed by the presidential administration; widened military bases and strategic crossroads in the Highlands and roads connect the Highlands with delta areas to serve the war purposes; encouraged comprador, army commanders to establish private-owned plantations in the Central Highlands. The authors argued the confiscation of the land by force and rejecting the traditional land ownership was the direct cause leading to discontents and protests of ethnic groups in the Central Highlands. Learned from the severe failure of Diệm regime, after coming to power, Nguyễn Văn Thiệu sought to increase the minorities' loyalty towards the government by making some remarkable improvements in his policies towards the minorities (Lợi, Đạo, & Hồng 2000).

March 2003, the Journal of historical research published an article entitled *Bàn thêm về vấn đề ruộng đất ở Bắc Tây Nguyên dưới thời Mỹ - Ngụy*

(1954–1975) (Some more ideas on land possession in North Highlands under the U.S. - RVN regime (1954–1975)) written by Nguyễn Thị Kim Vân. According to Vân, throughout the period from 1954 to 1963, Diệm government deprived of land ownership of highland natives, forced minority compatriots into resettlement camps, and uprooted massive people from coastal plains to establish Land Development Centers (Vietnamese: Khu Dinh điền)[53] in 1957 and the Agrovilles or Rural Community Development Centers (Vietnamese: Khu Trù mật) in 1959. In the next phases, experienced from Diệm's blunders, the succeeding administrations worked out a so-called Land-to-the-Tiller program[54] (Vietnamese: Người cày có ruộng). Through this plan, the ownership of lands, which had been passed by Montagnards' ancestors, was legalized. Moreover, the implementation of Land-to-the-Highlander Program achieved its two primary objectives, namely to contribute to reducing land disputes and strengthen the GVN's control over highland villages (Vân 2003). Five years later, in the book *Chuyển biến kinh tế - xã hội Bắc Tây Nguyên (1945–1995) (Socio-economic changes in North Highlands (1945–1995))* Nguyễn Thị Kim Vân also spent several pages on analyzing the U.S. and the GVN economic policy and the transformation in socio-economic lives of highland ethnic communities. According to Vân, after being stripped of traditional ownership of land, the Montagnards then were forced to move into resettlement camps and strategic hamlets[55]. The

---

53 The Land Development Center and the Agrovilles were critical socio-economic plans of the First Republic. By which, many Highlanders and the Việt people those living in plains were brought to the uncultivated regions for economic development, preventing the infiltration of VC and the PAVN forces from the North. These plans announced initially on 23rd April 1957. Accordingly, the population in lowland areas, especially the North migratory was regrouped to sparsely populated regions to expand cultivation. The government supplied residents with schools, clinics, and other infrastructures.

54 August 25th, 1969, President Nguyễn Văn Thiệu introduced a bill to parliament to discuss; including the withdrawal of land left for landlords to 15 hectares in the South Part, 5 hectares in Central Part and granted 1.5 million hectares of rice fields for more than 800 thousand farmers. September 9th, 1969, the U.S. President Richard Nixon dispatched I. Hogh, an expert on rural development in Asia, along with 35 Vietnamese and the U.S. experts to Saigon directly advised Land Reform Program. Also, some 40 million dollars (approximately 11 billion RVN currencies) spent by the U.S., the Second Republic government also spent 178 million RVN currencies on the draft law "Land-to-the-Tiller" (Sen 1996, 71).

55 The Strategic Hamlet Program (Vietnamese: Ấp chiến lược) was a program by the GVN and U.S. during the Vietnam War to combat the VC insurgency by pacifying the countryside and reducing the influence of the Communists among the rural population (Tucker 2011, 1070). Hamlet was a traditional smallest organized community

establishment of military bases and land development centers under Diệm period made the people in North Highlands indignant. The political instability in the Highlands, therefore, increased dramatically. Entering the period of 1964–1975, Diệm successors launched many measures to "buy off" the Highlanders, especially the dignitaries; and to control the notable individuals in the minority communities. The life of the highland compatriots, therefore, got some certain progress (Vân 2008).

Tracing the policies of Washington and Saigon implemented in Đắk Lắk Province, Nguyễn Duy Thụy had an article named *Mấy nét về chính sách kinh tế, xã hội của Mỹ và chính quyền Sài Gòn ở Đắk Lắk (Several features on socio-economic policies of the U.S. and Saigon government in Đắk Lắk Province)*, published in the Journal of Historical Research. Concerning the economic system, Thụy devoted especial attention to the programs of "Land Development Centers," "Plantations," "Land Surveying," etc. For the social policy, the article's author denounced that the GVN not only brutally suppressed the Communists, raiding movements of the masses, tried to abolish democratic freedoms, creating the divisions between religions but also carried out measures to enlist nobility, intellectuals, soldiers, founded pro-U.S. political organizations such as "Autonomous America," "Indigenous special force" (Thụy 2010).

Last but not least were the two articles of Nguyễn Văn Tiệp published in the Journal of Science and Technology Development, 2013 entitled: *Mấy nhận xét về chính sách dân tộc đối với các dân tộc thiểu số tây nguyên của chính quyền Việt Nam Cộng hòa dưới thời tổng thống Ngô Đình Diệm (1954-1963) (Some Remarks on the Ethnic Policies of the Republic of Vietnam towards the Highlanders under Ngô Đình Diệm Regime (1954-1963))* and *Mấy nhận xét về chính sách dân tộc của chính quyền đệ nhị Cộng Hòa đối với các dân tộc thiểu số Tây Nguyên (1964-1975) (Some Remarks on the Ethnic Policies of the Second Republic of Vietnam towards the Highlanders (1964-1975))*. According to Tiệp, Diệm considered the Highlands as a strategic area in the fields of political and military. After taking power in SVN, he implemented the forced assimilation policy of indigenous people to control the Highlands tightly. Nonetheless, due to a wrong economic system, which denied the land-collective ownership of villages, forced compatriots to move into sedentary farms, resettlement centers, and strategic hamlets. These fallibilities led to chaotic and poverty lives of the Montagnards.

---

in the rural SVN. Several hamlets (typically 3–5) formed a village. Aimed at getting sympathies from the people, in later years that program was renamed to the Ấp Đời mới (1964) and Ấp Tân sinh (1965), both meant the New Life Hamlet.

Simultaneously, the assimilation policy was implemented in multiple aspects of culture, education, law, etc. Moreover, the discrimination among Việt (Kinh) and Montagnard civil and military officers deepened the perpetual conflict and division between the Highlanders and the Lowlanders. The Bureau for Highland Affairs was established with the function of advising the government in solving problems related to the mountainous people but worked only superficially. All those unreasonable points in Diệm ethnic strategies led to the discontent and the uprisings of the Highlanders during Diệm regime (Tiệp 2013b).

Experienced from Diệm's failure, Nguyễn Văn Thiệu and his administration made an effort to reconstruct and improve ethnic policies. Beginning with the undertaking what so-called Ethnic harmony, co-development in a united nation, and then the policies of "Nation, harmony, and progress," the Thiệu-Kỳ regime achieved some significant successes, notably the commitment to cooperate with the government of FULRO. In addition to acknowledging the advances in the Second Republic's domination strategies, Tiệp also pointed out some of its shortcomings such as the process of policy-making was slow, sometimes was clumsy and coping. The implementation of the Saigon's strategy for the minorities, in practice, was challenging due to the ongoing severe fighting in the Central Highlands, the author finally concluded (Tiệp 2013a).

1.5 Structure of the Thesis

This thesis consists of 6 chapters those convey the main contents as follows:

The first chapter foremost introduces the process of decolonization and appearance of American politics in Vietnam. It then discusses reasons, for which the transformation of domination strategies in the Central Highlands from pre-colonialism over colonialism to American warfare under the decolonization and cold-war politics was chosen as the topic of my Ph.D. thesis. The remaining sections then mention purposes, issues of theoretical basis of this study, sources and research methods, and finally the structure of the thesis.

In Chapter 2, at first, a panorama of the Central Highlands is given. Based on differences in origins, the locations of residence, economic models, cultural traditions, languages, etc., the GVN divided the ethnic minorities over the South into three main groups including the Montagnards, the lowland minorities, and the minorities migrated from the North. Of those, the Montagnards was considered the most important minority group, and also the central object of the RVN's ethnic policies.

After presenting the key concepts of "Mọi", "ethnic minority," "Montagnards", "tribal peoples or tribes" and the criteria for ethnic classification applied in

Vietnam, the thesis author provides several main features of 19 tribes resided in the Central Highlands.

After reviewing the ethnic policies conducted by the Vietnamese feudal dynasties,

Chapter 3 presents main contents and changes in the French domination strategies in the Central Highlands; especially in the context of the decolonization process in Vietnam after the August Revolution of 1945. In this chapter, the author also gives a brief history of contact between the French (mainly missionaries, traders, explorers) and the indigenous peoples in the hinterland. That step paved the way for the entry of colonialism.

Chapter 4, first, attempts to provide a brief look into the role of the Americans in the creation of the First Republic and next steps of the nation-building process. After being chosen by Cardinal Francis Spellman and some politicians at the U.S. Department of State, Ngô Đình Diệm's life began a significant breakthrough, from an exiled politician became prime minister and then president of the First Republic of Vietnam. Of course, we should not forget that all American efforts to establish a pro-Western government in SVN were in the orbit of U.S. Containment Policy during the cold-war period.

The chapter also aims to explain that military and socioeconomic plans the Americans deployed in ethnic minority areas were to gain an ultimate purpose of controlling the strategic area of the Central Highlands. Also, the Americans repeatedly intervened in the course of formulation the GVN's ethnic policies such as taking control of the Montagnard armed units or pressing the Diệm government to release leaders of the BAJARAKA movement retained in prisons. This chapter then focuses on analyzing the Highland Affairs Policies including the strategy of merging the autonomous zone of Crown Domain into the national territory; on government-deployed programs in the minority regions to achieve goals of military, politics, economy, social welfare, culture[56]; and on the forced assimilation policy.

After commenting on impacts of those strategies on the lives of minorities, the rest sections summarize some of the minority-led struggle movements against the Diệm regime.

Chapter 5 deals with the American impacts on the policies of the Military Junta and the Second Republic towards the ethnic minorities in the Central Highlands. In the historical background sections, a perspective on the role of

---

56 Such as Land Reform Program, Land Development Program, Highlander Resettlement Program, Strategic Hamlet Program.

CIA and U.S. Ambassador in the selection of personnel and their sophisticated tactics for bringing selected characters to power, as well as, removing someone, who was no longer appropriate for American benefits, is given.

The following parts continue clarifying the U.S. influence on the RVN ethnic policies. Like in the previous stage, during the period 1964–1975, the Americans maintained the doctrine of "carrot and stick approach" to make the Saigon government perform counterinsurgency programs in form of "search and destroy" operations over minority and rural areas. The foundation of Domino Theory about the anti-communist outpost role of SVN remained unchanged until President Richard Nixon's visit to China in 1972[57].

Also in Chapter 5, some prominent projects and decree-laws on the adjustment and improvement of the GVN's domination strategies are analyzed. It can be said that those reforms, along with the American-led economic and social programs, created some positive impacts on various aspects of ethnic communities' lives. On the other hand, the deepest contradiction between the GVN and the minorities was the Highlanders' request for autonomy remained unresolved. Additionally, derived from several subjective and objective causes, many good points of the ethnic strategies during this period were not fully implemented while its mistakes and limitations arose. Those inadequacies led to several anti-government rebellions in the second half of the 1960s.

Chapter 6 summarizes the research results presented in previous episodes. By the conclusions drawn, the thesis author tries to point out that there was a remarkable transformation in the domination strategies in the Central Highlands from pre-colonialism to colonialism over post-colonialism. During the post-World War II and cold war periods, the policies of different political systems for the strategic area of Central Highlands though did not change as sharply as in the previous times but was more complicated and multi-dimensional under the influence of the decolonization and cold-war politics.

---

57 The historic handshake between leaders of these two world powers marked the opening of a new U.S. strategy in Southeast Asia. This turning point made the task of building an anti-communist outpost in Vietnam into a historical concept.

II An Overview of the Central Highlands

This chapter begins with ethnic classification criteria and the interpretation of terms adopted to refer to indigenous peoples in the Central Highlands by different political regimes in Vietnamese history. The following sections focus on the geographical features, topography, and population of the Central Highlands. Through discussing those characteristics, the thesis author attempts to answer a question: why did colonial and Postcolonial Strategists consider the Central Highlands as a geopolitical and military strategic area in Indochina and then in Southeast Asia?

2.1 Classification of Ethnic Minorities in Vietnam

The ethnic grouping of the ethnic minorities in the Central Highlands has been raising many as yet unsolved problems. Similar to the region name and the common label for the indigenous peoples, the ethnic classification changed over time. The process of ethnic classification even has been reactivated after the establishment of each new political system led to different results, depending on whether one approached the matter from ethnographic, linguistic or political standpoint[58] (Salemink 2002, 4). There is the fact that several lists of ethnic minorities in SVN co-existed in different records, in which the number of ethnicities and their names were relatively divergent. Each classification is mere "an arbitrary and convenient device" and that the generalizations made possible by it must be examined with extreme caution[59].

It is worth noting that during the wartime some ethnic minorities lived in disputed areas between the GVN and NLF[60]; and many had to relocate

---

58 Anthropologists like Georges Condominas and Gerald Hickey believed that tribal boundaries were fluid and permeable and ethnic identities were not fixed before the establishment of colonial rule. See: Condominas, G., *Classes sociales et groupes tribaux au Sud-Viêtnam, Cahiers Internationaux de Sociologie*, Vol. 40, 1966, pp. 161–70, and (Hickey 1982b, 4).
59 See: *Montagnard Tribal Groups of the Republic of South Vietnam*. P.1. In: TTU, VC, VA 23970404002.
60 Since June 8, 1969, the NLF upgraded to be the Provisional Revolutionary Government of the Republic of South Vietnam (Vietnamese: Chính phủ Cách mạng lâm thời Cộng hòa miền Nam Việt Nam). Six months after its establishment, this Provisional Government was recognized by 25 countries. See: *List of Countries Having Recognized the Provisional Revolutionary Government of the Republic of South Viet Nam*. In: TTU, VC, VA 2310605017.

continuously due to shelling from the two sides and the American bombing and defoliant spraying. Those circumstances caused extensive changes in the population structure of minorities[61]. Ethnic and linguistic studies on the Highlands, therefore, had never been carried out in the most favorable conditions. Also, a complete census of the Montagnard population in SVN even had never been made[62]. Consequently, all the various sources gave only approximate figures and tended to be somewhat tentative (Hickey 1967, 15, 22)&(Engelbert et al. 2015, 96).

In the graph below, we can see estimates of the population of the Montagnards carried out by the Special Commission For Highland Affairs in 1967 was pretty much lower than unofficial sources provided by the Summer Institute of Linguistics (SIL), FULRO, Catholic Yearbook, and Minority Rights Group. Those were 610.551, 927.000, 700.000, and 800.000, respectively[63].

Before discussing the policies towards ethnic minorities in Vietnam history, we need to clarify who the ethnic minorities in Vietnam are? According to the contemporary Vietnamese anthropologists, an "ethnic group" or "nation" (Vietnamese: Dân tộc or tộc người)[64] is "*A stable or relatively stable group of people formed over a historical period, with common territorial ties, economic activities and cultural characteristics. It was on the basis of these common ties that there arose an awareness of ethnic identity and a name of one's own*" (Vạn et al. 1998, 20). Or "*A stable community was one formed over a historical period, involving relationships of identity regarding language, habitat, socioeconomic activities and cultural characteristics and was also conscious of a shared ethnic identity*" (Giáo

---

61 For example, in the late 1960s and early 1970s, the Brou had been displaced from Quảng Trị to the zone of Buon Jat (Darlac Province); many Bahnar and Sédang were displaced into the territory of the Jarai in Cheo Reo (Phú Bổn Province); the Stieng of Bình Long, Phước Long and Tây Ninh had been transferred into the province of Lâm Đồng, among the Kaho. Therefore, the maps which show the distribution of the ethnic minorities also became inconsistent in different stages of the war because of those continuing displacements.
62 See: Health Data Publications, No. 5 (Revised), January 1966 – *The Republic of Viet-Nam (South Viet-Nam) - Department of Health Data, Division of Preventive Medicine*. In: TTU, VC, VA 16090119001.
63 Minority Rights Group - *The Montagnards of South Vietnam*. In: TTU, VC, VA 24990112002.
64 Those definitions are deeply influenced by Stalinist national theory. Accordingly, there is no distinction between "nation" (Vietnamese: dân tộc) and "ethnic group" (Vietnamese: tộc người).

Classification of Ethnic Minorities in Vietnam

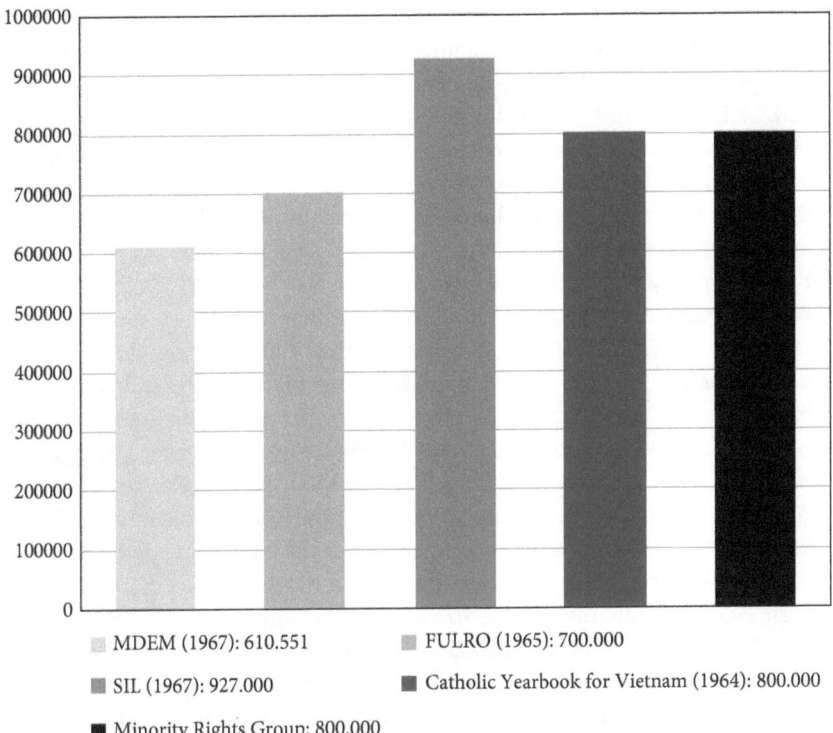

Fig. 1: Estimates of Total Populations of Montagnards by Various Sources. Sources: Minority Rights Group - The Montagnards of South Vietnam. In: TTU, VC, VA 24990112002.

et al. 1997, 6)&(Ba et al. 2002, 5). From these definitions, five ethnic classification criteria including language, habitat, economic activities, cultural characteristics, and self-identification can be listed (Giáo et al. 1997, 96–116)[65].

---

[65] However, after applying this set of criteria to field work for years, Vietnamese ethnologists concluded that habitat and economic activities have not been widely suitable. For example, in the Central Highlands, the tribal groups tended to have a shared territory and almost undertook the same economic activities, which were based on dry cultivation and supplemented by hunting, gathering and making traditional crafts. Therefore, only three criteria of classification as language, cultural characteristics, and the conscious of a shared ethnic identity are applied (or self-identification) (Chiến 2015) & (Salemink 2002, 4).

Also according to the current regulations of the Vietnamese government, the term *"ethnic minority"* (Vietnamese: dân tộc thiểu số) refers to an ethnic whose population less than fifty percent of total population of a country, as far as the national census[66]. Following the state requirements, a National Program of ethnic classification was first conducted since the 1960s by DRV ethnologists led by the Hanoi Institute of Ethnology. As a result of that long-term project, in 1979 a list of 54 ethnic groups living in the Socialist Republic of Vietnam was first presented. Of 54 ethnicities, the Việt (Kinh) is the vast majority, accounting for approximately 87 percent. The rest 13 percent is divided into 53 other groups, those who were officially classified as ethnic minorities. As we can see from that list, the tribes in the Central Highlands consist of nineteen ethnic minorities, categorized into two linguistic groups. Four Malayo-Polynesian speaking ethnicities are Ê Đê, Gia Rai, Raglay, and Chu Ru. The remaining fifteen ones are Mon-Khmer-speaking peoples includes Ba Na, Cơ Ho, Xơ Đăng, Mnông, Giẻ Triêng, Hrê, Mạ, Cơ Tu, Tà Ôi, Xtiêng, Bru-Vân Kiều, Co, Chơ Ro, Rơ Măm, and Brâu[67] (Trình 2007a, 5). Regarding terminology, the term "ethnic minority" was first used in SVN administrative documents since the early phase of the national state formation process. In particular, since Diem enacted Decree No. 21 on 11th March 1955, officially merged the Crown Domain into the Central Part of the State of Vietnam, all non-Việt peoples living in the territory of SVN were officially considered the ethnic minority (including the lowlander minorities such as the Cham, the Khmer, the Chinese and the Highlanders). Thus, the term ethnic minority has a broader meaning than "Montagnard" or "tribe". As we have earlier addressed, Montagnard and tribe are only words used by the French and Americans to refer to ethnic minorities living in the southern highlands of Indochina, mainly in SVN (the Central Highlands).

In another account, *Minority groups in the Republic of Vietnam*, written by a group of American researchers. Though did not give clear classification criteria, the authors pointed out that the minorities in SVN comprised of eighteen tribal groups such as the Bahnar, the Bru, the Cua, the Halang, the Hre, the Hroi, the Jarai, the Jeh, the Katu, the Koho, the Ma, the M'nong, the Muong, the Raglai, the Rengao, the Rhade, the Sédang, and the Stieng; and other minority groups

---

66 Decree 05/2011/ND-CP on Ethnic Affairs of Vietnam government, issued on 14th January 2011.

67 See more in: *Danh mục các thành phần dân tộc Việt Nam (The list of Vietnam ethnic composition)*. Journal of Ethnology, January 1979. P. 60.

including the Bình Xuyên, the Cao Đài, the Hòa Hảo, the Cham, the Chinese, the Khmer, the Indians and the Pakistanis (Schrock et al. 1966)[68].

During the wartime, anthropologists like Gerald C. Hickey and specialists of the Summer Institute of Linguistics (SIL), listed the minorities scattering from 17th parallel southwards into three main groups: the Cham, the Khmer, and the Highlanders. Of those, the last group consisted of 35 minorities such as the Bahnar, the Brou, the Chrau, the Chru, the Cil, the Cua, the Duan, the Halang, the Hre, the Hroy, the Jarai, the Jeh, the Kalop, the Katu, the Kayong, the Laya, the Ma, the Mnong, the Monam, the Nop, the Pacoh, the Phuong, the Rai, the Rengao, the Rahadé, the Rion, the Roglai, the Sédang, the Sop, the Sre, the Stieng, the Takua, the Tala, the Todra, the Tring (Hickey 1967, 13, 16–22).

In a research completed in 1966, U.S. Special Warfare School offered a record of 14 tribes[69].

Despite remaining confusion over ethnic identities, the official ethnic classification based on ethnolinguistic differences, which had been developed by ethnologists and then adopted by the MDEM (Ministry for Development of Ethnic Minorities - SVN), was considered the most logical classification before 1975. The result of this ethnic classification, therefore, is chosen to present in my thesis. As the announcement of the MDEM, there were twenty-eight ethnic minorities in the SVN categorized into three groups such as:

– Nineteen tribes (Montagnards), in which fourteen ethnicities speak Mon-Khmer language including the Pacoh, the K'tu, the Hré, the Dié, the Halang, the Sédang, the Bahnar, the Mnong, the Cill, the Kaho, the Maa, the Chroo, the Stieng, the Cua; five remaining ones speak Malayo-Polynesian language as the Jarai, the Hroi, the Rahde, the Churu and the Roglai.

---

68 From our point of view, this classification does not make sense. Firstly, the authors referred to the Muong (Mường) as a tribal group in the Central Highlands while ignoring the other five remaining ethnic minorities those, like the Muong, also migrated from the North after 1954 such as the Hmong, the Tai, the Nùng, the Tày, and the Dao. Second, the Indians and the Pakistanis should not be ranked alongside other ethnic minorities as RVN had never officially recognized these groups as its ethnic minorities. Third, the two armed religious-political groups Cao Đài and Hòa Hảo and the gangster party Bình Xuyên should also not to be listed as minority groups here, besides these parties, there were many other religious or political organizations in SVN who were not mentioned in the study.

69 See: *Montagnard Tribal Groups of the Republic of South Vietnam*. In: TTU, VC, VA 23970404002.

- Three ethnicities inhabited in the central coastal plains, Saigon, and Mekong River Delta: the Cham, the Hoa (Chinese), and the Khmer.
- Six northern-originated minorities: the Hmong (Mèo), the Tai (Black Tai and White Tai), the Nùng, the Mường, the Tày, and the Dao (Mán)[70] (MDEM 1972).

The map and graph below present the distribution of ethnic minorities by areas and estimates of the populations by groups in the late 1960s and early 1970s in the South.

2.2 Background Information on the Central Highlands

2.2.1 A Brief Introduction to the Central Highlands

During the Vietnam War (1954–1975), the Central Highlands was a territorial area of RVN that located between $11^{0}00$ and $15^{0}30$ North, $105^{0}30$ East[71]. As a 65.000 square-kilometer territory, accounting for 37,34 percent of SVN, the Highlands were composed of granite plateaus on the southern part of the Long Mountain Range[72], which was adjacent to Bùng River (Quảng Nam Province) to the north; with Đồng Nai and Saigon river plains to the south; with the Central Coast plains to the east; and with Attapeu (Laos), Ratanakiri and Mondulkiri (Cambodia) to the west (Giang & Ánh 1974, 43) & (Salemink 2018).

---

70 Those ethnicities migrated from Northern provinces of Vietnam to settle in the South after the Geneva Accords of 1954.

71 In some recent researches, the term "Highlands" has been used to mention about the region where the indigenous groups (tribes) resided. To what extent, its spatial scope is far different from the geographical area of the current Central Highlands. According to the General Statistics Office of Vietnam, the Central Highlands nowadays consists of five provinces including Gia Lai, Kon Tum, Đắk Lắk, Đắk Nông and Lâm Đồng with a total area of 54.641 km², accounting for 16.8 percent of the whole national natural area. See: *Diện tích, dân số và mật độ dân số năm 2011 phân theo địa phương (Area, population and population density in 2011 by province)*. Sources: http://www.gso.gov.vn/default.aspx?tabid=387&idmid=3&ItemID=12875. (Accessed 2nd April 2018).

72 In essence, the Central Highlands is not an only but a series of adjoining plateaus. Those are the Kontum plateau at the height of 500 m high, the plateaus Kon Plông Kon Hà Nừng, Pleiku of about 800 me, plateaus M'Drak and Buôn Mê Thuột with the height of 500 m, plateau M'nong at around 800–1000 m, plateau Lang Bian (Lâm Viên) of approximately 1500 m, and plateau Di Linh of about 900–1000 m. All of these plateaus are bounded to the east by high mountain ranges and massif (South-Long Mountain Range).

Fig. 2: Distribution of Ethnic Minorities in SVN. Sources: Author.

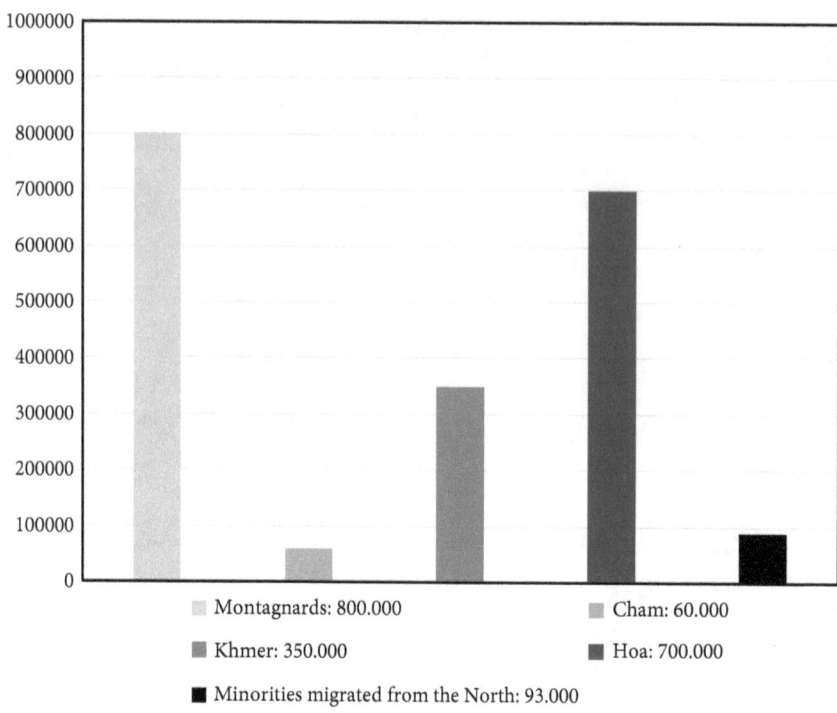

Fig. 3: Estimates of Populations of Different Minority Groups. Sources: Minority Rights Group - The Montagnards of South Vietnam. P. 3-4. In: TTU, VC, VA 24990112002.

According to geologists, geologic movements during the tectonic crust, which began on Earth between 3 and 3.5 billion years ago, created many cracks in the surface of the plateau. After volcanic eruptions, layers of lava covered rocks' surface forming red and fertile strips of land. Also, the craters turned into romantic lakes lying intermingled slopes, majestic ridges, and year-round flowing waterfalls. Vertical movements of the crust, on the other hand, caused the fall in coastal areas, forming the curved bows like mountains in the western Pacific.

The scenery was diverse from the north to the southern Highlands. While great granite blocks with dense and mysterious jungles were characteristic of Kontum region, sharp vertical mountains with green pine forests created a harmony, romantic dreaming Lang Bian. Unlike dry, bare lands in deep valleys separated by huge-sandstone slabs within the Ba Biên Giới zone (the bordering area among Cambodge, Cochinchine, and Annam), the low hilly regions positioned in the northwest of Darlac, southwest of Pleiku, or in M'Drak and Mnong plateaus were full of grass and wild animals. Accounting for 80 percent of the whole natural area, the forests in the hinterlands were considered as endless reserves of the biosphere as well as hunting resources, both regarding species and quantity. In dense forests, in addition to large animals which fascinated marksmen like elephants, tigers, bison, buffalo, leopards, bears, etc., there also was the Min (Scientific name: Bos gaurus laosiensis or Bos gaurus readei), one of the world largest gaurs with average height and length of up to 1.8 m and 2.8 m, respectively[73]. Smaller animals like deer, rabbit, etc., on the contrary, tended to be plentiful in sparse forests and grasslands those spanned between mountains and the central coast (Giang & Ánh 1974, 58, 59, 71)&(Salemink 2018).

The land was considered the primary natural resources in Central Highlands, facilitating the improvement of agriculture and forestry. With an area of approximately one million hectares, the fertile red soil in the plateaus of Kontum, Pleiku, M'nong, and Buôn Mê Thuột was perfect for various tropical crops like rubber, coffee, tea, pepper, and cashew. Besides, millions of hectares of yellow-red and gray soils lay on southwest hillsides and in valleys; alluvial soils along rivers were suitable for food crops.

Locates in the tropical savanna, the climate in the Central Highlands is divided into two seasons: the rainy season from May to October and the dry one from November to April, in which March and April were two hottest and driest months. Also according to the diversity in topography and climate, the Central Highlands could be divided into three sub-regions, including North Central Highlands (consisted of Kontum and Pleiku); Middle Central Highlands (including Darlac and Phú Bổn); South Central Highlands (comprised Tuyên Đức, Quảng Đức, Lâm Đồng). Among those sub-regions, Middle Central Highlands had lower altitude; therefore, it's average temperature higher than that of other two sub-regions[74].

The Central Highlands owned many broad rivers like the Ba River, Ia Yun Pa, Pô Cô, Krông Ana, Krong Nô, Đạ Đờn, La Ngà. With total surface water flows was about 50 billion cubic meters, the flow regime deeply affected by the climate (Giang & Ánh 1974, 53–56)&(Trình 2007a, 2–4).

The map below displays the provinces of the Central Highlands in 1967.

---

73 See also Viễn Sự, Sơn Lâm. *Bò tót - tiếng kêu bên bờ vực - Kỳ 1: Chiếc kèn motova cuối cùng. (Min- the cries on the brink - Part 1: The last motova)*. Tuoi Tre News. Sources: https://tuoitre.vn/bo-tot-tieng-keu-ben-bo-vuc-ky-1-chiec-ken-motova-cuoi-cung-663889.htm. (Accessed 9th April 2018).

74 See in Fig. 4.

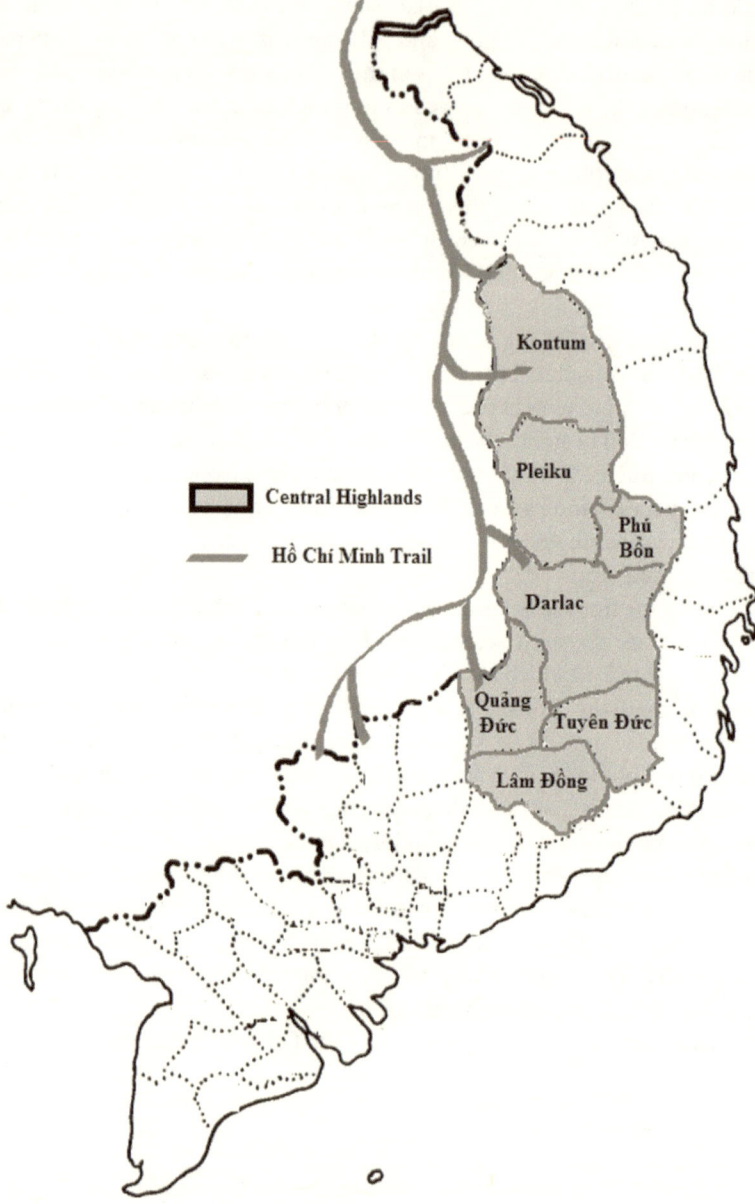

Fig. 4: Provinces of the Central Highlands in 1967. Sources: Author.

2.2.2 Indigenous Peoples of the Central Highlands

It is known that the "tribal groups" (the tribes, Montagnards) were native inhabitants who scattered over a mountainous region stretching from mountainous areas of the central province of Quảng Bình to the western regions of Bình Phước and Tây Ninh Provinces. As estimated by the Special Commission For Highland Affairs in 1967, the population of the Montagnards was 610.551[75].

According to anthropologists, Vietnam has a unique geopolitical and geo-cultural position. This country is located between the two world great civilizations: India and China; on the intersection of the critical maritime routes linking the Pacific and the Indian Ocean; and on the bridge between Mainland Southeast Asia and Maritime Southeast Asia. So, since ancient times, Vietnam has become the meeting place of many peoples, leading to the blending of blood between different ethnic groups (Janse 1941, 247)&(Vượng et al., 2009, 23)&(Dĩ 1972, 3).

Studies show that the first inhabitants, those who had the Negroid characteristics like a low figure, black hair, dark skin, appeared in the Central Highlands about 10.000 to 5.000 years ago. The second migration from coastal and islands to the Central Highlands occurred about 6.000–5.000 years ago is of the Austroasiatic language speaking peoples. This group carries main typical features of the Melanesians such as low figure, swarthy, black and wavy hair. The third earliest residents of the Central Highlands are the Indonesian people coming from Indus River (India) between 5.000 and 2.500 years before the present. The general appearance of Indonesian people is tall, with wavy black hair, dark skin. A complicated process of blending of blood among these groups created current indigenous communities in the Central Highlands. Although belonging to two different language families, Mon-Khmer[76] and

---

75 Ibid. Minority Rights Group - *The Montagnards of South Vietnam*. In: TTU, VC, VA 24990112002.
76 Mon-Khmer speaking residents reside throughout Southeast Asia, especially in Mainland Southeast Asia, including northeastern India and southern China for a long time. According to the 2009 National Population and Housing Census, the Mon-Khmer language group in Vietnam has 21 ethnic groups with nearly 2.6 million people, spreading from the Northwest through Long Mountain-Central Highlands to the Southern parts. See: Vietnamese Museum of Ethnology, the Mon-Khmer. Sources: http://www.vme.org.vn/trung-bay-thuong-xuyen/cac-dan-toc-viet-nam/nhom-mon-khme/. (Accessed 6th April 2018).

Malayo-Polynesian[77], the ethnic minorities have much in common in traditional economic and cultural life such as heavy dependence on forest resources; adopting the slash-and-burn farming method (rotational shifting cultivation); mastering techniques of making ceramic utensils, weaving fabrics, and forging rudimentary working tools; way of setting up village (plei), building stilt house and tomb house; festivals with buffalo sacrifice and gong performance show follow cycles of people's life and cycle of crops; custom of celebrating a new home, worshipping water wharf, dispelling diseases; animism, etc. (Salemink 2018)&(Vạn & Hùng 1988, 49)&(Thịnh 2006, 50)&(Giang & Ánh 1974, 15–20)&(Trình 2007a, 5)&(Lệ & Mạnh 2017).

According to the French ethnologist, the Montagnards in the 1950s were still in the so-called primitive state. They, therefore, "are witnesses of the past of mankind, showing us what we were like in the old days"; "looking at them, we see a unique and compelling picture of ourselves in the past" (Dambo 2002, 4, 8). Also under French ethnographers' eyes, not only the hinterlands appeared as "a wonderland," "a dreaming region"[78] but the people there were also extraordinary. To understand them, outsiders needed to have deep sympathy, respect and love their way of thinking, simple lifestyle and the mysterious natural scenery where they were living.

As for the number of groups and ethnic names

There had been a controversy among scholars on the number of tribal groups and their ethnic names. In RVN official documents, the indigenous peoples those who lived permanently in the Central Highlands were collectively mentioned as Đồng bào Thượng (the Compatriots of the Highlands) or Các sắc tộc Thượng (Colored peoples of the Highlands).

---

77 Malayo-Polynesian speaking peoples live in Vietnam, Cambodia, Thailand, Indonesia, East Timor, Malaysia, Philippines, Singapore, Brunei, Madagascar, Micronesia, Polynesia, Melanesia, New Guinea, and Taiwan. In Vietnam, there are five Malayo-Polynesian ethnic groups with a total population of over one million (2009). See: Vietnamese Museum of Ethnology, the Malayo-Polynesian. Sources: http://www.vme.org.vn/trung-bay-thuong-xuyen/cac-dan-toc-viet-nam/nhom-nam-djo/. (Accessed 6th April 2018).

78 Words used in the books *Les populations montagnardes du sud-indochinois*, and *Forêt, femme, folie - Une traversée de l'imaginaire joraï* of Jacques Dournes.

In pre-colonial times, the Highlanders were called *Mọi* by the Việt (Kinh)[79], Phnong (or Pnong) by the Khmer and Kha by the Laotian which could be translated roughly as "savage," and, of course, were deeply distasteful to them. In early colonial times, the French would simply borrow the term *Mọi* and called the tribes "Les Mois" or "sauvages" "savages" before changing to "Montagnards"[80] or "Mountaineers" (literally "mountain dwellers"). Accordingly, the mountainous peoples were subject to the conceptions such as primitive, backward, superstitious, unstable, conservative, or even ignorant. That affirmation served as a pretext for the outsiders to deprive the tribes of their land or exploit them[81]. After 1955 the Americans inherited the word Montagnards and translated into English as the Highlanders (Salemink 2002, 3).

As for the term "Mọi," Nguyên Ngọc, the best-known translator for translations of French ethnographers' works on ethnic minorities in Indochina, points out a different critical meaning. According to him, "Mọi" in Bahnar language originally does not have an adverse meaning. Particularly, the term "tơ-moi" only means "guest." For example, when the Jarai or the Sédang come to the Bahnar land, they are called "tơ-moi Gia-rai" or "tơ-moi Sédang."[82] In the late 19th and early 20th centuries, the Bahnar in Kontum often called themselves "tơ-moi," when they came to see French missionaries. The missionaries, however, misunderstood and thought that the visitors were introducing their ethnic identity.

---

79   Mentioning about the Việt (Kinh) people in Vietnam Western scholars often used the terminology "Vietnamese" or "Annamese." See: for example, Hickey (1967&1982), Schrock (1966). That notion is somewhat inappropriate and might confuse readers. Literally, Vietnamese "is a person from Vietnam" that means a Vietnamese can be a member of any ethnic groups living anywhere in the territory of Vietnam. Likewise, an Annamese is a native or inhabitant of Annam. During French colonial era, "Annam" was only the central part of Vietnam, distinguished from Tonkin and Cochinchine. Therefore, the term "Annamese" could not be a synonym of "Vietnamese," and, of course, could also not be used to refer to the Việt people in general.

   To avoid misunderstanding, in this thesis, I consistently use the term "the Việt" instead of "the Vietnamese" or "the Annamese" when mentioning to the Việt or Kinh ethnic group.

80   Montagnards is a term used by the French to refer to hill-dwelling peoples in Southeast Asia, especially those living in the highlands of Vietnam.

81   Minority Rights Group - *The Montagnards of South Vietnam*. Pp. 24–25. In: TTU, VC, VA 24990112002. See also Manual, Michigan State University Viet-Nam Advisory Group - *A Study of Montagnard Names in Vietnam*. P. 6. In: TTU, VC, VA 21940102001.

82   See also Chi, N. K., & Chi, N. Đ. (2011). *Người Ba-Na ở Kontum (The Bahnar People in Kontum)*. Hanoi: Knowledge Publishing House.

Years later, because Vietnamese is a single syllable language, the prefix "tơ" was gradually lost, only "moi" existed. Henceforth, "Mọi" automatically became the common name of the tribal groups. The Việt called *the Mọi (not Moi)*; the French called *Les Mois*. Ngọc also asserted that the term "Mọi" only carried bad meaning since the relation between the Việt and the Highlanders tinged with scorn color and when it was paired with one other Chinese-Vietnamese word *"rợ"* to be *"Mọi rợ,"* that resembled *"savage"* (Maitre 2008, 19–20).

The inconsistency derived from the fact that some researchers recorded the self-claiming ethnic names while others based on the list of minorities provided by administrative authorities[83]. Besides, the discrepancy in the principles of transcribing ethnic identity names data resources also created troubles. In some documents, ethnic names were recorded by French letters while others were written in English, Vietnamese, and Montagnard native languages.

The list of native ethnic minorities in the Central Highlands is presented in Tab. 1 below somewhat reveals that complexity.

Some key features of each tribal group

To give an overview of 19 tribes in the Central Highlands, in this section, I will introduce some basic information of each such as the ethnic name, population, places of residence, and prominent cultural-economic activities. As presented above, there were fourteen ethnic groups those who spoke Mon-Khmer language such as the Pacoh, the K'tu, the Hré, the Dié, the Halang, the Sédang, the Bahnar, the Mnong, the Cill, the Kaho, the Maa, the Chroo, the Stieng, and the Cua; five others those who spoke Malayo-Polynesian language as the Jarai, the Hroi, the Rahde, the Churu and the Roglai.

---

83 According to Đặng Nghiêm Vạn, in the Central Highlands, sometimes subgroups claimed themselves to belong to an ethnic. However, after that one or more members of those subgroups might redefine themselves as a subset of another ethnicity. Even in one clan, while some individuals recognized themselves as members of an ethnicity, their cousins believed they belonged to another (Vạn 1981, 28). Regarding this issue, Đinh Quang Du gave a typical example that some minority groups such in Quảng Bình Province called themselves as Mày, Sách, Rục, Khùa, while those names have not ever appeared in the list of 54 ethnic groups announced by the Vietnam government. Likewise, the Chil people in the province of Lâm Đồng has self-recognized as a separate ethnic minority while the government only categorized them as a subgroup (local group) of the Koho. See more in: Đinh Quang Du, *Identifying and preserving ethnic identity, cultural development of ethnic minorities until 2020*, Journal of Vietnam Ethnic Minorities Commission. June 12th, 2012.

Tab. 1: Names of Native Ethnic Minorities in the Central Highlands. (This list only includes ethnic groups living in southern Vietnam before 1975. After 1975, many other minority groups departed from northern mountainous provinces to the south part of the country, especially to the Central Highlands to live in government-built New Economic Zones). Sources: General Statistics Office of Vietnam. Danh mục các dân tộc Việt Nam. Ban hành theo Quyết định số 121-TCTK/PPCĐ ngày 02 tháng 3 năm 1979) (List of ethnic groups in Vietnam. Issued together with Decision No. 121-TCTK/PPCĐ of March 2, 1979). Http://www.gso.gov.vn/default.aspx?tabid= 405&idmid=5&ItemID=1851. (Accessed 20th December 2017)

Nr.	Ethnic name	Some other different names	Nr.	Ethnic name	Some other different names
1	Ba Na	Gơ Lar, Tơ Lô, Giơ Lâng, (Y lăng), Rơ ngao, Krem, Roh, ConKđe, A La Công, Kpăng Công, Bơ Nâm.	11	Giẻ-Triêng	Đgiéh, Ta Riêng, Ve (Veh), Giang Rẫy Pin, Triêng, Treng, Ca Tang, La Ve, Bnoong (Mnoong), Cà Tang.
2	Cơ Ho	Xrê, Nốp (Tu Lốp), Cơ Don, Chil, Lat (Lach), Tơ Ring.	12	Co	Cor, Col, Cùa, Trầu.
3	Xơ Đăng	Xơ Teng, Hđang, Tơ Đra, Mơ Nâm, Ha Lăng, Ca Dong, Kmrâng, Con Lan, Bri La, Tang, Tà Trĩ, Châu.	13	Chơ Ro	Dơ Ro, Châu Ro, Chro, Thượng.
4	Hrê	Chăm Rê, Mọi Chom, Krẹ, Luỹ, Thượng Ba Tơ, Mọi Lũy, Mọi Sơn Phòng, Mọi Đá Vách, Chăm Quảng Ngãi, Man Thạch Bích.	14	Rơ Măm	
5	Mnông	Pnông, Mnông Nông, Mnông Pré, Mnông Bu đăng, ĐiPri, Biat, Mnông Gar, Mnông Rơ Lam, Mnông Chil, Mnông Kuênh, Mnông Đíp, Mnông Bu Nor, Mnông Bu Đêh.	15	Brâu	Brao
6	Xtiêng	Xa Điêng, Xa Chiêng, Bù Lơ, Bù Đek (Bù Đêh), Bù Biêk.	16	RaGlay	Ra Clây, Rai, La Oang, Noang.
7	Bru Vân Kiều	Măng Coong, Tri Khùa.	17	Chu Ru	Chơ Ru, Chu, Kru, Thượng
8	Cơ Tu	Ca Tu, Cao, Hạ, Phương, Ca Tang.	18	Gia Rai	Giơ Rai, Tơ Buăn, Chơ Rai, Hđrung (Hbau, Chor), Aráp, Mthur.

(continued on next page)

Tab. 1: Continued

Nr.	Ethnic name	Some other different names	Nr.	Ethnic name	Some other different names
9	Tà Ôi	Tôi Ôi, Pa Co, Pa Hi (Ba Hi), Kan Tua, Tà Uốt.	19	Ê Đê	Ra Đê, Ê Đê Êgar, Đê, Kpa, A Dham, Krung, Ktul, Đliê Huruê, Blô, Kah, Kdrao, Dong Kay, Dong Mak, Ening, Arul, Hwing, Ktlê, Êpan, Mdhur, Bih.
10	Mạ	Châu Mạ, Chô Mạ, Chê Mạ, Mạ Ngăn, Mạ Xóp, Mạ Tô, Mạ Krung.			

First, you can see the official estimates of the distribution of nineteen tribal groups by provinces in 1967 in the table below.

The Mon-Khmer language family

1 The Pacoh

The Pacoh, also called the Bru, Brâu, the Vân-Kiều, the Tôi-Ôi, the Teu, resided mostly in Quảng Trị uplands, bordering area between the RVN and Laos, northern district of Nam Hòa, Thừa Thiên Province and in the north of the 17th parallel (MDEM 1972, 21). The estimated population of this ethnicity in 1967 was at 28.954[84]. The Pacoh people were relatively qualified in agriculture. In the past, they inhabited concentrated in central Laos. However, actual changes taken place for centuries forced them to scatter to other locations. Some moved northwest to Thailand; others went east on settlement in the western mountainous areas of Quảng Bình, Quảng Trị and Thừa Thiên Huế of Vietnam. Pacoh legends recounted that, while entering Vietnam their ancestors built a village around a mountain that named Vân Kiều which later was given this ethnic group to be Pahco-Vân Kiều or the Bru-Vân Kiều (Dĩ 1972, 11–15).

2 The K'tu

With a population of about 25.836[85], the K'tu was also known as the Kha, the We, the Katua and the Phương. This ethnic group resided mostly in the provinces

---

[84] See Fig. 5: Estimates of Population of the Montagnards by Provinces in 1967.
[85] See Fig. 5.

of Quảng Nam and Quảng Tín of SVN, near the Laos border and, in Dak Glei, Dak Pek Districts of Kontum (MDEM 1972, 22). The K'tu cultivated upland rice, corn, and manioc by slash-and-burn method. Other economic activities included weaving and knitting. Besides that, they also kept ways of hunting and gathering forest products which were passed by forefather generations. Farming tools were relatively poor with axes, knives and wooden sticks. Under the influences of Việt people, the K'tu started using a monetary system; however, they still almost depended on barter (Dĩ 1972, 16–18).

3 The Hré

The Hré resided in remote districts such as Sơn Hà, Minh Long, An Lão, and the densest in Ba Tơ, Quảng Ngãi Province[86]. They were surrounded and had close relationships with the Cua, the Bahnar, and the Sédang. With an approximate population of 43.015[87], this ethnic group also had different names as Kré, Khét, Karé (MDEM 1972, 22). The majority of the Hré cultivated wet rice. Their farming method was similar to the Việt in the south-central region of Vietnam, who used a plow or a harrow pulled by a pair of buffaloes, sowed and transplanted, adopted sickles to harvest, etc. On the contrary, the remaining small portion depended on dry farming with the slash-and-burn method, used simple farming tools including axes, ballistic knife, sticks, grass scraper and bare hands to thresh rice while harvesting (Dĩ 1972, 24–25).

4 The Dié

This Montagnard group was also called the Đgiéh, Ta Reh, Giàng Rây, Pin, Triêng, Treng, Ta Liêng, Ve, La-Ve, Bnoong, Ca Tang. The Dié tribe in SVN had about 7.582[88] people, mostly lived in the territory of Dakto District, northwestern Kontum Province. This ethnicity mainly practiced shifting agriculture; moreover, they also did hunting, fishing, gathering forest vegetables, berries, mushrooms, etc., and breeding buffaloes, cows, pigs, chickens, but mostly used for sacrifice. The Dié tribal men wore loincloths while women were garbed in skirts. Both men and women had long hair with a comb inserted in the bun (MDEM 1972, 23)&(Dĩ 1972, 26–28).

---

86 See: *Montagnard Tribal Groups of the Republic of South Vietnam*. P. 61. In: TTU, VC, VA 23970404002.
87 See Fig. 5.
88 See Fig. 5.

Province	Pacoh	K'tu	Hre	Die	Halang	Sedang	Bahnar	Mnong	Cill	Kaho	Maa	Chroo	Stieng	Cua	Jarai	Hroi	Rahde	Churu	Roglai	Total
Quang Tri	24,254	0	0	0	0	0	0	0	0	0	0	0	0	0	0	0	0	0	0	24,254
Thua Thien	4,700	4,221	0	0	0	0	0	0	0	0	0	0	0	0	0	0	0	0	0	8,921
Quang Nam	0	9,038	0	0	0	0	0	0	0	0	0	0	0	0	0	0	0	0	0	9,038
Quang Tin	0	12,277	0	(5000)	0	0	0	0	0	0	0	0	0	0	0	0	0	0	0	12,277
Quang Ngai	0	0	43,015	0	0	0	0	0	0	0	0	0	0	11,562	0	0	0	0	0	54,577
Binh Dinh	0	0	0	0	0	0	43,491	0	0	0	0	0	0	0	0	450	0	0	0	43,941
Phu Yen	0	0	0	0	0	0	0	0	0	0	0	0	0	0	0	6,385	8,679	0	0	15,064
Khanh Hoa	0	0	0	0	0	0	0	14,177	0	194	0	0	0	0	0	0	6,451	0	9,607	30,429
Ninh Thuan	0	0	0	0	0	0	0	0	46	443	0	0	0	0	0	0	0	939	11,294	12,722
Binh Thuan	0	0	0	0	0	0	0	0	0	180	0	0	0	0	0	0	0	0	4,306	4,486
Kontum	0	300	0	7,582	3,064	29,390	17,398	0	0	0	0	0	0	0	10,920	0	0	0	0	68,654
Pleiku	0	0	0	0	0	0	5,803	0	0	0	0	0	0	0	96,196	0	571	0	0	102,570
Phu Bon	0	0	0	0	0	0	1,260	0	0	0	0	0	0	0	22,146	798	3,489	0	0	27,693
Darlac	0	0	0	0	0	0	0	0	0	0	0	0	0	0	5,276	0	63,474	0	0	68,750
Quang Duc	0	0	0	0	0	0	0	13,553	0	4	4,581	0	0	0	0	0	1,070	0	0	19,208
Tuyen Duc	0	0	0	0	0	0	4	0	10,479	8,473	4,609	0	0	0	0	0	6	4,059	0	27,710
Lam Dong	0	0	0	0	0	0	0	0	0	10,327	15,039	0	0	0	0	0	0	0	0	27,747
Binh Tuy	0	0	0	0	0	0	0	0	0	4,409	0	426	0	0	0	0	0	0	3,129	7,964
Long Khanh	0	0	0	0	0	0	0	0	0	0	1,841	5,429	1,379	0	0	0	0	90	0	8,649
Phuoc Tuy	0	0	0	0	0	0	0	0	0	0	0	(3000)	0	0	0	0	0	2,381	0	0
Phuoc Long	0	0	0	0	0	0	0	0	0	0	0	0	21,528	0	0	0	0	0	0	21,528
Binh Long	0	0	0	0	0	0	0	0	0	0	0	573	13,794	0	0	0	0	0	0	14,367
Bien Hoa	0	0	0	0	0	0	0	0	0	0	0	(3000)	0	0	0	0	0	0	0	0
Total	28,954	25,836	43,015	7,582	3,064	29,390	67,956	27,730	10,525	24,030	26,070	6,428	36,701	11,562	134,538	7,633	83,740	4,998	30,809	610,551

Fig. 5: Estimates of Population of the Montagnards by Provinces in 1967. Sources: The Vietnam Center and Archive, Texas Tech University. Minority Rights Group - The Montagnards of South Vietnam. Pp. 24–25. In: TTU, VC, VA 24990112002; Manual, Michigan State University Viet-Nam Advisory Group - A Study of Montagnard Names in Vietnam. P. 6. In: TTU, VC, VA 21940102001.

5 The Halang

The Halang was a minority ethnic inhabited mainly in Laos, where the Laotian people called them Saleng. It was estimated that there were 3.064 Halang inhabitants[89] in SVN. This ethnicity lived in the southwest of Kontum where they had mutual relations with neighboring tribes such as the Sédang, the Dié, the Jarai and the Banhnar-Rongao. There were many similarities among the language and customs of the Halang with the Sédang's ones, those more or less influenced by the Jarai and Bahnar. Because of these features, some researchers considered the Halang a subgroup of the Sédang. Cultivation skills of this minority were underdeveloped, their crops and corn depended heavily on monsoon rain (Schrock et al. 1966, 125).

6 The Sédang

Numbering about 29.390[90], the Sédang resided concentratedly over the districts of Dakto, Daksut and Toum'rong in northern Kontum. This ethnicity was also known as the Strieng, the Dedrah, the Ko-Krang, the Kadong, and the Bri La Teng. While almost Sédang people depended on dry farming, its subgroup Mo-nam lived on wet rice cultivation. Nevertheless, there was a somewhat unusual in the farming habit of this local group. Instead of using buffalos to pull plows, as usual, the Mo-nam only had human, and buffalos were trampling their land. Besides crops, the Sédang also bred livestock and poultry and made handicrafts such as knitting, weaving, forging.

With a strong characteristic, Sédang tribal men were regarded as warlike, good at making bows and swords and fond of hunting. The Sédang displayed a wary demeanor in contact with strangers, however, when someone had been familiar to their community, would be treated honestly, kindly and thoughtfully (MDEM 1972, 24)& (Giang & Ánh 1974, 265–285).

7 The Bahnar

The Bahnar was also known as the Bonam, the Hrui, the Jơlong, the Konko, the Krem, the Roh, the Tolo, the Mownam, the Rowngao and the Alakong[91]. As one of the largest minority groups in SVN with a population of 67.956[92], the Bahnar

---

89 See Fig. 5.
90 See Fig. 5.
91 See: *Montagnard Tribal Groups of the Republic of South Vietnam*. Pp. 20–21. In: TTU, VC, VA 23970404002.
92 See Fig. 5.

mainly lived in Pleiku and Kontum Provinces (Schrock et al. 1966, 1–2). The tribe's livelihood was based on agriculture, in which primarily was dry cultivation. Along with the crops, each household usually bred poultry and livestock like cattle, goats, pigs, and chickens. Almost every village had its own smithy while only some communities could produce simple kinds of potteries. In the Bahnar communal life, the labor source naturally attributed. The women weaved fabric to provide for their households while the men created sedge mats, nets and all kinds of baskets. The purchase and sale applied a principle of barter. There were some items usually used as commodity equivalents such as chicken, ax, a basket of paddy, pig, copper pot, jar, gong, and buffalo (Giang & Ánh 1974, 288–292).

8 *The Mnong*

This Montagnard group resided primarily in the left bank Krong Ana and Serepok Rivers with the center was Quảng Đức Province. Some scattered in northeastern Cambodia. There were about 27.730[93] Mnong people in SVN, who was known as multiple names, for example, the Nong, the Budong, the Gar, the Preh, the Rlan (MDEM 1972, 25)&(Giang & Ánh 1974, 369–378). Each Mnong village often had a few dozen families, in which the community's chief performed a significant role and was respected by villagers.

The Mnong people were rural residents over generations. In traditional economic activities, the method of slash-and-burn kept a dominant position. Their primary food crop was ordinary rice. The glutinous rice was also grown, but it accounted for a negligible portion and was used only on special occasions as worshiping ceremonies. Besides, the Mnong planted corn, potato, and cassava on upland as an additive food source and especially for raising pigs and chickens (Condominas 1994).

9 *The Cill*

As a small mountainous group with the population of about 10.525[94], the Cill primarily lived in the north of Đà Lạt. Their area of residence of was a sunken zone, surrounded by mountains as Yang-Sin, Bidoup, and Liang-Biang (MDEM 1972, 25). In Kaho language, the term "Cill" had the negative meaning as "backward people." On this point, Jacques Dournes claimed that the Ma, the Sre, and the Noang considered the Cill as "Mọi" (savage), this prejudice was similar to the

---

93 See Fig. 5.
94 See Fig. 5.

way the Việt looked down at the Montagnards (Dambo 2001, 112). Contrary to the above conception of the Kaho, the MDEM argued that in comparison with other minority groups the Cill people were healthier, wiser, franker, and courageous and had tall stature (MDEM 1972, 25).

The Cill tribespeople dwelled concentratedly in separate residential units, called "Bons" (villages). Their society organized following the tradition of matrilineal and matrilocal, in which each family had its own land boundary. Head of a family or a village was an elder man who knew about the extent of land owned by residents and also became the witnesses of occurred disputes. As the same as many other tribal groups, the Cill depended on swidden cultivation. However, due to they did not use fertilizers, after a few harvest seasons, the soil became unproductive. The villagers then abandoned their old land and moved to a forested zone to begin a new cycle of slash-and-burn (Dĩ 1972, 45–47).

10 The Kaho

The Kaho had an estimated population of 24.030[95], who distributed from the province of Tuyên Đức to the province of Long Khánh. The Kaho also called Koho including tribes influenced by the Cham as the Lat (Lach), the Sré and the Loang (Noang) (MDEM 1972, 25). In economic forms of Kaho Lat and Kaho Sré, wet rice cultivation was considered to be the most important. Kaho Lat's fields were concentrated in valleys and along streams. The farming depended heavily on the weather; thus, they only cultivated one crop in a year. In the past, the Kaho Lat customarily chose muddy lands where water was available, but later they gradually realized those were low-yield rice fields. Through experience learning from the Chu Ru's irrigation, the Kaho Lat changed to cultivate in higher lands, terraced fields. The Kaho Sré had two types of rice fields; this distinction was based on the geography feature of the grounds. While *srê lơngơn* located in level terrain, close to rivers and streams, where water was always available, *srê đang* based in a higher position, where it only had water when in the raining season or thanks to the irrigation system[96] (Giang & Ánh 1974, 395–413).

Before having acculturation process to the Việt people, Kaho men wore indigo loincloth and Kroh jacket, wrapped black scarves around the head and fastened brooch and inserted comb in the bun while the tribal women dressed Ntiêng,

---

95 See Fig. 5.
96 See more in: Nguyễn Tuấn Tài, *Người Kaho ở Đà Lạt (The Kaho in Đà Lạt)* in Địa chí Đà Lạt (Unification Records of Đà Lạt). Http://www.lamdong.gov.vn/viVN/a/book/Pages/books/diachidalat/ Tongluan/bai9.htm. (Accessed 4th August 2017).

what looked like the Việt women's Yếm, draped shawl from left to right and also wrapped scarf around the head. Traditional costume of Kaho women was dyed with white and indigo colors. Since 1954, because of living near towns, major roads and having more contact with the Việt people in resettlement centers, the lifestyle of this tribe had been many changes. Many of Kaho traditional customs faded steadily due to affecting the majority culture (Dĩ 1972, 48, 50).

11 The Maa (Ma)

The Maa also known as the Châu Mạ, the Mạ, which comprised several subgroups as the To (Cho To), the Ro (Cho Ro), the J Sop (Cho Sop), the Borse, the Tou, the Da Dong, the Wang, the Daa Guy and the Krung (Schrock et al. 1966, 436). According to an announcement of the Saigon government in 1967, the Ma group had about 26.070 inhabitants[97] who mainly resided in a vast territory of western Đồng Nai Thượng Province. In addition, there were scattered Maa villages in Quảng Đức and northern Bình Tuy Provinces. During the 1970s, this ethnicity was only a small tribe. However, in the past, they had established a state of their own, coexisted with the countries Chân Lạp of the Khmer and Chiêm Thành of the Cham (MDEM 1972, 26).

Because of residing near the Đồng Nai River and in steep terrain, the Maa cultivated both wet rice and dry rice. Also, they cropped corn, hunted and fished for an additional food source. The Maa tribal men made wooden canoes, forged iron, gathered clay while their women made pottery, cloth, and baskets (Schrock et al. 1966, 446). The livestock and poultry in Maa families were underdeveloped. They often raised pigs, goats, cows, buffaloes, chickens, and ducks but mostly for sacrificial purposes. They celebrated sacrifices to the gods of the forest and agriculture after harvesting crops, as well as when unfortunate things occurred to their families or villages such as sickness, disease, funeral, natural disaster (Dĩ 1972, 53–54).

12 The Chroo

With estimated inhabitants of 6428[98], the Chroo was also called the Chrau or the Ro. Like other aboriginal groups in the Central Highlands, this minority also comprised several subgroups including the Jro, the Mru, the Butwa, the Hà Giêng and the Chahla, those who scattered over the provinces of Long Khánh, Bình Tuy, Bình Phước and Biên Hòa (MDEM 1972, 27). Economic activities, as

---

97 See Fig. 5.
98 See Fig. 5.

well as customs and traditional culture of the Chroo, were believed to be quite similar to which of the Kaho, though more or less influenced by the Roglai. Due to acculturation with the Việt and mainly resulted from the forced assimilation policy under Ngô Đình Diệm regime, Chroo tribespeople dressed in clothes like the Việt while going out. However, they kept wearing loincloth when they stayed at home.

13 The Stieng

Statistics of the Saigon government showed that the Stieng was the second largest tribal group in SVN with 36.701 people[99]. The Stieng comprised some subgroups such as the Ray, the Tàmun, the Bà-tá and the Dalmer. This ethnicity resided along the border between RVN and Cambodia, from the southwestern province of Quảng Đức to Tây Ninh Province. The most concentrated density belonged to the provinces of Phước Long and Bình Long while a small number lived in the territories of Biên Hòa and Thủ Dầu Một (MDEM 1972, 27).

Stieng's economy was primarily based on dry rice cultivation with the traditional method of slash-and-burn. It also was supplemented by hunting and fishing (Schrock et al. 1966, 767). The characteristic of Stieng people was identified as agile, energetic hospitality but also impatient and belligerent. They had long hair, tied it in a bun at the nape of the neck and inserted into that bun one of the various decorations. In the 1970s, although there had many advances in the cultural life, the Stieng tribespeople still retained some practices adversely affected to their health such as piercing and elongating earlobes, eating raw meat, taking food with bare hands in the meals, (Giang & Ánh 1974, 379–394).

14 The Cua

With a population estimated at 11.562[100], the Cua inhabited in the districts of Trà Bồng, Sơn Hà in Quảng Ngãi Province; in southern Quảng Tín Province; and in northeastern Kontum Province (MDEM 1972, 22). This tribe was one of the least known Montagnard groups in SVN that were also called the Khua, the Cor and the Traw[101]. The Cua had a relatively different appearance from other ethnic groups belonging to the Mon-Khmer speaking group. Their faces tended to be

---

99 See Fig. 5.
100 See Fig. 5.
101 See: *Montagnard Tribal Groups of the Republic of South Vietnam*. P. 55. In: TTU, VC, VA 23970404002.

round, with full cheeks and wide-bridged noses, although long and thin-faced tribesmen were seen (Schrock et al. 1966, 98)&(Dĩ 1972, 21–22).

The livelihood of the Cua was mainly based on dry rice cultivation, with the slash-and-burn method. Nevertheless, there were also a few villages lived along valleys, where rudimentary irrigation systems were used during the rainy season. Also, hunting, gathering and fishing activities were retained to provide the supplemental source of food, especially in crop failure periods.

The Malayo-Polynesian language family

1 The Jarai

The Jarai was a significant minority group that had critical cultural impacts on other tribes in the Central Highlands through the role of the King of Water, and the King of Fire[102]. Numbering approximately 134.538 people[103], this tribe was also known as the Djirai, the Chrérai, and the Jarai. The Jarai had three subgroups such as the Arap, the Hdung and the Tòbuan. The Jarai people resided in the provinces of Pleiku, Phú Bổn, and a small portion lived in the southwest near the provincial center of Kontum; in the northern district of Ealeo, Daclarc Province (MDEM 1972, 28).

Like most of the Highlanders, the Jarai people had a subsistence economy that was based on the slash-and-burn cultivation of dry rice. Together with swidden agriculture, they also engaged in hunting, fishing and a primitive level of trade (Schrock et al. 1966, 257). Although the Jarai people were relatively tempered and traditionally warlike, they were also rustic, gullible and hospitality, in particular with the guests who relatively knew and respected customary laws as well as taboos of the host community (Giang & Ánh 1974, 316–317).

---

102 King of Water and King of Fire were also known with other names Water Lord and Fire Lord. In the Khmer language, they were called Sdet Tik and Sdet Phlong. The Laotian called Sadet Fai and Sadet Nam. Their name in Ede language was Mtao Ea and Mtao Pui. The Việt called them Thủy Xá and Hỏa Xá. The Jarai called Potao Ia and Potao Apui. The two emirates ruled Jarai tribal people in Pleiku Highland from the fifteenth century to the late nineteenth century. By the Nguyễn Dynasty, Nguyễn Emperors set up a closer relationship with the Highlands by establishing the diplomatic protocol with the two Jarai emirs. However, it is worth understanding that King of Water and King of Fire just were tribal leaders, who held spiritual power by owning a sacred object in agricultural religion which was a magic sword. Entirely different from other Kings, they had neither strong militaries nor secular forces (Dournes. J. 2013)&(Giang and Ánh 1974, 150)&(Maitre 2008, 179–80).

103 See Fig. 5.

2 The Hroi[104]

Numbering approximately 7.633[105], the Hroi inhabited in upland regions of Phú Yên Province, Western Phú Bổn Province and, in the district of Buôn Hồ, Dak Lak (Darlac) Province. This tribe also called M'Dhur or M'Thur. The language of the Hroi people was dramatically influenced by the Jarai and the Rhade (MDEM 1972, 29).

Like many other aboriginal groups in SVN, the Hroi earned for living by dry rice cultivation with the slash-and-burn technique. Their livelihood was supplemented by hunting, fishing, vegetable gardens and basket weaving. The Hroi dwelled in small villages, where every five to seven families lived together. The most significant community had merely twenty families. Each Hroi village was a little autonomous society, which all villagers followed matriarchy but a respectable man always held community political authority.

The Hroi tribespeople's nature was meek and rustic. Tribal men were often garbed in loincloths with bare-chested while women like wearing long-necked white dresses and jewelry made of silver or copper (Schrock et al. 1966, 217–256).

3 The Rhade

The Rahde was also called Edé (Ê Đê), was one of four largest minority ethnic groups in the Central Highlands. With a population estimated at 83.740[106], this tribe composed of subgroups such as the Tring, the Adham, the Dlié Rué, the Édé, the Krung and the Bih. Most of Rahde tribespeople lived in the province of Darlac, the few remaining scattered in Khánh Dương (M'Drack) District, Khánh Hòa Province; in the southern area of Pleiku Province; Phú Bổn Province; and northern Tuyên Đức Province (MDEM 1972, 30).

The Rahde economy was primarily based on swidden cultivation, excepting the Bih people, those who planted wet rice following a primitive style. Their farming technique was entirely unconventional because it used buffaloes to trample the land instead of plowing. Also, their livelihood was supplemented by animal farming, hunting, gathering, fishing, knitting, and weaving. On upland fields, outside the main crop as rice, the Rahde tribesmen cultivated corn, potato, gourd, tobacco, squash, onion, pepper, cotton as well. The characteristic of Rahde

---

104 In the official list of ethnic groups in Vietnam announced in 1979 (see Fig. 4), the Hroi is classified as a local group of the Cham.
105 See Fig. 5.
106 See Fig. 5.

agriculture was rotational cultivation. This meant, besides arable lands, some other fallow fields were forsaken intentionally to restore soil's fertility[107].

The Rahde people were regarded as honest, uncomplaining in desperate circumstances, hardworking and enthusiastic in their work. However, they also tended to be excitable to rebel against oppression. The active participation of Rahde tribesmen in BAJARAKA Movement and FULRO uprising during the 1950s and 1960s was vivid evidence for this claim (Dĩ 1972, 74–77).

4 The Churu

The Churu resided mainly in the district of Đơn Dươngg, Tuyên Đức Province. Some scattered villages could be found in northwestern areas of Ninh Thuận Province. With a population of about 4.998[108], their oral language was similar to that of the Roglai, Rahde and Jarai people. However, due to resided nearby the Kaho people's territory and had cultural exchanges with them for generations, one portion of the Churu spoke Kaho language that belonged to Mon-Khmer speaking branch (MDEM 1972, 31). The Churu was also known as the Cru, the Cado, the Kơdu, the P'nông chàm.

The Churu had the sedentary livelihood that was based on their traditional agriculture. They cultivated both muddy and dry fields. The irrigation system was built carefully with ditches, dikes, dams and so on. Livestock and poultry breeding were widespread in most household. Furthermore, hunting, gathering, and fishing were also maintained as part of daily life supplementation. Traditional handicrafts were relatively well-developed, including textile weaving, plaiting and making somewhat coarse pottery.

In Churu society, the matriarchal social structure, where women assumed the more prominent role in the families and were inheritors, was dominant. Children there were named after their mother's line.

The Churu people favored metaphor style in communication, even in small talks, they also using rhyme. They were considered as smart, agile and more advanced than other aboriginal groups in Central Highlands (Dĩ 1972, 81–84).

5 The Roglai

The Roglai resided along the upland from the district of Diên Khánh, Khánh Hòa Province to the province of Bình Thuận; and an area of between the provinces

---

107 See: Summary Report, USOM - The Rhadé Tribe One of the Longer Group of Montagnard in the High Plateau of South Vietnam. In: TTU, VC, VA 0880204002.

108 See Fig. 5.

of Ninh Thuận and Bình Thuận surrounded by the traditional territory of the Cham. With a population of approximately 30.809[109], this tribe was also known as the Agglai, the Raglai, the Tring, the Sré and so on (MDEM 1972, 31).

In the distant past, the Roglai was often referred to as a nomadic ethnic group, but in fact, their economy was based on rotational swidden cultivation[110]. Dry rice and corn were their primary grain sources. Due to the process of long-term cultural interchange with the Cham, this ethnic group learned the technique of wet rice farming. Along with agricultural products, hunting, gathering activities and traditional craft like forging, knitting also played a significant role in the livelihood of most Churu Roglai household.

As the result of frequent acculturation with the Cham, a more civilized community, the Roglai manners were greatly affected. Overall, the Roglai tribesmen were very hospitable, especially with those who understood and complied with their taboos (Schrock et al. 1966, 579–580).

In short, as mentioned earlier, this is only an overview of the nineteen indigenous groups those who lived in the Central Highlands during the Vietnam War. By indicating some critical features of each group, this section could be possibly helpful for researchers who are new in the field of ethnic minorities in Vietnam.

---

109 See Fig. 5.
110 In this type of planting, new fields were cleared, farmed for several years and then left to lie fallow for a period of between ten and twenty years before being brought back into cultivation (Jones et al. 2002, 14).

III French Domination Strategies in the Central Highlands

Research materials point out that except for the Tây Sơn, all most Vietnamese feudal dynasties tended to be interested in the coastal plains while having a hesitant attitude towards the hinterlands. In nominal terms, before France established its colonial regime in Indochina, the Central Highlands was placed in the custody of the Nguyễn. However, the interaction between the central government and the tribes there was relatively loose, even after the establishment of the Sơn Phòng Trấn[111] (Defense systems against the infiltration of minorities). Until the late nineteenth century, there were very few Việt people living in the hinterlands and the Nguyễn court merely put there some postal stations and military posts. Though tributary relations were being maintained over centuries, the dependence between the highland Kings of Water and Fire and the Nguyễn mainly existed in nominal (Salemink 2002, 6).

Since the seventeenth century, long before the French-Spanish alliance opened fire on Sơn Trà estuary in Đà Nẵng (Tourane) in 1858, Western missionaries had known the Montagnard community, especially after the born of Missions Étrangères de Paris (MEP) in 1658. It is evident that the appearance of Catholic clergy changed the power relations among the ethnic groups in the hinterland. Together with missionaries, the discoveries of French explorers gradually unveiled a lot of mystery in the mountains of Indochina.

In order to prepare for the "pacification" of the mountainous areas in Indochina, in 1880 Governor Le Myre de Vilers set out the first highland affairs policies. Due to a keen opposition of indigenous peoples, the French domination strategies were subsequently adjusted for several times. Of these, most notably were the ethnic policies of Pierre Marie Antoine Pasquier in 1923 and Georges Thierry d'Argenlieu which was born in the context of decolonization in Vietnam after the August Revolution of 1945. Despite last efforts of France in maintaining its colonial power in the minority regions of Vietnam, until very end of the first Indochina War of 1954, most objectives of the socio-economic development programs for the Montagnards had not been fully achieved.

---

111 Sơn Phòng Trấn was an administrative unit formed by the Nguyễn Lords, which ran along the Trường Sơn range and consisted mountainous districts of five provinces from Quảng Nam to Bình Thuận.

3.1 The Ethnic Policies in Pre-colonial Times

As mentioned above, the majority of the ethnic minorities in southern Vietnam inhabited in the western highlands, where the Việt considered abode of evil spirits and poisoned water. The tribal groups such as Sédang, Bahnar, and Jarai had been given no attention until their tributary relation to Xứ Đàng Trong[112] of Nguyễn Lords was established in 1558 (Dournes 2013, 28)[113]. During earlier centuries, after raiding on Cham forces in the Highlands, Kings of Đại Việt always quickly withdrew their army without setting garrison or ruler system. Perhaps for this reason, the feudal dynasties left very few archival documents about the Montagnards.

According to ethnographers, the earliest records on the Highlanders discovered so far are inscriptions of the Cham, dating back over 1000 years. This source reveals that the King of Champa Jaya Harivarman I defeated tribes in the western mountains as Rhade, Mada (probably Mdhur) and others that the Cham collectively called "Kiratas" in 1160 (Maitre 2008, 188). Although once thought to be a powerful kingdom, after several attacks by the Đại Việt feudal dynasties as Lê Đại Hành in 982, Lý Thánh Tông in 1069, Hồ Quý Ly in 1402 and especially Lê Thánh Tông in 1471[114] (Liên et al. 2001, 469)[115], Champa steadily weakened

---

112 Xứ Đàng Trong was also known as Cochinchine, Cochin Chin, Caupchy, Canglan, was a portion of the territory of Đại Việt (Great Vietnam) controlled by Nguyễn Lords, where was determined from the Gianh River of Quảng Bình Province southwards.

113 Regarding the starting point of tributary relation between the Nguyễn and the two Highlander Kings (King of Water and King of Fire), Hickey was sensible to assume that the year1558 were too early. At that time (1558), Nguyễn Hoàng was newly appointed as governor of Thuận Hóa in a situation of being knocked out of the Thăng Long administration. Therefore, he could not have an enough strong military force to win the tribal groups. Also, there was no Nguyễn court until the eighth lord of Nguyễn, Võ Vương (Nguyễn Phúc Khoát) assumed power in 1738 and then nominated himself as King in 1744. During 1558–1774 the Nguyễn Lords remained to recognize the Lê-Trịnh sovereignty of the Thăng Long court over Xứ Đàng Trong (Hickey 1982, 158–9).

114 See Po Dharma. *Ts. Po Dharma nói gì về lịch sử Champa trong ngày đại hội 2015 (The speech of Dr. Po Dharma on the Champa history on the 2015 convention).* Sources: http://champaka.info/index.php/quandiem/quandiemlichsu/1246-quan. (Accessed 14th August 2017).

115 Ibid. *"On January 7 of the Tân Mão year (1471), the king led himself by more than 1.000 boats, more than 700.000 men to two seaports Tân Áp and Cựu Tọa, raised the flag of heaven… On March 1, defeated Chà Bàn capital citadel, caught more than 30.000 people, cut more than 4.000 heads, captured King Trà Toàn and retreated"* (Liên et al. 2001, 469). About 700.000 Đại Việt troops, the translation notes: *"Translated literally,*

and its realm gradually shrunk southwards. Ultimately, in 1692 King of Champa named Bà Tranh made his highest attempt to recover territory by putting all Cham forces to attack Diên Khánh Citadel (Khánh Hòa), but was abortive. The Cham later suffered heavy losses, Bà Tranh was captured in 1693, the entire royal family fled to Cambodia or arrested. Lord Nguyễn renamed the Champa territory to Thuận Phủ, forced the former royal Cham to used clothes as the Việt. Over the next year, Thuận Phủ was changed to Thuận Thành. In the year Đinh Sửu (1697) Lord Nguyễn set Bình Thuận province, the Champa Kingdom terminated its existence as a nation (Kim 1950, 136)&(Khoang 1969, 392–3)&(Trình 2007b, 19–20)&(Ninh 2004, 220). Since then, all tribal groups who were being ruled by Cham became dependent on Nguyễn Lords. The Việt contact with Highlanders took place for the most part on two levels. First, there was the level of the Việt settlers and traders who penetrated the valleys and in particular cases the higher elevations adjacent to the coastal plain where the Montagnards lived. Then there was the level of the Việt civil-military administration that was always organized in newly gained territories and had as one of its goals strict control over any contact between Việt and Highlanders.

In Vietnamese official documents, the designation for expansion of Đại Việt territory to the south was called the process of advance southward (Vietnamese: Nam tiến). Since 1780, traditional realm of the Khmer in the Mekong River Delta was also under control of the court of Phú Xuân, which later became the capital city of Huế (since 1802). According to the Đại Việt feudal historians, by the tenth century since regaining independence from the Chinese rulers, the Việt people ought to quickly expand their territory southward to meet the demand of the development of paddy agriculture and the concomitant increase in population. With a disadvantaged terrain: the North was adjacent to the unfriendly neighbor China; forests and mountains limited the West; while the East Sea blocked the East, advance southward was regarded as the only way to expand the territory of the Việt people.

After being appointed as Admiral General (First Governor) of military-administration of Quảng Nam (Vietnamese: Bắc quân đô đốc Phủ chưởng phủ sự) by King Lê Trang Tông in 1546, Bùi Tá Hán set up military posts and bulwarks in the western areas of Quảng Nam, Quảng Ngãi. This action not only aimed at self-defense against attacks of Mọi Đá Vách (the ethnic minorities living in west Quảng Ngãi) but created favorable conditions for a stable trade

---

this number is probably not accurate." Regarding that event, historian Trần Trọng Kim recorded that King Lê Thánh Tông led 200.000 troops (Kim 1950, 101).

between the Lowlanders and the Uplanders. To establish an initial administration for the minorities in his realm of governing, Hán created four subdistricts (Vietnamese: Nguyên) including Cù Bà, Đà Bồng, Cự Đà, and Ba Tơ in the mountainous interior of Chương Nghĩa and Mộ Đức Districts. Hán also appointed native chiefs as heads of these subdistricts. Payment tax on these areas was set but mostly in kind[116] (Cung and Tấn 1998, 50, 60–61)&(Vũ 2008)&(Thị 1996, 23–25)&(Maitre 2008, 197). This policy of local authority, however, exclusively affected buffer zones between coastal plains and western uplands. Practically, during the Lê regime, the central court had no significant ties with ethnic minorities in the Central Highlands.

It is commonly acknowledged that the policies towards ethnic minorities of feudal families as Lý, Trần, Hồ, and Lê could be summed up in the two highlights: granted the privilege for local chiefs in mountainous and bordered areas (Vietnamese: Nhu viễn), but severely punished disobedient ones. Namely, the central government usually sought to bind leaders of hilly and frontier minorities (especially northern boundary) by intermarriage relation with the royal members as well as granting them title and money. In appreciation, these local leaders would have to swear allegiance to the King and willing to sacrifice to defend national territory.

Since the Nguyễn era, the state continued establishing and maintaining diplomatic relationships with the Kings of Fire and Water, whom they considered as their vassals. However, the Nguyễn Lords discouraged any connection between the Vietnamese and Highlanders. This policy latter was legalized when Nguyễn Ánh unified the whole country. Article 16, Volume 7 (State Laws on Marriage) of the Gia Long Code[117] determined that any Việt individuals who contracted marriage with a member "of savage ethnicities" could be sentenced to one hundred blows by a rod[118] (Thành et al. 1994, 350). This restriction, nevertheless, did not apply to the military personnel who kept security for the frontier and the trading agents who conducted commercial relations with the Highlanders.

---

116 According to Maitre, the payment tax and fees that the four subdistricts had to contribute to the central court were 1470 piasters annually, of which Cù Bà 370 piasters, Đà Bồng 600 piasters, Cự Đà 140 piasters, and Ba Tơ 360 piasters, respectively (Maitre 2008, 198).
117 Gia Long Code was the official Vietnamese law code of the Nguyễn Dynasty issued by King Gia Long (Nguyễn Ánh) in 1815.
118 This draconian perhaps derived from the fact that the tribal groups had earlier supported strongly for the Tây Sơn movement against Nguyễn Ánh.

With respect to the relation between the Nguyễn Lords and the two Kings of the Jarai people, Annals of Nguyễn Dynasty records that since 1751[119]Thủy Xá and Hỏa Xá (Kings of Water and Fire, respectively) initiated tributary relations with Nguyễn Lords in Phú Xuân. In return, the two emirates were also rewarded regularly by the Phú Xuân court. Lê Quý Đôn had noted this issue in his publication named Phủ Biên Tạp Lục[120] (Frontier Chronicles). According to Đôn, every five years Nguyễn Lords dispatched officers of Phú Yên Province as chief and deputy envoy to the basin of Ba River to visit the Emirates whom they would give brocade coat, crown, copper pot, iron buckle, porcelain, bowls, plates and at the same time demanding paid tribute and taxes (Đôn 1972, 213–214). Researchers at Vietnam National Historical Institute added that the vassal convention was kept faithfully until 1841 when the Montagnards rebelled against King Thiệu Trị, excepting a disruptive period during the Tây Sơn Uprising[121] (Maitre 2008, 200). And, after Nguyễn Ánh assumed the throne in 1802, the frequency of tribute shortened from every five years to every three years[122] (Institute of History 1962, 172). The issue was also implemented by Nghiêm Thẩm, a renowned anthropologist in the South. According to Thẩm, until 1868 by the fortieth birthday of King Tự Đức, the Kings of Water and Fire still sent gifts and ivories to Phú Yên. And, the Nguyễn Emperor also instructed local officials to receive. According to Nghiêm Thẩm, the tributary relation only finished in 1883, after the death

---

119 See more in: Nghiêm Thẩm, *Tìm hiểu đồng bào Thượng (Understanding the Montagnard compatriots)*, Quê hương, No. 31 (1962), p. 137.
120 The volume consisted of eight books divided into two parts, in which Lê Quý Đôn recorded most valuable information about economy and society of Cochin - Southern of Đại Việt (Xứ Đàng Trong) in nearly 200 years, from the late sixteenth century to the year 1776.
121 The Tây Sơn peasant movement (also known as the Tây Sơn uprising) is a peasant rebellion and decentralized dynasties of the figurehead Later Lê (Lê Sơ) Dynasty and the two rival feudal families holding real political power were Trịnh Lords in Tonkin (Đàng Ngoài) and Nguyễn Lords in Cochin - Southern (Đàng Trong) between 1771 and 1802 (Dutton 2006, 1–2).
122 In essence, the relationship between the Nguyễn Lords (or later Nguyễn Emperors) and the Kings of Water and Fire was as the same as the system of suzerainty (upper-sovereign) in Europe. The term suzerainty was first used to refer to the dominant position of the Ottoman Empire about its surrounding regions. In that case, the Ottoman Empire was the dominator, and the relationship was suzerainty. The term then is used commonly to refer to any link in which one region or person controls the foreign policy and international relations of a tributary state while allowing the tributary nation to have internal autonomy.

of King Tự Đức and Vietnam lost its independence to the French (Thẩm 1962, 147–8).

Belonged to the Đại Việt feudal orbit but the Tây Sơn's policies towards ethnic minority groups was unlike other dynasties' one. The Tây Sơn movement arose in 1771 in the northern mountainous area of An Khê[123] (Dutton 2006, 1), where the majority of residents were Bahnar and Sédang peoples. Shortly after launching the uprising, Nguyễn Nhạc, the supreme leader of the peasant movement and his wife named Ya Đố[124], quickly formed a coalition with leaders of Sédang, Bahnar, Jarai in Cheo Reo, Pleiku, Kontum and the Hre in western Quảng Ngãi (Quang 2006, 197). The Central Highlands not only became the insurgent army's base but also supplied food and foodstuff as well as sources of militant recruitment. Historical sources pointed out that the Tây Sơn's Montagnard followers increased significantly after Nguyễn Nhạc declared to establish his dynasty in 1778; notably, the cavalry unit of 2.000 outstanding soldiers in the army of Nguyễn Huệ[125] (Quang 2006, 197–198). In the Kỷ Dậu military operations (1789) to expel the invasive Qing (Chinese), the Tượng Binh unit (Elephantry)[126] of the Highlanders always served as the pioneering force. Apart from the tribal groups, historical documents of Nguyễn Dynasty also mentioned to a queen of the Cham named Thị Hỏa in Phú Yên, another Cham officer in Bình Thuận and the two Chinese traders called Lí Tài, Tập Đình, those who volunteering supported the Tây Sơn movement (Dutton 2006, 5)&(Quang 2006, 171)&(Li 1998). Additionally, according to Murray, Nguyễn Huệ was also the second man, after Zheng Chenggong[127], who could conquer and use entire force of pirates in southern China in his mighty army (Murray 1987).

Regarding the reason why the Tây Sơn movement would attract a vast number of followers[128], Nguyễn Phan Quang claimed that it was because the Tây Sơn brothers promptly announced and implemented populist policies. When the

---

123 An Khê currently belongs to Gia Lai Province.
124 A daughter of a Bahnar local chief.
125 Nguyễn Huệ was Nhạc's younger brother, born in Bình Định a central province of Đại Việt in 1753 and died in Phú Xuân in 1792. He was regarded as one of the most successful military commanders in Vietnam's history.
126 A military unit with warriors who ride war elephants while going to battlefields
127 Zheng Chenggong is known as one of the most loyalists of the Ming Dynasty who resisted the Qing conquering of China in the seventeenth century. He led a struggle against the Qing regime in China's southeastern coastal areas for 16 rest years of his life.
128 In the early phase of the uprising, most of the followers were tribesmen.

Nguyễn Lords government dramatically weaken due to its poor leadership, internal contradictions together with cumbersome and overlapping taxation policy, the uprising was, therefore, considered as a new hope which could help Great Vietnam get rid of the turmoil condition (Quang 2006, 162–167)&(Dutton 2004)[129].

3.2 French Domination Strategies in the Central Highlands

3.2.1 Primal Contacts between Westerners and Ethnic Minorities

In the late sixteenth and early seventeenth centuries, merchants from Western countries like Portugal, England, France, and Asian countries like Japan began to establish commercial relationships with Vietnam to exchange goods and military hardware. At that time, Catholicism also launched large-scale evangelism around the world, including the Far East of Asia. *Khâm định Việt sử Thông giám Cương mục* is a collection of the history of the Nguyễn Dynasty, compiled under the reign of King Tự Đức. According to this account, since 1533, Catholicism was first transmitted "sneakily" at the villages of Ninh Cường and Quần Anh, Nam Chân District and the village of Trà Lũ, Giao Thủy District (Nam Định Province) by a Western missionary named I-ni-khu (National Historiographer's Office of Nguyễn Dynasty 2001, 720). Despite many difficulties and challenges[130], the number of Catholic followers increased continuously, some large parishes were established; especially since the born of Missions Étrangères de Paris (MEP) in 1658, and was accepted in 1664 by Pope Alexander VII (Hồng 1959).

In 1802, Nguyễn Phúc Ánh (King Gia Long, reigned: 1802–1820), the first Emperor of the Nguyễn Dynasty, took the throne. To express his gratitude to Bishop Pigneau de Behaine[131] (also known as Bá Đa Lộc), Gia Long generously allowed Catholicism to spread in his country. However, since the reign of King Minh Mạng (reigned: 1820–1841) onward, the Catholicism was banned stringently. The missionaries, therefore, had to move to the Highlands for refuging and also for seeking to spread the faith in God in the minority regions. The

---

129 According to Georges Dutton, the favorable view of the Tây Sơn movement and regime could be both the product of the antipathy that the people had towards the Nguyễn Lords and the actual collective memory of the Tây Sơn.
130 Such as differences in languages; the precaution of the government system of Great Vietnam; and stiff resistance from the indigenous folk beliefs and religions originated from India and China those spread in this country for centuries.
131 Pigneau de Behaine was a French missionary who support Nguyễn Ánh actively to regain power from the Tây Sơn in the late eighteenth century (Khoang 1961, 55–73).

intrusion of the French and later the Việt into the hinterland is the premise of the cooperation or opposition of the Montagnards.

In fact, far long before the Nguyễn Emperors issued banning edicts on Catholicism, since the seventeenth century Western missionaries had known the Montagnard community. In a memoir written in 1621, missionary Cristophoro Borri collectively called minority groups dwelling in the north of Cochinchina as Kemoy (Vietnamese: Kẻ Mọi)[132]. The documentaries on mission history in Vietnam reveal that Father Marini Romain first mentioned about the Kings of Water and Fire in 1646; Father Alexandre de Rhodes affirmed the Rumoi Country (or the Forests of the Savages) (Vietnamese: Rú Mọi) located between Laos and Annam in 1651. In 1790, Father João de Loureira published the book *De nigris Moi et Champanensibus (About the Dark Moi and Champa People)* in Lisbon. Also during this time, Father De La Bissachère traveled along the Mekong to the north and explored the tribal groups living along the river's banks. In 1765, Father Pigues went to the upstream of Prek Chlong River (Cambodia). After contacting with the minorities such as Stieng, Proue, Queraie, Penong, etc., he returned to the coastal plain and never came back again. In 1770, Father Juguet went to Prek Chlong to preach to the Stieng and died of exhaustion, etc. At the early nineteenth century, although the knowledge of the missionaries on the Central Highlands was increasing, the effectiveness of evangelism remained very modest (Maitre 2008, 212–215)&(Lam, Cadière, & Tố 1944)&(Hồng 1959)&(Salemink 2002, 6).

During the reign of Emperor Tự Đức (Reigned: October 5th, 1847–July 19th, 1883), when the religious persecution became intense in the plains, the clergy's effort in finding a way to the plateau revitalized[133]. In Cochinchine, in 1857, Bishop Lefèbvre sent a man to the Stieng's living space (north-west of Gia Định) to seek shelter. In 1861, priest Azémar founded the Brơlam monastery (Bình Long) that would be burned down by Pou Kombo (a Khmer French-resisted leader) in 1867. After escaping the persecution in Phan Rang in 1865, Father Vuillaume ran to the Di Linh Plateau to live with the Maa and Sré (Lam, Cadière, & Tố 1944)&(Hồng 1959).

---

132 See more in: Cristophoro Borri, Translated by Hồng Nhuệ, Nguyễn Khắc Xuyên, & Nguyễn Nghị (2017). *Xứ đàng trong năm 1621 (The Cochinchine in 1621)*.

133 In 1854 the authorities in Bình Định ordered the administrative and military officers in the Highlands to capture all the clergy. However, none of the Montagnards served as the guide, they even deliberately misled. As a result, the troops sent had to give up and retreat after being starved in the forest (Giang & Ánh 1974, 102).

The discovery of the Central Highlands and Montagnards would only be scaled up since the mid nineteenth century. In 1848, the bishop of the eastern Cochinchine diocese (Quy Nhơn), Etienne Théodore Cuénot, sent Nguyễn Do, a Vietnamese follower, from Trạm Gò to the territory of the Jarai in An Khê. In 1850, Nguyễn Do led four French missionaries (Combes, Fontaine, Dourisboure, and Besombes) to the residence of the Bahnar, Rengao, and Sédang. Upon returning to the plains, each priest drew maps and detailed notes of the contacted ethnic groups' custom. Two years after its establishment, in 1851 the Kontum mission developed a solid base in four villages near the confluence of the Bla and Poco Rivers (Giang & Ánh 1974, 100–101).

As described by missionaries, during the mid-nineteenth century the Sédang, Jarai, and Stieng were "very aggressive". These tribes often captured the Rengao Bahnar, Sédang Halang, and Mnong Bhiet who later would be sold to Siamese and Laotians as slavery (Maitre 2008, 245). In 1862, when smallpox raged, Montagnard shamans concluded that the Church was causes of Jang's (the gods) wrath and punishment. These shamans, therefore, incited a rebellion to expel the clergy. As a consequence, about 400 Sédang tribesmen from the north Kontum moved down to attack the Bahnar Catholic villages. Similarly, in 1871, a flock of locusts devastated most of the Highlanders' crops, causing widespread famine. The chiefs of Jarai and Sédang urged their people to burn Bahnar Catholic villages. Before that permanent threat, French missionaries helped the Bahnar to establish an armed self-defense force of 1.200 men in 1883[134].

It can be said that the appearance of Catholic clergy changed the power relations among the ethnic groups in the Central Highlands. And, the impact of Christian mission was an ambivalent one: on the one hand modernization, on the other hand, control. Bahnar people, who had been victims of the Jarai and Sédang, could defend themselves efficiently. Also, the Việt missionaries taught the Bahnar intensive farming techniques and raise livestock. This tribe, therefore, became an influential group. The slavery since then has no longer been mentioned in the Central Highlands (Giang & Ánh 1974, 103).

---

134 Nguyễn Văn Huy. *Cộng đồng người Thượng trên cao nguyên miền Trung (The Montagnard community in the Central Highlands)*. Sources: https://nghiencuulichsu.com/2016/08/31/cong-dong-nguoi-thuong-tren-cao-nguyen-mien-trung/ (Accessed 26th February 2018).

3.2.2 French Surveys in the Central Highlands

Together with missionaries, the discoveries of French explorers gradually unveiled a lot of mystery in mountains of Indochina where had earlier been considered "land of evil spirit forests and poisoned water" (Vietnamese: rừng thiêng nước độc). During voyages, explorers also found abundant natural resources neglected in the Central Highlands. The adventurers' reports were an essential basis for Governor General of Indochina (French: Gouverneur-général de l'Indochine française), Paul Doumer, building program colonial exploitation in the late nineteenth century, and other socio-economic programs later deployed in the Highlands.

After France occupied Cochinchine, Governor Le Myre de Vilers ordered Lieutenant Amédée Gautier to investigate the northeastern border of this country. In 1881, Gautier departed from Trị An waterfall, going upstream Đồng Nai river. After a long journey, according to the guide's direction, he stopped to survey the Stieng people in Bù Đăng in the basin of Da Glun River (a tributary of the Bé River) (Giang & Ánh 1974, 124–128).

In preparation for fighting against troubles caused by Siam in the bordering areas between Vietnam-China, and Vietnam-Cambodia, Auguste Pavie was tasked to conduct geological and military surveillance and map Indochina. In years 1890, 1891, under the charge of Pavie, two survey teams whose responsibility was examining the Central Highlands were formed. The first team consisted of two captains, De Malglaive and Tunnelet Faber, who were assigned to investigate Sébang-biên area. The other, which included Captains Cupet and Cogniard, Lieutenant Dugast, and Inspector Garnier, would survey the region from Pleiku to Kontum (Giang & Ánh 1974, 124–128).

In July 1890, Dr. Alexandre Yersin planned a road trip from Nha Trang to the Highlands, then back to Saigon. Could not find any guide in Nha Trang, he went to Phan Rí (Bình Thuận Province), where he later was led to Di Linh. After returning to Nha Trang, in April 1892, he again organized another trip from Nha Trang to Stung Treng (Cambodia). This journey lasted three months, along with the route: Nha Trang-Ninh Hòa-M'drao-M'Siao-Bandon-Long Path-Stung Ttreng. In March 1893, one more time, Doctor Alexandre Yersin organized an observation trip from Nha Trang to Phan Thiết. On June 21st of the same year, he reached the Langbian Highlands and was much attracted by the terrain, landscape, and climate of there. Based on this finding, in 1899 he advised Governor General Doumer to choose Đà Lạt as a convalescent center for French military and administrative officers in southern Indochina (Giang & Ánh 1974, 124–128).

In 1904 inspector Prosper D'Odend'hal, who had earlier joined Pavie's expedition, left Phan Rang for Langbian and Darlac. On the way, D'Odend'hal stopped at Cheo Reo to contact with King of Fire (named Oi Ât), who welcomed him very warmly. However, due to his illness, the investigators refused the host's offer to drink wine and eat chicken. Also, he insisted on seeing the sacred saber which should be only seen by "the King."[135] These gestures created a hostile suspicion for the French inspector. The incident was even more severe when Odend'hal sent a letter to the chief of the Cheo Reo military garrison. Assuming it was a request for reinforcements to harm his community, King of Fire ordered his subordinates to kill the explorer on April 7th, 1904 (Dournes 2013, 32–33).

Last but not least, the explorer Henri Maitre who surveyed Buôn Mê Thuột and the surrounding plateaus within three years to write the book *Les Régions Mọi du Sud Indochinois*, and later *Les Jungles Mọi*. Besides the role of an adventurer, the writer Maitre was also a ruler. Because of this role, in August 1914 he was ambushed and killed by Nơ Trang Lơng, a well-known Mnong chief, to revenge for his wife and children, who had been murdered by soldiers stationed in Bou Sra Pou (a Maitre-created garrison) (Maitre 2008, 547)&(Giang & Ánh 1974, 124–128)&(Lâm et al. 2000, 206).

3.2.3 The Transformation of the French Domination Strategies from Colonization to Decolonization Era

The domination strategies in early colonial times

In order to prepare for the pacification of the mountainous areas in Indochina, in 1880 Governor Le Myre de Vilers set out the first highland affairs policies including three main contents:

1. Survey the terrain and traditional customs in the areas of revolt or prepared occupation.
2. Build one or more military posts to influence and set up an administrative representation to govern each area.
3. Find the areas where people are willing to cooperate, use friendly measures to attract them, avoid using forceful actions (Giang & Ánh 1974, 128–129).

These domination strategies were implemented within the years 1881 and 1885 but did not produce meaningful results. Aggressive tribes like the Stieng always

---

135 The Jarai people believed that their whole community would be punished by gods if anyone, except "the King" saw the sacred saber.

fought back, while more gentle ones like the Maa were trying to avoid the rulers. Also, during this period, anti-French activities continued to break out, so the Montagnards generally refused to cooperate with the protectorate government.

Under the pretext that Trường Sơn (Long Mountain) had been the resistance base of Sơn Phòng of Cần Vương insurgent army the French forced the Huế royal court to sign a decree in 1888. According to this ordinance, foreigners in Annam with permanent residence status had the right to own and to transfer estates[136] over the Long Mountain range without payment or only a token amount. Eleven years later, in a decree issued on 28th April 1899, the Huế court agreed to hand over the right to grant land title to the French colonial government (Khoang 1961, 409)&(Hickey 1982b, 274). October 16th the same year, the French compelled King Đồng Khánh (reigned: 1885–1889) to sign a proclamation giving them the full right to organize the colonial administrative system and directly ruled ethnic minorities in the Central Highlands[137] (Chi 2006, 401–449)&(Giang & Ánh 1974, 132).

Also during that period, King of Siam, after controlling southern Laos, began claiming some of the lands near the Central Highlands those held by the French. In this context, a French-Corsican named Charles-Marie David de Mayréna proposed for permission to go exploring the Central Highlands in an attempt to reach the ethnic minorities, and finally gained the approval of Governor-General of Indochina, Ernest Constans in 1888. Thanks to skills of shooting, fencing, and rhetorical, some villages offered Mayréna to serve as village head during his stay in Kontum. With the help of Catholic clergies such as Pierre Irigoyen (1856–1935) and Jean Baptiste Guerlach (1858–1912), he convinced the Bahnar and Sédang people that they could separate to form an independent kingdom. As a result, on 3rd June 1888, the Kingdom of Sédang (French: Royaume des Sédangs) was born with its own national flag, banknote, and legal regulations; Mayréna made herself as the First King Marie of the Sédang (French: Marie Premier, Roi des Sédangs).

In order to regain control of the Central Highlands, on the occasion of Mayréna's return to Europe to ask for aid from the Western powers, the French government sent F. Guiomar (1889–1890), provincial résident of Quy Nhơn

---

136 As a result of this law; many plantations were put up. For example, paddy fields and sugar cane estates of Borel and Richardson in An Diệm; paddy fields and cinnamon farms organized by two French brothers in Trà My; coffee and rubber estates named Delignon-Paris in An Khê; or a rice and tobacco farm near Quy Nhơn, etc.

137 See more in: Dương Kinh Quốc (2006). *Việt Nam những sự kiện lịch sử 1958–1918 (Vietnam Historical Events 1958–1918)*. Education Publishing House. Hà Nội.

(Vietnamese: Công sứ Quy Nhơn), to take over the Kingdom of Sédang. After returning to Europe to seek aid for his kingdom Mayréna was banned from entering Indochina by the French government. His death shortly after that put an end to his power adventure in the Montagnard region. The Kingdom of Sédang was dissolved, and the Central Highlands since 1889 was placed under the administration of Quy Nhơn provincial résident (Chi 2006, 401–449)[138].

Make the best use of regulatory regime transformation, the French résident superior[139] deposed Việt agents, who had been serving as intermediaries in the operating trade but were alleged to abuse the credulity of the Highlanders. Henceforth, the French provincial officers[140] directly handled with the local communities (Nứr 1966, 74–75). They only retained some of Việt agents as translators in complex negotiations. To promote commercial activities between Highlanders and Lowlanders, some markets were planned to establish and would be placed under the supervision of representatives of provincial résident (Hickey 1982b, 274).

In the early twentieth century, France consistently established military posts and administrative offices to govern ethnic minority areas. In 1900 An Lão station was built. In the following year, France set up an executive office in Trà My, a military post at Ba Tơ, then in Lang Ri, Minh Long, Nước Vong to control the Montagnards. In 1904, M'drac administrative posts were set up in Ninh Hòa to rule the minorities in Khánh Hòa Province. In 1905 Sơn Phòng Trấn, the

---

138 See also Jean Marquet. *Un aventurier du XIXè siècle: Marie 1er, roi des Sédangs (1888–1890)*. BAVH, vol 14, nos 1–2 (1–6/1927). Pp. 1–13.
139 Résident of Supérieur de l'Annam (Vietnamese: Khâm sứ Trung kỳ) was an official representative of the French protectorate government in Annam under French colonial. Nominally, this officer had no internal political power, but he ruled Annam in practice. Résident of Supérieur de l'Annam even had the right to approve all the edicts of Nguyễn Emperors.
140 Since 1897, to implement the policy of "Divide and rule," the French established the Federation of French Indochina, dividing Vietnam into three territorial parts with different political systems. Of those, Tonkin (Vietnamese: Bắc kỳ) demarcated from Ninh Bình Province to north, was put under the French protectorate; Annam (Vietnamese: Trung kỳ) determined from Thanh Hóa to Bình Thuận Province, was placed under the French semi-colonial regime; Cochinchine (Vietnamese: Nam kỳ) stretched from Đồng Nai to Hà Tiên Province, was separated to be a French colony. Excepting the colonial Cochinchine, where governance principle applied like a French province. In Tonkin and Annam, the French took power only from provincial level upwards; the local administrative system in the meantime was still under the management of Nguyễn Dynasty (Khánh 1999, 12).

defense systems against the infiltration of minorities were officially abolished (Giang & Ánh 1974, 132–133). In areas, where the pacification had achieved considerable success, the colonizers transformed military-administrative posts into civil-administrative ones.

The colonial socio-economic policies in the Central Highlands

Aimed to increase Indochinese budget quickly, after being named as Governor General of Indochina in early 1897, Paul Doumer adopted a new taxation policy. As a result, essential commodities in highland-lowland commerce as cinnamon, anise, salt, and wood were applied a very high tax rate. Payment of taxes in kind applied before then would be replaced by new annual fees of 1,00 to 1,50 piasters depending on the living condition in each locality. This amount imposed to all Montagnards from the ages of eighteen to sixty years old (Hickey 1982b, 273, 300).

In the agricultural sector, the French governors claimed that the traditional method of slash-and-burn cultivation of Highlanders could cause soil erosion and deforestation. For this reason, they encouraged the villagers to switch to cultivate rice permanently in areas favorable for irrigation. Also, the farming kitchen gardens were considered as a supplement to a stable settlement.

To avoid unwanted conflict with the indigenous people over land title, the governors advocated respecting the areas claimed by Highlanders, particularly the land they inherited from their ancestors. Notably, the French landowners established plantations side by the side of tribal villages to share productive land resources. By this method, the colonizers made Highlanders believe that they would not seek to force villagers out of their ancestral territory. To what extent, the colonial government land policy is thought to be wiser than that of Ngô Đình Diệm administration after 1954.

Considered the network of roads as "The great means of civilization and pacification," the French renovated footpaths through forests over the Central Highlands. And, in order to strengthen public administration as well as to develop the colonial economy, some modern multifunction towns[141] were formed in the geographic center like Kontum, Pleiku, Buôn Mê Thuột and Đà Lạt.

---

[141] There is a fact that traditional Vietnamese society is a closed rustic social style. For centuries, the feudal governments focused only on agriculture, disregarded commodity economy (Vietnamese: trọng nông ức thương). So, the urban system had no favorable condition to develop. Even the capital cities of Thăng Long (lasted from the tenth century to the end of the nineteenth century) and Huế (from 1802 to 1945) was merely single-function urban as administrative centers, somewhat simultaneously

Being equipped with basic knowledge about customs of ethnic minorities before taking office, French provincial résidents seemed to be good at dealing with the Montagnards. Understanding the autonomous tradition of tribal groups, in which each local chief performed the decisive role in his own communities' important activities. Traditionally, each Montagnard village was a relatively independent and closed community, where a village elder (village headman) always served as the judge in all disputes arising based on the rules prescribed in customary law[142]. Those meant, who got the support of local leaders that person could easily control all the villagers. By giving benefit and formally offering local chiefs the mandate of authority, which derived from "the mother country," France then used village elders as its lowest civil servants in the mountains. Since 1904 the French began implementing administrative innovations in parochial level. Many village elders accepted the French proposal and, subsequently served as intermediaries between their people and the rulers. They took responsibility of tax collectors and corvée organizers for colonial administration. In order to break the traditional autonomy of minority villages, the colonial rulers also regularly gathered pro-French local chiefs in various forms of ritual activities. By this way, they hoped to gradually weaken awareness of small, independent communities and build up a new notion of ethnic Highlander identity. In addition, they were also interested in propaganda to make Highlanders believe that "the mandate of gods" had been transmitted to the French administration instead of being held by local leaders as before (Hickey 1982b, 261, 291, 294).

July 13th, 1913, Résident Superior Albert Sarraut approved the proposal of Huế court on maintaining customary law and the highland law judicial system. This token gesture of "respecting local culture" somewhat helped the

---

    played the role of a cultural center. This feature was contrary to multifunction cities of Western countries, where trade role was considered the most prominent.

142 Customary law (also known as traditional law, unwritten law) was unwritten code formed in local communities in Central Highlands during the long history. It aimed to guide, adjust and regulate social relations, relations between human being and their surrounding environment. The application of customary law in deciding cases was quite straightforward and fast. Specifically, after listening to plaintiff and defendant presented, the judge would intone an appropriate provision of customary law which provided bases to make a best suitable decision in the interests of both parties. However, it should be added that, due to be formed in a condition of people's poor scientific knowledge and was transmitted through generations verbally, some contents of the customary laws inevitably contained inconsistent points, lacked strict logics or expressed superstition.

colonizers speed up pacification operations in the hinterlands. However, to make those oral regulations in line with the colonial interest, the French lawmakers in Indochina conducted some adjustments in customary law. In a little more detail, they focused on provisions relating to obligations of indigenous people, which included providing corvée for the construction of roads, plantations and paying taxes.

Aiming at gradually apply the French laws into the Central Highlands, on 8th July 1925 Résident Fournier recommend the Huế court to issue a proclamation reorganizing the highland law courts. Accordingly, a customary court should be run by a Montagnard judge, a representative of provincial résident and ten local chiefs acting as assistant judges (Hickey 1982b, 294). Apparently, in the new model of customary law courts, the judicial power of highland judges was shrunk significantly. This organizational model looks somewhat different from the judicature in Tonkin and Annam, wherein with the principle of the protectorate, the verdicts still were pronounced by Vietnamese officials, although their declared judgments only took effect after having the approval of French provincial résidents[143].

Concerning French education system in minority regions in southern Vietnam, the French believed education was the best means for the Highlanders to defend themselves before the dominant of outsiders including the Cambodian, Laotian and Việt people. Education was also thought to be the most efficient ways to spread "French civilization" as well as to train senior staff, those who could assist France to exploit natural and low-cost labor resources efficiently. To "Frenchify" the Indochinese education system, the colonizers carried out two reforms in the years 1906 and 1917[144]. As a result, some primary schools such as

---

[143] As for the judicial system in Cochinchine, on 25th July 1864, the French Cochinchina governor issued the first decree on the organization of two types of judicial courts. According to this document, French court judged French and other European offenders using the laws of France while Vietnamese court decided natives and Asian criminals using the law of Annam (the Gia Long Code). On 25th May 1881 French President decreed to depose the Vietnamese court there, assigned the French court in districts to judge the natives, but with condescension to the terms of Annam law.

[144] Previously, the education system in the Central Highlands was pretty simple. The first elementary school was opened in Kontum by Father Vialleton in 1892. Nevertheless, in the early years, the number of students attending this school was very modest. A long time later, in 1908 Cuénot School, the second elementary school for the Montagnards, named after Bishop Cuénot, was established (Lam, Cadière, & Tố 1944)&(Hồng 1959). See also Diocese of Kontum, *100th Anniversary of Yao Phu Cuénot School (1908–2008)*, Sources: https://gpkontum.wordpress.com/2011/02/20/k%E1%BB%B7-y%E1%BA%BFu-nam-thanh-yao-phu/.; Kon Tum Provincial

Franco-Rhade, Franco-Bahnar, and Franco-Vietnamese were opened in Pleiku, Buôn Mê Thuột, and Đà Lạt those would be ready to enroll students for the first academic year, 1917. Six years later, thanks to the positive impact of Pierre Pasquier's ethnic policies, the primary education program was extended to six years instead of three years as it used to be. As of the 1929–1930 school years, there were some 229 students of ethnic Jarai, Bahna, Sédang, and Rhade in the Franco-Montagnard schools (Báu 2008, 20).

The ethnic strategies of Pierre Marie Antoine Pasquier

On 30th July 1923, Résident of Supérieur de l'Annam (Vietnamese: Khâm sứ Trung kỳ) Pierre Marie Antoine Pasquier issued Decree No. 578-ca on the French policies towards the Highlanders. This decree stipulated the principle of supporting the Montagnards; preventing the Việt from settling in the Highlands; and restricting the over labor exploitation of plantation owners. In a little more detail, for pacified areas, the French sought to sever the relations between the Montagnards and outsiders (including the Việt, the Khmer, the Cham, the Laotian, the Hoa (Chinese), the Tay, and Catholic church); respected customs and traditions of the Montagnards; built roads, schools, markets; fixed places of residence and trained the people useful techniques in cultivation; adjusted the amount of corvée and land for industrial plantations; recruited and trained Montagnard soldiers, personnel; set up military posts and administrative apparatus; suppressed movements for rebellion and autonomy; and held the annual traditional ceremony to accept the Montagnards' surrender (Giang & Ánh 1974, 133).

Pasquier set Darlac region where had been ruling by Sabatier as a pattern for other French officials in the Central Highlands. Since he had been sent to Darlac in 1912, Sabatier advocated *"Highland land to the Montagnards"* and did not allow outsiders to exploit (Chi 2006, 407–450). During his 16 years in office, he lived like a Rhade. The ruler communicated, handled administrative affairs in Rhade language, and even married a daughter of local chief Kun Yu Nob. Sabatier also organized the construction of schools, roads, hospitals, and power plants in Darlac. During 1923–1925, received Darlac Résident's encouragement, a Rhade teacher at Franco-Rhade elementary school in Buôn Mê Thuột named Y

Committee for Propaganda and Training, *Những sự kiện lịch sử tháng 01 ở Kon Tum (Historical events in January in Kon Tum)*, Sources: http://www.tuyengiaokontum.org.vn/Lich-su/nhung-su-kien-lich-su-thang-01-o-kon-tum-344.html. (Accessed 17th April 2018).

Jut[145] and his two colleagues, Y Jut Hwing and Y Ut Nie Buon Rit devised Rhade alphabet on the basis of Latinization Rhade spoken language. Also in 1923, Sabatier inspired Y Say recorded the Rhade customary law while he witnessed a judge manipulated all the Rhade customs in a highland law court. Based on these records, in 1927 Y Say, and Y Ut published the formal Rhade customary law in both Rhade and French languages[146] (Hickey 1982b, 298)&(Giang & Ánh 1974, 134).

In order to call for local capital in new projects, as soon as being appointed as the first provincial résident of Darlac in 1923, Sabatier sought to raise tax rates from the Highlanders. Hence, the annual tax revenue of this province reached to 30.000 piasters in comparison with an amount of 3000 to 4000 per year before the World War I (Hickey 1982b, 273, 300).

Entering the 1930s, to reduce the burden of world economic crisis, the French colonial government, as well as the plantation owners, increased various forms of exploitation and oppression in Indochina. Taxes and corvée which had been being heavy then became overload. The average daily working hours of plantation workers extended reaching to sixteen while their wages reduced significantly. The native intellectuals and civil servants were disdained and mistreated[147], graduated students encountered unemployment risk, etc. In this context, the rise of nationalist movements in Vietnam, especially the establishment and expansion of Indochinese Communist Party seriously undermined the influence of French colonizers in the hinterlands. In many minority areas, the revolutionaries confiscated plantations and property of the imperialists and the pro-French capitalists to distribute to the poor. As mentioned earlier, except the local chiefs who received benefits from the French, the Montagnards were not willing to cooperate with France to avoid being dependent (Lacouture 1968, 48–50)&(Hickey 1982b, 325).

Among the Highlanders, the Rhade was a large group and got enthusiastic support from the French. This ethnicity, therefore, became the most elite one. The Jarai and Sédang, although were also populous and strong, were not granted privileges because they had fought against the French. Whether holding different positions in the colonizers' concern, these three great communities were

---

145 Y Jut also was initiator and leader of a minority intellectual movement against the French in the Central Highlands during the years 1925–1926.
146 Sabatier's attempt on "Highland land to the Montagnards" was finally fail because the Indochinese authorities sent him away to pave the way for the plantation owners.
147 French civil servants were always ranked and earning much higher salaries than Vietnamese those who had the same qualifications (Lâm et al. 2000, 221).

the principal objects of their ethnic policies on the plateau. The young of the Rhade, Jarai, and Sédang were recruited into cultural, medical and military training courses to serve as intermediaries between the colonial government and the Montagnards. The French also taught them to distrust, hate, and when necessary, fight against the Việt. The relationship between the Lowlanders and the Highlanders during this period hence were troubled as the French wanted[148].

In 1932, the first regular battalion of Montagnard soldiers (le Bataillon des Tirailleurs Montagnards du Sud Annam) was formed. This battalion consisted of a Rhade company stationed in Buôn Mê Thuột, a Rhade company stationed in Buon Djen Drom, a Jarai company stationed in Pleiku, and a Sédang company stationed in Kontum. The regular unit would be responsible for assisting the French officers in training newly recruited combatants. From 1933 to 1942, five other regular battalions with 2.172 men of all the tribal groups were created to serve the colonial government in pacifying the Highlands[149].

To suppress the protest movement broke out in northern Vietnam between 1930–1931 the French authority shot on demonstrators killing hundreds of protesters. That repression was subsequently denounced to cause ten thousand deaths and fifty thousand deportations (Hickey 1982b, 359). In 1932 there were over ten thousand political prisoners detained in French prisons throughout Vietnam. Some of the jails located in Long Mountain like Dakto (Kontum), Lao Bảo (Quảng Trị), Dak Pek, Buôn Mê Thuột, etc. Also during this period, the Battalion of Highlander Riflemen of South Annam was organized in Buôn Mê Thuột (Hickey 1982b, 360).

Since 1940 the situation became more robust with the French when the Japanese jumped on Indochina. With the purpose of maintaining a fragile French autonomy, the Vichy government signed the Protocol Concerning Joint Defense and Joint Military Cooperation (Protocole concernant la Défense encommun de l'Indochine Francaise) on 29th July 1941. This treaty then defined the Franco-Japanese relations for Indochina until the Japanese revoked it by carrying out a military coup on 9th March 1945. Accordingly, Japan was given the right to use all the airports and seaports of Indochina, all the Indochinese logistic, financial

---

148 Ibid. Nguyễn Văn Huy. *Cộng đồng người Thượng trên cao nguyên miền Trung (The Montagnard community in the Central Highlands).*
149 Ibid. Nguyễn Văn Huy. *Cộng đồng người Thượng trên cao nguyên miền Trung (The Montagnard community in the Central Highlands).*

system and human resource for military purposes; France also allowed Japan to have more troops present in Indochina[150] (Salemink 2002, 6).

In the Central Highlands, Japanese troops directly controlled all French-trained Montagnard soldiers, and the entire transport system. Japanese then equipped some Montagnard villages to guide their armed forces moving in thick forests. The slogan "Asia of Asians" was responded by some of the minority intellectuals until Japan surrendered to the Allies in the mid-August 1945.

Also, after the coup of March 9th, 1945, Vietnamese political prisoners detained by the French were released. Of those, Việt Minh cadres stayed in Highlands to mobilize Montagnard intellectuals and soldiers to join them against the French. With the promise of autonomy, the Việt Minh movement attracted the Highlanders' enthusiastic participation, especially of the Rhade and Jarai elite. Montagnard intellectuals and soldiers urged their people to occupy the French military and administrative facilities left by Japan and to join interim administration committees[151].

The domination strategies of Georges Thierry d'Argenlieu in the context of decolonization in Vietnam

August 1945, French President appointed Admiral Georges Thierry d'Argenlieu as High Commissioner (to replace for the title of Governor General), and General Philippe Leclerc de Hauteclocque as commander of the French expeditionary force in Indochina. Merely three weeks after the independent ceremony of Vietnam, with the help of the British army, the French troops opened fire to seize control of Saigon on 23rd September 1945 aiming to reoccupy this peninsular[152].

---

150 See more in: David G. Marr. (1997). *Vietnam 1945: The quest for power*. University of California Press.
151 Ibid. Nguyễn Văn Huy. *Cộng đồng người Thượng trên cao nguyên miền Trung (The Montagnard community in the Central Highlands)*.
152 In his famous study about the First Indochina War, Norwegian historian Stein Tonnesson presents a perspective, which is considered exciting and novel, on the reasons for the outbreak of the war. According to Tonnesson, the Chinese Kuomintang generals significantly contributed to the brokerage of both sides (France and Vietnam), negotiating for a preliminary agreement signed on 6th March 1946. Despite the fact that after 1945, Paris only wanted to protect French interests in the South, French officials in Indochina planned to gain control of the whole Vietnam in the long run when they moved north to replace the Chinese Kuomintang troops. Without the Chinese Kuomintang strong pressures on both sides to sign the preliminary agreement, the war might have exploded in early 1946. Also according to Tonnesson, French officials in

During the First Indochina War (1946-1954), the Highlanders became the "People in between." On the one hand, the Việt Minh government called to establish an autonomous zone over the Central Highlands under their control. On the contrary, the French wished to reactivate their rule and to turn this region into an essential pawn in their strategy.

With dominance in equipment, the French Expeditionary Force quickly dispatched maneuver battalions to recapture southern Annam and Cochinchina. Late June 1946, France mobilized the 1st Far East Brigade and Highlander Battalion to reoccupy the remaining portions of the high plateau such as Buôn Mê Thuột, Kontum, Pleiku, Cheo Reo, An Khê, etc. (Giang & Ánh 1974, 136). Confronting the elite troops, Việt Minh force actively selected guerrilla tactics. They intensively recruited highland militants; organized to training their military personnel in remote areas and suddenly ambushed to undermine their enemy's strength and willpower.

To break the national unity of the Vietnamese, D'Argenlieu thoroughly applied the policy of divide and rule. On October 31st, 1945, right after arriving in Saigon, the first High Commissioner reorganized the Indochinese Federation, placing Indochina in the French Union (French: Union française). He also established Autonomous Republic of Cochinchina (French: République autonome de Cochinchine) on 26th May 1946 (Thêm 1966, 23-24).

For the Central Highlands, on 27th May 1946, D'Argenlieu issued a proclamation giving this region a *"Special Administrative Circumscription,"* better known as the autonomous region for the Montagnards[153] (French: Pays Montagnard du Sud Indochinois), that would be administered by a special French delegate (French: Commissariat des Populations Montagnardes du Sud-Indochinois: P.M.S.I.). On the other hand, on 16th May 1946 d'Argenlieu departed for Buôn Mê Thuột to organize an oath ceremony, in which some pro-French minority chiefs as Nay Nui, Y Ut Nie Buon Rit, and Khunjanob swore allegiance to France. It is believed that the d'Argenlieu's ordinance marked the beginning of a period during which the Highlands would be a pawn in French political strategy. The decree also officially detached the high plateau from Annam and put it into the orbit of French directly control likewise "The

---

Indochina had deliberately acted against the French government's instructions when they provoked the Việt Minh government into attacking first. The Việt Minh Army tried not to retaliate for provocations of the French Army for some time, but finally, they lost the temper and started firing on December 19th (Tonnesson 2009).

153 This special administrative zone consisted of Darlac, Haut Donnai, Lang Bian, Pleiku, and Kontum Provinces. Its administrative center would be located in Buôn Mê Thuột.

Autonomous Republic of Cochinchine" (Hickey 1982b, 393)&(Giang & Ánh 1974, 136–137)&(Thêm 1966, 24).

To train indigenous military officers, the French established a military academy in Huế in December 1948, which two years later was relocated in Đà Lạt with new the name École Militaire Interarmes (the Combined Arms School). Also during that period, the founding of the Ecole de l'Air and a naval center in Nha Trang marked the birth of the air force and navy of Vietnam National Army (Vietnamese: Quân đội Quốc gia Việt Nam).

Similar to previous periods, after the Second World War, the French government resumed funding for studies on ethnic minorities in southern Indochina. As part of research projects of the *Centre des Recherches Scientifique et Coloniale (Center of Scientific Research and Colonial)*, Georges Condominas returned to the Central Highlands in 1948 to conduct ethnographic research on Mnong Gar in Sar Luk, a remote village in Southern Darlac. With his proficiency in the native language, Condominas could attend villagers' daily activities and conduct all the surveys without interpreters. From the knowledge and experience collected through the field works, he later wrote many scientific works on Mnong Gar people. Two of those were highly appreciated by ethnographers worldwide such as *"Nous avons mangé la forêt (We have eaten the forest)* and *L'exotique est quotidien: Sar Luk, Vietnam Central"* (The exotic is daily: Sar Luk, Central Vietnam).

After the August Revolution, most of the workers in plantations, civil servants and teachers left the colonial rulers to adhere to Việt Minh forces. At this stage, the Montagnard elite were distinctly divided. Some followed the French such as Y Sok Eban, Y Tuic Mlo Duon Du, Y Bih Aleo, Y Blieng Hmok, Touprong Hiou, Touprong Ya Ba, Touneh Han Din, Ya Yu Sahau, Bahnaria Ya Don; while others, for example, Y Ngong, Y Wang, Y Nue, Y Tlam, Phem, Depp, etc., chose Việt Minh side[154] (Hickey 1982b, 390).

In this context, in April 1946 Việt Minh convened a "Southern Fraternal Minority Peoples" conference in Kontum where was still under their control. At the meeting, a letter of President Hồ Chí Minh was released explaining about the Việt Minh government's stance towards ethnic groups in southern Vietnam. Accordingly, those such as Pacoh, the K'tu, the Cua, the Hré, the Dié, the Halang, the Sédang, the Bahnar, the Mnong, the Cill, the Kaho, and so on, would be treated as "blood brothers and sisters" of the Việt and other ethnic minorities

---

154 Ibid. Nguyễn Văn Huy. *Cộng đồng người Thượng trên cao nguyên miền Trung (The Montagnard community in the Central Highlands).*

across the country[155]. Previously, the Việt Minh government had already established the Department for National Minorities to take charge of minority and mountainous areas. The ethnic minorities were also promised the right to learn their native languages in primary schools, as well as, to maintain their traditional law courts. Moreover, representatives of ethnic minorities were entitled to participate in parliamentary elections by law[156] (Đạo et al. 2006, 249).

Entering the 1950s, the escalation of the First Indochina War made France to withdraw most of its Expeditionary Force in the Central Highlands to reinforce northern battlefield. In order to prevent attacks of Việt Minh in highland towns such as Buôn Mê Thuột, Kontum, Pleiku, Đà Lạt, together with the construction of more new outposts, March 1951 the colonial government created Vietnamese Light Infantry Division (also known as the "Division Montagnarde" or the 4th Division). This division operated stretching from Dak Pek (north of Kontum) to the Phan Thiết Province in the South of Highlands. Its 9.000 militants were arranged into three indigenous infantry battalions (the 1st, 2nd and 7th) and a mixed Vietnamese and Highlander battalion (the 28th) (Moore 2007, 70).

As a result of Elysée Accords, signed on 8th March 1949, the Highland Plateau became a "Crown Domain" under the governance of the former Emperor Bảo Đại. May 30th the same year, France ordained the management empower of the Central Highlands and the Montagnards in Southern Indochina to the government of State of Vietnam. A subsequent decree dated 15th April 1950 of Chief of State Bảo Đại separated the central plateau to establish a particular administrative zone called the Crown Domain of the Southern Highlander Country (Domaine de la Couronne du Pays Montagnards du Sud). In this territory, Bảo Đại was the Head of State and also remained as Emperor nominally (Dharma 2012, 11)&(Salemink 2002, 6).

On May 21, 1951, Chief of State Bảo Đại issued the Ordinance 16/QT/TD, regulating a *statut particulier* (special status) to the Crown Domain. The Ordinance granted the Highlanders "eminent rights" to develop in accordance with their own customs. It also encouraged the Highlanders to participate in the administrative system of Crown Domain like taking part in highland law

---

155 See: *Hồ Chí Minh Chronicles, Volume 3 (9/1945 – 12/1946)*. Http://dangcongsan.vn/tu-lieu-van-kien/ho-so-su-kien/books-191820154013456/index-1918201535758569.html. (Accessed 25th December 2017).
156 There were 34 ethnic minority deputies out of 333 delegates attended National Assembly in 1946. Some of them came from southern provinces as Y Ngong Nie Kdam, Y Wang Mlo Duon Du, Nay Phin, Recom Rock, Djouik John, Ouok, Tuprong Hieu, etc.

courts. Its provisions defined the role of provincial and district advisers, as well as, positions of the headmen of cantons and villages. The regulation then devoted attention to the issues of economy, health, and education. Accordingly, rights of landowners (Polan) would be respected; the authorities would verify all activities of sale or transfer of land in accordance with traditional custom and by consultation with the local chief. The training of Montagnard cadres in military, medical, administrative and educational fields would base on the needs of each locality. Like statutes enacted by the French previously, the teaching of ethnic minority languages would be maintained at the primary level. Finally, the regulation determined that the Montagnards only had to join the army[157] which garrisoned in the Highlands and served for protecting their own territories[158] (Giang & Ánh 1974, 138)&(Thêm 1966, 94)&(Thọ 1970, 92–97).

Thanks to that special regulation, the economy, culture and society of the Crown Domain were getting more support from the colonial government than other parts of Vietnam. On 4th April 1952, Chief of State continued to issue the second law decree on the highland affairs, Ordinance 27/QT/TD. Following this Ordinance, a Social and Economic Council for the Southern Highlander was formed under the cabinet of the Chief of State. This council swiftly came up with a socio-economic development program for the Central Highlands with two primary objectives. The first goal was "Struggle against the depopulation" by forming "Fixed, stable communities," with a modern farming method instead of shifting cultivation that heavily depended on nature. The second one was to create favorable conditions for Việt people in the overpopulated coastal migrating to the high plateau; considered migrants as pioneers in implementing the new economic policy[159] (Thêm 1966, 109). In order to achieve those objectives, some large-scale projects would be put into practice, in which the government provided capital for infrastructure including irrigation, roads, and electricity. At the same time, private capital was also called for investing in those long-term programs.

---

157 The imperial army consisted of only minority men, those who would be trained, equipped and commanded by French officers.
158 Dụ số 16/QT/TD (Ordinance No. 16/QT/TD). In: Hồ sơ về các hoạt động của Cao nguyên miền Nam 1952–1954 (Records of the activities of the Southern Highlands from 1950 to 1951). The National Archives Center IV, Da Lat city. Dossier code 66, V1.
159 Dụ số 27/QT/TD (Ordinance No. 16/QT/TD). In: Hồ sơ về các hoạt động của Cao nguyên miền Nam 1952–1954 (Records of the activities of the Southern Highlands from 1952 to 1954). The National Archives Center IV, Da Lat city. Dossier code 66, V2.

According to governmental plans, many coffees, tea, rubber, sugar cane plantations would be expanded or established to productively exploit basalt soil and tropical climate of the Central Highlands. Along with economic goals, those programs also focused on improving villagers' way of life by encouraging them to use lamps, sewing clothes, household items and soap. The healing methods based on scientific therapy would steadily replace the shamanic procedures in prevention and treatment of diseases. Each village should have its own school, market, communal house, infirmary, and shops.

Although the French nominally recognized Vietnamese sovereignty over the high plateau since the Crown Domain formed, they maintained a "Statute particular." Bound and determined by the "Special obligations," the French continued to direct this mountainous zone through their special delegate. With the Bảo Đại solution, the French were relatively successful in taking advantage of the former emperor and the traditional relationship between the Huế court and Kings of Water and Fire to group pro-French highland chiefs. As a result of the gathering of local leaders in inter-village events and their offsprings in the French schools or the Division Montagnarde, a common identity of being Highlanders was formed and strengthened gradually. That was primarily the process of exchanging of language and culture among ethnic groups and the establishment of the intermarriage relations among elite families. And more importantly, in the upper-class, French culture as the same as a sense of cooperation with colonizers increasingly diffused.

It can be said that the trend of decolonization after the Second World War was an inevitable one. Despite last efforts of France in maintaining its colonial power in the minority regions of Vietnam, until the end of the first Indochina War of 1954, most objectives of the socio-economic development program for the Montagnards had not been fully achieved. And, it is not difficult to realize the racially prejudiced view of policymakers in the Bảo Đại administration when they determined the prominent role of Vietnamese migrants in *"helping the Montagnards fight off their backwardness and superstition"*. However, to some extent, it is abundantly clear that the ethnic strategies of the Crown Domain regime towards the ethnic minorities in the Central Highlands were much more progress than which of the previous administrations.

3.2.4 Struggle Movements of the Montagnard Groups against French Colonialism

Not willing to be dominated as well as the Việt, ethnic minorities in the Central Highlands soon rose up against French colonialists. Since the Giáp Thân Peace

Treaty of 1884 (also known as Patenôtre Treaty, Treaty of Huế or Protectorate Treat), Vietnam was placed under French control. From then onwards, their military and administrative posts were established gradually in the Central Highlands. However, the anti-French movement of the Montagnards indeed began two decades earlier.

Sooner after the French attacked the Cochinchine, in 1861, Trương Định (a military mandarin of the Nguyễn Dynasty) launched the first resistance attracting the warm support from various minority groups (Giang & Ánh 1974, 111-112). In particular, the Stieng in Biên Hòa, north of Thủ Dầu Một and the Chrau in Bà Rịa cooperated actively with insurgents, forming the jaws around North and Northeast of Saigon. These forces took mountainous areas as bases, thoroughly promoting the guerrilla tactics that caused the French army much hardships and casualties. However, eventually, most of the insurgents were suppressed and destroyed by French forces. In 1864, Trương Quyền (Son of Trương Định) continued to rise against the French. Like his father, Trương Quyền received valuable help from Stieng and Mnong tribes including food supplies, liaisons, and combatants. In 1869, the Stieng revolt against France again, this time the resistance base was located in Tây Ninh. Insurgents often ambush resupply missions (cattle) from Cambodia and many French garrisons in the plains. After several raids carried out by inspectors Reinhart, and his assistant, Quản Tấn, many insurgents surrendered, while the rest fled to Cambodia (Giang & Ánh 1974, 111-112).

Since 1885, under the great help of Regent Tôn Thất Thuyết, King Hàm Nghi called for the Cần Vương Movement[160] whose bases placed in Sơn Phòng, Tân Sở (Quảng Trị Province). Responding to that call, respected intellectuals and Vietnamese officials in the French protectorate government uprose throughout the country. Of those, the resistance forces operated in the mountains was supported strongly by the Montagnards. In 1894, two squads of French troops marched in the Valley of Ba River, and Năng River headed for Darlac but encountered the Mdhur (a subgroup of the Rhade). Those forces finally must return to the plain (Giang & Ánh 1974, 114).

Since 1898, France took over the defensive system - Sơn Phòng Trấn of the Nguyễn Dynasty. Direct French control, which was replaced for the previously

---

160 Cần Vương is a patriotic movement of a large group of officials in the French protectorate administration, led by Regent Tôn Thất Thuyết. This movement broke out in 1885, aiming to support King Hàm Nghi against the French to recover independence of Vietnam but failed in 1896.

relatively loose ties to the Huế court, making Montagnard peoples stand up against the new ruler. In the following years, there were uprisings of various ethnic groups such as of the Sédang in 1901 at the T-junction between Psi River and Poko River, the Bahnar in 1905 in Kon Chorah (An Khê), and in 1907 in Pleipang, etc. (Giang & Ánh 1974, 116)&(Thưởng 2008). Also in June 1901, the K'tu people in A Sơ, A Dong and A Bạc attacked military post An Điềm (Đại Lộc, Quảng Nam), injuring several soldiers. In 1903, the Hré led by Tổng Ren and Tia Các raided garrisons Mang Gia, Nước Vong và Nước Dinh (Quảng Ngãi); in April 1907, they attacked Đức Phổ, and in November the same year seized Đồng Mít military post (Quảng Ngãi) and was only suppressed in late 1910. In 1911, Tà Ôi (Bru-Vân Kiều) rebels killed many French officers and soldiers on the upstream of the Sé Pouc River in Quảng Trị and Thừa Thiên[161].

On the bordering areas between Attopeu (Laos) and Kontum, the Sédang fought violently against the French intrusion from 1900 to 1910. In 1900, a local chief named Thăng Mậu led the Sédang militia to attack Catholic villages along the banks of Psi and Poko rivers in Kontum, wounding some French soldiers. In May and June 1901, the Sédang continued attacking the military post in Psi, injured chief of station named Robert. Other Catholic villages in areas of Dak Drei, Dakto, and Krong Kno were also regularly assaulted until 1902 when the French regular troops defeated the rebellion[162].

In Kontum, thanks to the intermediary role of the clergy, the Bahnar were more cooperative than other ethnic groups. However, after being excessively exploited (corvée and land), especially being hatred by other Montagnard tribes, this group also rose up against the French[163]. In January 1901, they occupied Kon Chorah village (An Khê, Bình Định) and later retreated to their camp in Plei Bring village (near Chợ Đồn). Another attack of the Bahnar broke out in January 1907 repulsing the French army from the community of Kon Klot. Here, a plantation director named Delignon-Paris was shot dead, and many other soldiers

---

161 Ibid. Nguyễn Văn Huy. *Cộng đồng người Thượng trên cao nguyên miền Trung (The Montagnard community in the Central Highlands)*.
162 Ibid. Nguyễn Văn Huy. *Cộng đồng người Thượng trên cao nguyên miền Trung (The Montagnard community in the Central Highlands)*.
163 According to Bùi Minh Đạo, in the late nineteenth and early twentieth centuries, the imposed corvée for each Bahnar peasant was 20 days; sometimes, that amount even reached to 50–100 days. If not to do corvée, each person had to pay 0.35 piaster per day. In addition to corvée, the capitation was 0.1 piaster per person in 1898 and increased to 3.2 piasters (equivalent to 100 kg unmilled rice) in 1940 (Đạo et al. 2006, 245).

were wounded. In the years from 1918 to 1922, the Bahnar Halakong regularly raided plantations around An Khê[164]. After the August Revolution of 1945, the Bahnar resistance movement continued to break out under the leadership of the Viet Minh; many Bahnar villages such as Kong Hoa, Xã Nam, An Khê, etc., became resistance villages (Đạo et al. 2006, 245–247, 251).

As soon as the French army organized earliest operations in Pleiku between 1894 and 1897, it faced the Jarai's stiff resistance. These resistance activities were sustained in first years of the twentieth century when the French continued to advance to Kontum and Pleiku. After killing inspector Prosper Odend'hal on 7th April 1904, King of Fire Oi Ât had to leave An Khê to find a shelter in Ayun River upstream. On 12th the same month, at the request of the Supreme Council of Indochina, Governor General Paul Beau signed a decree to establish Darlac province with the lower level villages of ethnic minorities, and move the provincial capital from Bandon to Buôn Mê Thuột; appointed Bardin as provincial résident[165]. In order to watch over the Jarai, Bardin built Plei Tour and Chợ Đồn military posts in early 1905. Catholic villages in the area, however, were continuously attacked by the Jarai. The French then provided arms to some Việt Catholics to organize retaliatory operations. The chaotic situation would only be handled when Captain of Chợ Đồn garrison, Renard, arranged with two Jarai chieftain Tay and Khun (leaders of 28 Jarai villages in Pleiku and An Khê) promising not to pursue the King of Fire.

The Rhade community was known in 1894 when the expedition led by Doctor Yersin was attacked at the Poko River by a group of Rhade Pih. In 1899, Attopeu Attorney, Bourgeois established Bandon garrison and recruited Phet Lasa, a Lao chief at Bandon, and Khun Jonob, a Mnong leader in the region. These two chiefs then helped the French capture other Rhade Kpa leaders like Me Wal and Me Kheune in 1900; and repeatedly defeat Rhade Pih led by Ngeuh in Ban Tour, Ban Trap and Ban Tieuah in 1903. In upstream of the Năng River (an auxiliary to Đà Rằng River), the Rhade Mdhur ambushed the French troops

---

164 Ibid. Nguyễn Văn Huy. *Cộng đồng người Thượng trên cao nguyên miền Trung (The Montagnard community in the Central Highlands)*.

165 Prior to that, in 1899 the Indochinese Governor Paul Doumer signed a decree to set up an autonomous province of Darlac installing administrative base in Bandon and naming Bourgeois provincial résident. See: Lan Anh – Giang Nam, *Buôn Mê Thuột - từ dấu tích cổ xưa đến thành phố trẻ năng động (Buôn Mê Thuột - from ancient vestiges to an active young city)*. Newspaper of Dak Lak, Sources: Http://www.baodaklak.vn/channel/3721/201502/buon-ma-thuot-tu-dau-tich-co-xua-den-thanh-pho-tre-nang-dong-2371928/. (Accessed 25th December 2017).

at A Mai village (near M'Drack and Cheo Reo) in 1901, causing a severe wound to Lieutenant Péroux. In 1905, another leader of the Rhad Mdhur named Me Sao seized Bandon. The French troops there had to retreat to Buôn Mê Thuột, and Bandon was merely retaken in 1907 when Henri Maitre defeated Me Sao at Me Leap village[166].

From 1905 to 1908, the French established a system of interconnected outposts: Sré Lvi, Sré Ktum, Sré Onès, La Palkei, Le Rolland, Snoul, Bù Đăng, Bù Đốp, An Bình, Bà Rá, Bà Đen, Chứa Chan, Tà Lài, Bù Nông, Bù Tiên, Bou Pou Sra, Bou Méra, etc. French garrisons surrounded the living space of the Stieng and Mnong but did not dare to enter. In July 1914, Henri Maitre was killed by Nơ Trang Long[167], the Montagnards since then controlled the Ba Biên Giới zone (the border between Cambodge, Cochinchine, and Annam) until the year 1933[168].

After World War I, French colonizers promoting a large-scale program of colonial exploitation in the Central Highlands. Accordingly, many new plantations were established together with an expansion of the existing ones[169] (Salemink 2002, 6). This process led to the increase of agricultural workers (the French called them coolies) in plantations, those who were forced to work hard and could be tortured mercilessly by estate owners. In response to that brutal oppression and exploitation, farm workers repeatedly organized struggles in various forms, notably, the protests of plantation workers in Maillot plantation in 1927, Rossi and CHPI in 1933, respectively. Besides, there were also some political movements made by highland civil servants, intellectuals, and students against the policies of divide and rule, despising indigenous people of French authority. Prominently was the struggle of intellectuals led by the two young patriotic Ede teachers named Y Jut and Y Ut, in the years 1925–1926 (Lâm et al. 2000, 206).

---

166 Ibid. Nguyễn Văn Huy. *Cộng đồng người Thượng trên cao nguyên miền Trung (The Montagnard community in the Central Highlands)*.
167 Nơ Trang Long (also N'Trang Lơng) (1870 – 1935) was a chief of the Mnong ethnic group. He revolted against the French in the South Highlands (bordering Cambodia) during 24 years of the early twentieth century (1911 – 1935) (Lâm et al. 2000, 206).
168 Ibid. Nguyễn Văn Huy. *Cộng đồng người Thượng trên cao nguyên miền Trung (The Montagnard community in the Central Highlands)*.
169 Regarding rubber plantations, during the second colonial exploitation of France in Vietnam (1918–1930), the land used for rubber plantations increased sharply from 15.000 up to 120.000 hectares (eight times). Many large companies trading rubber products launched such as Đất Đỏ, Cây Trồng Nhiệt Đới, and Michelin (Lâm et al. 2000, 213).

From 1929, the French planned to explore the Mnong Plateau[170] to establish plantations and to build roads serving the task of pacification over mountainous regions in South Indochina. As in many other lands, the entry of the French into the Mnong Plateau and the opening of the 14th National Highway linking Saigon with Buôn Mê Thuột and Kontum encountered stiff resistance from native tribes. There were some typical events such as the Mnong people ambushed and killed Captain Gatille, who was tasked to construct roads through Sré Khtum and La Pankei in May 1931; the armed attack on military posts Bou Djeng Drom and Le Rolland in January 1933, but failed (Giang & Ánh 1974, 121–22)&(Thưởng 2008).

In the late 1930s, many minorities including Sédang, Dié, Bahnar, Hré, etc., cut off all contacts with the French authorities. Furthermore, after the Sédang rebels attacked some French garrisons in early 1938, ethnic groups in Phú Yên and Bình Định Provinces also repeatedly organized sieges of the French military and administrative offices. However, like many previous uprisings, derived from various causes such as sporadic outbursts, defective equipment, famine, and so on, all anti-French activities finally were defeated. In May 1935, Nơ Trang Long was arrested and executed, the anti-French movement temporarily subsided (Giang & Ánh 1974, 124).

In summary, as a part of the colonial strategy, the domination strategies of the French for minority groups in the south of Vietnam aimed to support their invasion and exploitative plans. It is evident that massive taxation system together with corvée, which was considered "leprosy of the Highlands," became heavier since many projects of opening new roads or repairing old paths had been deploying (Harris 2016, 16). Those, along with the disregard attitude of colonial officials while contacting with indigenous peoples repeatedly triggered political and armed struggles. The establishment and operation of the Division Montagnarde brought many casualties to tribal men, who were forced to fight in a war for the benefit of the French colonists. And, it is thought that the proliferation of Catholicism and Protestantism under the patronage of the colonial administration also undermined the indigenous polytheism[171].

---

170 The Mnong Plateau with an elevation ranging from 600 to 1000 m, locates in the southwest of Darlac Plateau and west of Dalat Plateau, between Vietnam and Cambodia.
171 By 1944 Kontum Province, where was home to 150.000 Highlanders and 7.000 Vietnamese, was considered the fastest growing locality of Christian in the Central Highlands. At that time there were over 22.000 Christians in the mission. Of those people, 4.500 were Bahnar Jolong; 6000 Sédang; 5.800 Rengao; and 6.300 Vietnamese. Bishop Sion presided over 24 districts with 165 Highlander and 37 Vietnamese

To meet the demand for spreading French culture, missionary work and training native officials the colonial government opened several primary schools in upland towns until the early twenty century. Though up to the 1940s, some secondary schools and normal schools were also established in Buôn Mê Thuột and Đà Lạt, the opportunity to access the colonial education system was not equal among highland children. In other words, that was only the privilege of offspring of pro-French local chiefs and wealthy landowners.

Like many social developments, colonialism produced ambivalent results: oppression and modernization at the same time. Although unintended by the rulers, to some extent, the "French civilization" brought advancement in farming practices as well as in cultural activities of the Highlanders. The trans-Indochina expeditions created perspective for the network of roads connecting remote areas, where previously had been considered mysterious and dangerous over centuries. The emergence of multi-function towns also contributed a new appearance to the high plateau. Apart from Catholic clergy, those played pioneering roles, newly trained intellectuals from French schools became critical cultural bridges between the French and the Highlanders. The hospitals were built in Buôn Mê Thuột, Kontum, An Khê, Dran, Di Linh, and Đà Lạt together with Catholic nursing centers somewhat replaced traditional shamanic methods. Last but not least, the ethnological records conducted by French ethnographers were invaluable contributions. Those monographs provided not only abundant sources of materials for researchers but also the scientific basis for the policymakers in planning development schemes for ethnic regions in southern Vietnam.

---

congregations that gathered in 26 churches and 135 chapels. Among the clergy, there were 16 French, 13 Vietnamese and 3 Bahnar priests (Hickey 1982b, 370–71).

IV The Policies of the First Republic toward Ethnic Minorities in the Central Highlands (1954–1963)

In the transformation of domination strategies in the Central Highlands under decolonization and cold-war politics, the first president of SVN, Ngô Đình Diệm, played a crucial role. After the French, with cooperation with former Emperor Bảo Đại, repeatedly failed in the attempts of breaking down the fledgling Vietnamese communist-led government, the U.S. increasingly intervened into the Indochina War and prepared to crowd France out of the Indochina peninsula. Following the French defeat at Điện Biên Phủ in early May 1954, the Americans thought it was time to have an anti-communist nationalist leader in SVN to undermine the attractiveness of Hồ Chí Minh. According to some U.S. diplomats, at the time, Ngô Đình Diệm was emerging as the brightest star among the nationalists who was believed to hold required qualifications to cope with the rapid expansion of communism in the country of Vietnam.

For many countries in Southeast Asia, the integration of much and varied ethnolinguistic states was considered as one of the most critical goals after the Second World War. With the establishment of the RVN in 1955, the Highlanders then were classified as ethnic minorities in their own homeland. Aimed at building a unified political entity in SVN, Diệm asserted that the ethnic minorities including the Highlanders, the Cham, the Khmer and the Chinese would have to be assimilated into the Vietnamese cultural sphere. The president's objective then was institutionalized by a decree, issued on June 12th, 1955, marking the beginning of formulation of the First Republic's Highland Affairs Policies (Vietnamese: Chính sách Thượng vụ). While abolishing some crucial privileges of the Montagnards, the new ethnic policies imposed to them new obligations. Also, purposes of pacification and counterinsurgency strategies often were integrated into socio-economic development programs causing severe disorder in the lives of the Montagnards. These political mistakes along with the maturation of awareness among some French-trained minority intellectuals eventually led to the birth of the organized struggle movement BAJARAKA.

4.1 The U.S. and the Path to Power of Ngô Đình Diệm

After the assassination of President Ngô Đình Diệm and his younger brother Ngô Đình Nhu in 1963, many historians and other writers described him as the U.S. best hope. With Diệm, the American Containment Policy against the Communism was believed to be most effectively deployed in SVN. However, the reason why and how Diệm could come to such critical position still has been in a controversy (Miller 2004, 433). The following explanations hope to close that question.

Through his activities during the tenure in power (1954-1963), Diệm was believed to be erected and backed by the Americans as a political figurehead, who helped the U.S. in carrying out its strategic goals in the Cold War in Southeast Asia. And, the perseverance of Ngô clan against the deployment of the American Expeditionary troops into Vietnam merely derived from the traditional perspective. Diệm did not wish to lose "Mandate of Heaven" (Vietnamese: Thiên mệnh or mệnh trời) and "National sentiment" (Vietnamese: Tinh thần dân tộc) those were believed to bring him the masses' support. With a Confucian intellectual like Diệm, the loyalty towards his nation was always considered the highest criterion of personal dignity. Although the feudal institutions officially collapsed in Vietnam after the August Revolution of 1945, during the 1950s, Confucian intellectuals still kept dominant in the Vietnamese intelligentsia. Furthermore, Diệm, with his erudite knowledge, of course, knew that in the thousand-year-history of Vietnam, there was an unprecedented political regime that existed permanently basing on sponsorship of foreign military forces, who came to suppress and kill Vietnamese compatriots[172] (Dung 2008, 4)&(Catton 2002, 2).

On the contrary, some of the works, especially those were written from the 1960s onwards showed an opposite point of view. While acknowledging Diệm regime was nourished thanks to the U.S. financial aid and military equipment, these authors argued that the Ngô clan fought hard to deny receiving American advisors, and the alliance between Saigon and Washington finally fell (Miller 2004, 433). Even, some deemed Diệm as a strong-willed patriotic intellectual who was ready to fight for his ideal at any cost (Phương 1957, 66-69)&(Luận 1982).

Thus, although researchers have not reached a consensus on assessing Ngô Đình Diệm in several aspects, the greater part admitted the American arrangement for his political career. Based on collected research materials, I wholeheartedly endorse the idea that Diệm, though sometimes expressed his disagreement with Washington in methods of conducting the war in Vietnam or governing SVN, was only a political puppet. Fact showed that as a U.S. political pawn, Diệm finally could not avoid being replaced when the U.S. lost their control over

---

172 See more in: Cao Huy Thuần, *Toàn trị và ngoại thuộc (Totalitarian and foreign dependence)*, Hoa Sen Library, 2011.

him and realized that the conflict could not be won with him. The approval, which White House[173] gave to the Revolutionary Military Council (RMC)[174] in the November 1st, 1963 coup d'état, proved the affinity between the Americans and Ngô clan was over. In turn, the generals who had carried out the coup to depose Ngô Đình Diệm also be replaced after only three months of taking power because they were incompetent in pleasing the U.S.

This section focuses on clarifying the U.S. operations during the first four years of the 1950s to turn Ngô Đình Diệm from an exiled politician to be the prime minister of SVN, or the Americans' role in Diệm political career, in other words.

Documents point out that two people who played the decisive role in bringing Ngô Đình Diệm back to SVN were Senator Mike Mansfield and Cardinal Spellman, the Archbishop of New York. Moreover, Diệm also received emotional support from the U.S. President, John F. Kennedy. Before becoming the boss of the White House, Kennedy had ever joined a club named "Organization of American Friends of Vietnam" in 1955. He even possibly had met Diệm since 1951 in the role of a senator (Dung 2008)&(Congressional Research Service 1984, 93).

In the book *"The American Pope: The Life and Times of Francis Cardinal Spellman,"* John Cooney also insisted the Americans prominent role in creating Premier Ngô Đình Diệm. Based on sources from the personal diary of Cardinal Spellman, Federal Bureau of Investigation (FBI) classified documents and interviews, Cooney launched assessments on Ngô Đình Diệm, which later have been considered believable and valuable. According to John Cooney, although

---

173 In the memoir named *Việt Nam máu lửa quê hương tôi (Vietnam blood and fire)*, Major General Đỗ Mậu, who participated in the coup, wrote on page 816 that followed the command of Edward Lansdale, the U.S. Ambassador in Saigon, Major Lucien Conein brought 3 million Vietnam currency to the Joint Staff giving for the coup party. This money was prepared for the purpose of "Buying off the opposition side." It was spent as a request of Generals who were going to implement the coup. Regarding this, William J. Rust also wrote that on 05th October, Conein met privately with General Dương Văn Minh (Big Minh), head of the coup d'état group, to pledge that the Americans "Will not sabotage the coup" and "Will continue aiding for SVN after the success of the coup faction" (Rust 1985, 148).

174 The so-called Revolutionary Military Council of Vietnam, established on November 1st, 1963 by a group of generals, who took power after the coup. The Council consisted of 20 members, took office nearly one year between 01st November 1963 and 26th October 1964. The council chairman was General Dương Văn Minh, the first vice president was General Trần Văn Đôn and the second vice president was General Tôn Thất Đính.

not many people knew the truth that Cardinal Spellman took a critical role in creating the political career of a man who had been in a seminary in New York, just became premier of SVN. At Diệm, Spellman saw all standards that he desired in a leader: ardent Catholic and extreme anti-communist (Cooney 1985, 307). The first meeting between Spellman and Diệm took place in New York, in 1950 under the arrangement of Pastor Fred McGuire. As a former missionary in Asia, McGuire possessed a profound knowledge of the Far East region that was respected by the State Department officials. After coming to the U.S., thanks to the intercession of Bishop Ngô Đình Thục, Diệm was accepted to live in Maryknoll Seminary in Ossining, New York.

The historic meeting later changed the life of this Vietnamese Catholic. October 1950, Diệm and Thục met with State Department officials at the Mayflower Hotel. In this session, Ngô brothers were accompanied by McGuire and three other political staff members of the Church (Father Emmanuel Jacque, Bishop Howard Carroll, and Edmund Walsh) when it was working to stop Communism at Georgetown University. The purpose of this gathering was to ask Diệm and Thục about their country and to determine their political beliefs. In the meeting, Ngô brothers confidently asserted that Diệm was capable of ruling their nation (Cooney 1985, 307–14).

Though opposing the view that Diệm was a political figurehead of the U.S. in SVN, Edward Miller, nevertheless, admitted in the early 1950s Diệm won the backing of many influential figures. Those included a Roman Catholic Cardinal (Francis Spellman), an American Supreme Court Justice (William O. Douglas), at least half a dozen members of Parliament, numerous journalists, some critical scholars and even the founder and director of Office of Strategic Services (OSS) (William J. Donovan) (Miller 2004, 444)&(Congressional Research Service 1984, 93). During 1951, most of the U.S. government officials who involved in the policy of intervention in Vietnam reaching a consensus that the Bảo Đại government must be replaced by another one with stronger support from the masses and began promoting actions to achieve that goal. In the viewpoint of these policymakers, the head of new cabinet should be an anti-French politician because the Vietnamese people had a belief that what related to France also linked to colonialism, in general (Congressional Research Service 1984, 91–92).

From late 1953 to mid-1954, Ngô Đình Nhu assumed the role of liaison between CIA and his brother. Through Nhu, CIA grasped all Diệm's intentions as well as future ambitions of Ngô family. For this reason, Ahern asserted Nhu had established a strategic relationship with CIA prior Diệm took office (Ahern 2000, 20).

Since the end of the Second World War, concerned about Vietnam, on the one hand, Truman began providing financial support for the French Expeditionary Troops in Indochina. In the meantime, the U.S. State Department officials paid attention to seek top anti-communist leaders (Ahern 2000, 1–2). This plan was discreetly preparing while the Americans recognized the French influence in Indochina relentlessly declined. After Điện Biên Phủ, Eisenhower would prefer to create an expanded government rather than maintain the administration of Bảo Đại, whom the Vietnamese people did not support and regarded as a puppet of France. The Americans thought it was time to have an elite nationalist leader in SVN to weaken the attractiveness of Hồ Chí Minh. Therefore, they pressured the former emperor to accept Diệm as prime minister replacing the pro-French courtier Prince Bửu Lộc (Cooney 1985, 307–314). After three weeks since the previous Emperor Bảo Đại signed the decision of appointment Ngô Đình Diệm as Premier, on July 7th, 1954, he officially established the new government with a cabinet of 18 members.

Although Diệm did not have any outstanding achievements as well as an active political organization of his followers, he still became the best choice of both France[175] and the U.S. and later became an anti-communist bulwark in SVN. According to Thomas L. Ahern Jr, who had been a former CIA agent working years in SVN battlefield, that was simply Diệm had rare standards for most indigenous leaders at that time, such as anti-communist spirit, a pious Catholic, and the possibility to understand English[176]. Furthermore, Diệm demonstrated his anti-colonialist thought from his early age when he refused the offer of continuing to serve as the interior minister in the French protectorate government in 1933. He then also accumulated Western political experiences during the time he lived in the U.S. and European countries (Ahern 2000, 9).

From above arguments, it can be concluded that through Cardinal Spellman's discovery, the U.S. found Ngô Đình Diệm as a cornerstone of the "Free World" in

---

175 According to Nguyễn Gia Kiểng, Diệm took power following a French plan, and he was supported enthusiastically and considerately by the French. Thanks for that help; Diệm gained victory in the conflicts with General Nguyễn Văn Hinh (Chief of Vietnam National Army), the Bình Xuyên, Cao Đài and Hòa Hảo opposition armed forces. See: Nguyễn Gia Kiểng, *Ông Ngô Đình Diệm lên cầm quyền như thế nào (How did Ngô Đình Diệm come to power)* at http://sachhiem.net/ THOISU_CT/ ChuN/ Nguyen GiaKieng_0.php. (Accessed 10th July 2017).

176 Agreeing with this view, Stanley Karnow claims: Diệm was chosen because the Americans "knew of no one better" or "They could find no alternative" (Karnow 1984, 214).

Asia. In accordance with the arrangement among the Americans, the French and Chief of State Bảo Đại, Diệm became premier of State of Vietnam in mid-June 1954. In response to that tremendous support, at least in the early years in power, Diệm proved that he was an excellent choice of the Americans for deploying their Containment Policy in Southeast Asia. In a speech made during the visit to the U.S. on May 13th, 1957, President Ngô Đình Diệm expressed his gratitude to the Americans and self-determining to accompany them in the mission of protecting the Free World. Diệm even was enthusiastic about declaring that U.S. boundary expanded to SVN as a way to display his loyalty.[177]

On 23rd October 1955, the referendum of the State of Vietnam took place with an overwhelming triumph of Diệm after a one-sided agitation propaganda campaigns of the Personalist Labour Party (Vietnamese: Cần Lao Nhân Vị) led by Ngô Đình Nhu. Soon later, Diệm held for establishing the Constituent National Assembly. The Assembly enacted the National Constitution of Vietnam, renamed the State of Vietnam to RVN on October 26th, 1955 and elected Diệm as President of the First Republic.

Finally, with American cooperation, Diệm was able to gain most of his objectives and concentrate power over SVN by the end of 1955 (Chapman 2006, 672–3). Despite the fact that the poll was heavily manipulated, right after the vote the spokesman of U.S. Foreign Department indicated the American "objective attitude" towards its final result. *"The people of Vietnam have spoken and we, of course, recognize their decision,"* he declared (Brownell 1963, 158).

4.2 The Formulation of the Diệm Ethnic Policies

The French defeat in Điện Biên Phủ battlefield unquestionably was the beginning of a political process which led to the expulsion of France from more or less entire Indochina. In accordance with the Geneva Agreement, Vietnam would be temporarily divided into two regrouping areas at the 17th parallel. However, the status of separation would finish by an election to unify the country that expected to take place on July 21st, 1956. In the North, the process of building socialism was strengthened by the model of production cooperation following the rehabilitation of peace following the model of China which even sent advisers

---

[177] "Indeed, today, more than ever, the defense of freedom is essentially a common task. With regard to security, the frontiers of the United States do not stop at the Atlantic and Pacific Coasts, but extend, in South East Asia, to the Ben Hai River, which partitions Viet-Nam at the 17th parallel, and forms the threatened border of the Free World." See details at TTU, VC, VA 2321507006.

to accelerate the land reform. Meanwhile, two weeks earlier than the signing ceremony of the Geneva Accords, on 07th July 1954, Ngô Đình Diệm established a pro-American government and placed southern half of the country under the U.S. control.

There was the fact that the nation-building process of the Diệm government took place in a challenging and complicated context. The French rule transformed Indochina, destroyed "traditional" societal structures, but was far from achieving its goal of an Indochinese society associated deeply with France. Also, during the first two years in office, Diệm's political power was insufficient. It was because the authority did not concentrate in the State. The Second World War and the Japanese occupation had earlier played a crucial role in the fragmentation of the society, resulting to a power vacuum and the unclear future of a divided country. The French policy of divide and rule had also dispersed the power among competing factions including the army, the police, the secret service and interest groups such as French and Chinese business circles or Vietnamese landlords with extensive holdings in the Mekong river delta. Besides that, the security control of the capital city of Saigon was in the hands of Bình Xuyên forces, a gangster band, which was nourished by the business of casinos and prostitution dens. Simultaneously, Diệm government had to encounter the strong opposition of two armed sects Cao Đài and Hòa Hảo backed by the French (Hickey 1982a, 2). Furthermore, practical activities of Việt Minh political cadres, who stayed in the South after the Geneva Agreement, contributed to the disintegration of the people's support for the GVN significantly. Last but not least, Diệm government had inherited a crumbling economy after a protracted war between Vietnam and France. Though agriculture was considered the critical field but stagnated at that time, many rice fields and plantations had been abandoned for a long time (Hickey 1982a, 2)&(Latham 2006).

With American help, Diệm gradually phased out the influence of the French, gained the control of the national army and eliminate armed opposition groups. More than a year after coming to power, Diệm deposed Emperor Bảo Đại in a referendum then self-declared as president of the RVN. Along with spreading rumors of the Việt Minh's revenge plan for Catholics to entice Christian believers migrating to the South, the GVN declared to refuse the general election to unify the country.

As mentioned above, since 1950, as a result of a French decree, the Central Highlands was detached as the Crown Domain (Vietnamese: Hoàng Triều Cương Thổ). This territory thenceforward was placed directly under the rule of Bảo Đại and belonged to the French Indochina, but not as a part of the other realms of Bảo Đại, notably Annam and Tonkin. The Crown Domain nominally was an autonomous zone, but all the right to make decisions was in the hands of the French. In other words, the Central Highlands was only an autonomous region in the French Indochina.

In order to stabilize political security in the Central Highlands, as soon as he took office, Ngô Đình Diệm devoted particular attention to reorganizing the management on every aspect of politics, military, social-economy, and culture. With the establishment of the RVN in 1955, Highlanders then were classified as ethnic minorities in their own homeland. Aiming at building a unified political entity in SVN, Diệm concluded that the ethnic minorities including the Highlanders, the Cham, the Khmer and the Chinese would have to be assimilated into the Vietnamese cultural sphere. The president objective was then institutionalized by a decree, issued on June 12th, 1955 the GVN, commonly known as the Highland Affairs Policies (Vietnamese: Chính sách Thượng vụ).

In order to implement his domination strategies, Ngô Đình Diệm established the Standing Advisory Office (Vietnamese: Văn phòng Cố vấn Thượng Vụ) with the function of consulting issues associated with the Montagnards in 1956. One year later, the Standing Advisory Office was upgraded to be the Bureau for Highland Affairs (Vietnamese: Nha Công tác Xã hội Miền Thượng) set under the Presidency. Its headquarters was placed in Huế. In 1958, the Social Chamber (Vietnamese: Phòng Xã Hội) was established to help highland students to enroll in schools like Việt students. Both the Bureau for Highland Affairs and the Social Chamber existed until the Diệm regime collapsed in the military coup d'état of 1963 (Thêm 1966).

On the U.S. side, as far as they were aware of the importance of the Central Highlands, the Americans determined to occupy that strategic area at all costs[178]. Along with promoting the Strategic Hamlet Program (SHP), which was considered the backbone or the core of the U.S. and GNV's pacification strategy, CIA began to launch the Village Defense Program (VDP) over rural areas in SVN, firstly in Darlac since early 1961. These programs were considered effective means to confront the intense penetration of Communist forces into the Highlands. However, that direct intervention of the Americans, as well as their demand to bring the U.S. Armed Forces to SVN, made the GVN feel discontentment. It is believed that Diệm did not want Americans to intervene deeply in internal affairs of the RVN and to combat directly in the Vietnam War. His first priority at the time was to maintain the "Mandate of Heaven" and "National

---

178 The relationship between the U.S. and RVN got tense many times around the problems of Highlands and FULRO.

sentiments." Nonetheless, regardless of objections of the GVN, from mid-1962 the American military took over the VDP and then quickly changed it into an offensive operation.

The Americans created the most favorable conditions for spreading Protestantism. It was not by accident that the spread of Protestantism in the minority regions was sticky correlated with the American intrusion, especially during the Vietnam War. Although since 1924 this denomination began being preached in Khmer community in Châu Đốc and, in the late 1920s, a chapel established in the ethnic minority residential area in Khe So near Đà Nẵng, up until 1929 the goal of evangelization for minorities became a concern of the Christian and Missionary Alliance (C&MA). Studies indicate that before the August Revolution the French administration restricted the expansion of Protestantism to the Central Highlands to avoid clashes with Catholics or to protect the Catholic missionary privileges, in other words (Đ. Q. Hưng 2011). That constraint made the efforts of missionaries only result in the cities like Đà Lạt, Buôn Mê Thuột instead of in areas along the national highway where ethnic minorities inhabited densely. Despite efforts of the French, the position of those two denominations was inverted from 1954 to 1975. The influence of Protestantism grew up in parallel with the increase of the U.S. Army in the Highlands. According to estimation, till 1975, there were some 38.965 Montagnards out of 200.000 Protestants in southern Vietnam[179] (N. V. Minh 2006, 52).

As assessed by the two evangelists named J. Fleming and R. Phillips who carried out a long-standing mission in the Rhade community, during the Vietnam War Protestantism in the Montagnard regions achieved three key ambitions:

1. Creating a political force, a "people's movement";
2. Training an active missionary system besides the nuclear class of local pastors;
3. Developing on three aspects: (1) promoting existing chapters; (2) exploiting the war circumstance to expand the mission; (3) taking advantage of opportunities when ethnic minority groups could not live separately and could

---

[179] Between the periods of 1954–1975, the evangelization of Protestantism among the ethnic minorities was considered to reach its peak. Missionary work received much support from the Christian and Missionary Alliance (C&MA) and the Vietnam General Confederation of Evangelical Churches. Thanks to that support, experienced pastors, as well as functional missionary supplies, were transferred to Vietnam. Since the Vietnam Evangelical Mission dissolved in 1959, in mid-1962, the Vietnam General Confederation of Evangelical Churches established the Central Missionary Committee in the Thirtieth Church Congress which then was assigned to direct the missionary activity in the ethnic minority regions (Hùng 2017) & (Phu 2010, 324).

not also be separated from the Việt people as before. After the Highlanders had come to new resettlement centers, the influences of many old divinities reduced considerably, and that was an excellent opportunity for new gods to take their place[180].

Some American programs contributed to enhancing economic and social development in the Central Highlands. Thanks to these programs, infrastructures such as roads, schools, and hospitals were constructed; some advanced farming techniques were introduced to the Montagnards; the scripts of some ethnic groups were created on the basis of Latinization of their dialects, etc. However, in general, just like their French predecessors, the Americans seemed to be concerned more about the purpose of taking advantage of the Highlanders for their strategic objectives than caring about the ethnonationalism or of the minorities' long-term interests. Thus, almost development programs that the U.S. had carried out in minority communities ended after Washington decided to sign the Paris Agreement of 1973.

4.3 Contents of the Diệm Highland Affairs Policies

4.3.1 Merging the Crown Domain into National Territory

Shortly after taking office Ngô Đình Diệm set the task of national unity in every aspect. Regarding territory, he proposed Emperor Bảo Đại to dissolve the Crown Domain of Southern Highlander Country and to merge this area into the territory of the State of Vietnam[181]. At that time, the Central Highlands consisted of five provinces such as Kontum, Pleiku, Darlac, Đồng Nai Thượng and Lâm Viên. Nguyễn Ngọc Thơ, Vice President under Diệm regime, revealed that Diệm considered abolishing Crown Domain status[182] was an efficient way to

---

180 Quoted by Đỗ Quang Hưng in *Một số vấn đề về Tin Lành ở Tây Nguyên (Some issues of Protestantism in the Central Highlands)*. Central Highlands' Journal of Social Science, Issue 2, Year 2011, pp. 3–12.
181 On October 23, 1956, the RVN President Ngô Đình Diệm signed Decree No. 143A/TTP renamed Bắc Việt (North Vietnam), Trung Việt (Central Vietnam), and Nam Việt (South Vietnam) to Bắc Phần (the North), Trung Phần (the Central), and Nam Phần (the South). The next day, he signed Decree No. 147-A/TTP continuously split Central into two domains of Cao Nguyên Trung Phần (Central Highlands) and Trung Nguyên Trung Phần (consisted of the central coastal provinces from Quảng Trị to Bình Thuận). Ibid. National Archives Center IV, Da Lat city, & (Thêm 1966, 204).
182 This particular status recognized the Crown Domain as an autonomous zone for indigenous peoples. Law acknowledged that the territorial sovereignty of the Crown Domain belonged to Huế court, but the land ownership there belonged to mountainous

remove influences of the French in the Highlands. According to him, the French maintained Crown Domain because they wanted to keep the Kinh (Việt) out of the Highlanders, by which they could develop plantations and exploit the valuable minerals (Hickey 1982a, 7).

On 11th March 1955, Ngô Đình Diệm enacted Decree No. 21, officially merged the Crown Domain into the Central Part of the State of Vietnam and terminated privileges of the French and Emperor Bảo Đại in the Central Highlands (MDEM 1972, 6–7). That same day, Decree No. 61 was issued to appoint Mr. Vĩnh Dự and Mr. Tôn Thất Hội as government representatives (Governors) in Buôn Mê Thuột and Đà Lạt, respectively. Thenceforth, the structure of administration, as well as military in the Central Highlands, was held under the system of national administrative management and national defense (Tiệp 2013b, 35).

Simultaneously with abolishing the Crown Domain regulation influence of nationalism, the GVN renamed the Cham people, who were living in the coastal areas of the provinces of Phan Rang, Phan Rí as Montagnards (Thượng) and Chams (Chàm). Both of these new groups, along with the tribal groups, the Khmer, the Chinese and northern migrant ethnic minorities were classified as "Ethnic minorities" (Vietnamese: Đồng bào Thượng) in their own home country.

Diệm also sought to reorganize administrative management apparatus in the Central Highlands to enhance the control over the Montagnards. Accordingly, the GVN established some new provinces by separating the old ones. Namely, on 19th May 1958, President Diệm enacted the Ordinance No. 170-NV[183] to rename Đồng Nai Thượng Province to Lâm Đồng (comprised two counties Bảo Lộc and Di Linh) and the Ordinance No. 261-NV[184] to establish Tuyên Đức Province (included three counties of Đơn Dương, Đức Trọng, and Lạc Dương), the town of Đà Lạt was provincial capital (Lan 2014, 32). On 23rd January 1959, the president issued Decree 24-NV, established Quảng Đức Province with the provincial

---

ethnicities (Article 1 and 3). Therefore, no one had the right to invade, transfer, lease lands in the Crown Domain without the consent of the indigenous peoples (Article 7), and no one had the right to divide the territory to cede to another country without the approval of the Huế court. Repealing Crown Domain regulation meant eliminating the autonomous status and revoking land ownership of the Highlanders. See Ibid. *Dụ số 27 QT/TD (Ordinance No. 27 QT/TD).*

183 See more in: *Địa chí Lâm Đồng (Unification Records of Lâm Đồng).* Http://www.lamdong.gov.vn/viVN/a/diachilamdong/Pages/chuong1p1.aspx#02. (Accessed 27th December 2017).

184 Ibid. *Địa chí Lâm Đồng (Unification Records of Lâm Đồng).*

capital located in Gia Nghĩa[185]. In accordance with the Order No. 186, issued on September 1st, 1962, Cheo Reo district (southern part of Pleiku) and the county of Thuần Mẫn, (northern part of Darlac) were merged to be the new province of Phú Bổn. This territory consisted of Hậu Bổn town and three counties of Phú Thiện, Phú Túc, and Thuần Mẫn[186].

In brief, the Central Highlands under Diệm regime was reorganized into seven provincial administrative units including Kontum, Pleiku, Darlac, Tuyên Đức, Quảng Đức, Lâm Đồng, and Phú Bổn. This organizational structure was retained until 1975.

As announced by the National Statistical Institute of Saigon, the population of Central Highlands in 1956 was 530.000, which increased to 604.000 in 1960 and 770.000 in 1966, respectively. To implement the policy of assimilation of ethnic minorities, in the first exodus of 1954 what so-called Operation Passage to Freedom, the GVN took about 54.551 migrants from the North to resettle in the Central Highlands[187]. This figure later would be supplemented by smaller evacuations in the next years. Also within the last five years of the 1950s, the government of SVN displaced some more 30.000 Việt people from the central coastal provinces to the Central Highlands (Chi 2006, 549–612).

---

185 President of the Republic of Vietnam (1959), *Sắc lệnh số 24-NV ngày, 23-1-1959 về việc thành lập tỉnh Quảng Đức (Ordinance No. 24-NV, dated 23rd January 1959, on the establishment of Tuyên Đức Province)*, the National Archives Center II, Ho Chi Minh City, dossier code Đệ I CH 3040.

186 President of the Republic of Vietnam (1962), *Sắc lệnh số 186-NV, ngày, 1 tháng 9 năm 1962 về việc thành lập tỉnh Phú Bổn (Ordinance No. 186-NV, dated 1st September 1962, on the establishment of Phú Bổn Province)*, the National Archives Center II, Ho Chi Minh City, dossier code Đệ I CH 3042.

187 On migration issues in Vietnam after 1954, in one of his researches about the struggles of the ethnic minorities in SVN, Po Dharma claims that Ngô Đình Diệm resettled entire 850.000 northern Vietnamese immigrants in the Central Highlands (Dharma 2012, 12). However, many studies, for example, (Dacy 1986, 2–3), (Hansen 2009, 173–211), (Fall 1965, 154), etc., indicate that immigrants from the North were resettled in many different areas in the South. After the period of temporary residence, migrants were transferred to settlements in the Saigon, Biên Hòa, Long Khánh, Cái Sắn (the area located within the provinces of Long Xuyên and Rạch Giá), and so on; fishers were moved to coastal regions. Resettlement sites were usually established in strategic locations and gateway to major cities. In the Central Highlands, Diệm government organized numerous resettlement sites surrounding Buôn Mê Thuột, Pleiku, and Đà Lạt.

Diệm believed the strategy of the relocation of anti-communist Catholic refugees could help his government to prevent the infiltration and movements of the VC over mountainous areas. Though the number of Việt people increased significantly since 1954, the population of ethnic minorities in the Highlands still accounted for 63.8 percent in 1960 (Vân 2003, 82). The Việt migrants often concentrated in towns or along national roads. It is thought that their presence caused disturbance for the traditional lifestyle of indigenous people, which made many cultural values of indigenous minority groups transfigured or faded over time.

4.3.2 Regarding Political and Armed Policies

With the ever-increasing level of the American assistant, by late 1954 Diệm declared to establish the "National Revolutionary Movement" that set out three targets: "Down the Communism" (Vietnamese: Diệt Cộng), "Throw out the French" (Vietnamese: Đả Thực) and "Throw Bảo Đại" (Vietnamese: Bài Phong). In other words, this program aimed at removing military, political organizations, which tended to be pro-French or royalists such as the paramilitary sects of Cao Đài, Hòa Hảo and the gangster group of Bình Xuyên from political arena; and, especially eliminating the Việt Minh forces. The National Revolutionary Movement impacted strongly upon almost social strata, putting the majority of people in rural areas in the state of panic. In particular, while local officials were considered remnants of the feudal government of Bảo Đại, those with degrees from Franco-Vietnamese schools was found to be colonial apparatuses, and relatives of Việt Minh followers were classified as the Communist's bases. To avoid of being denounced, imprisoned, even killed, social classes had no choice but "devoutly" took part in the National Revolutionary Movement to become anti-communists or participated in building Land Development Centers, Agrovilles, and Strategic Hamlets.

With the support from U.S. advisors, those who came from Michigan University (Michigan State University Group-MSUG), a police training center was built in Đà Lạt in 1957; the Military Academy there was also upgraded. At the same time, to meet the demand of training self-defense cadres and civil servants, the Directorate of Self-Defense under the Interior Ministry opened a training center in Buôn Mê Thuột (Thêm 1966)&(Latham 2006).

In another move, the U.S. embassy also called for long-term cooperation of the Montagnards in improving culture, society, health care system and religion to raise living standard. Accordingly, by October 1966, there were twenty-seven assistant agencies those operated 26 programs employing over 300 U.S. personnel,

Fig. 6: U.S. Technical Groups Trained Mountain Tribes in 1961. Sources: Training of Mountain Tribes, Vietnam. In: TTU, VC, VA 1780713024.

30 international, and over 500 Vietnamese many[188]. Delegations of social workers as U.S. Operations Mission (USOM), U.S. Agency for International Development (USAID), the Summer Institute of Linguistics (SIL), volunteer organizations, etc., came to instruct the Highlanders advanced methods to prevent and treat diseases; to transmit common sustainable agriculture techniques; to help building houses; to create alphabet based on Latinization of local dialects. Although only derived from the purpose of obtaining the Highlanders' loyalties, these supporting programs brought considerable benefits to the minorities. Many schools, in which local languages, Vietnamese and English were parallel taught, were founded in Buôn Mê Thuột, Pleiku, Kontum, and Đà Lạt. Also, multiple Cham and the Montagnards outstanding students enrolled to study at the University of Đà Lạt. The condition of medical examination and treatment for indigenous people also improved significantly[189].

While the pro-French and royalist political organizations were quickly eliminated by Diệm regime's suppression, in 1960, the National Front for the Liberation of South Vietnam (commonly known as the National Liberation Front - NLF) (Vietnamese: Mặt trận Giải phóng miền Nam Việt Nam), a political coalition of

---

188 *Programs of Technical Assistance in South Vietnam.* In: TTU, VC, VA 1780709052.
189 Ibid. *Programs of Technical Assistance in South Vietnam.*

left-wing nationalist, struggling to oppose Diệm policies and the intervention of the U.S., was founded and rapidly controlled large sections of countryside and mountains in SVN. In response to the development of national liberation movement and the rapid increase of insurgency in the South Vietnamese countryside[190], the U.S. decided to make a deeper intervention in Vietnam War. On 29th April 1961, the U.S. National Security Council approved the "Counterinsurgency Plan for Vietnam" (CIP) (FRUS 1988, 182–85). At the same time, President John F. Kennedy's administration decided to increase financial support for the Diệm government. Some 65 million dollars for military equipment and 136 million dollars for economic aid were delivered that year, and by December 3.200 U.S. troops were deployed in Vietnam. The U.S. Military Assistance Command, Vietnam (MACV) was formed under the command of General Paul D. Harkins in February 1962[191]. There also was a dramatic rise in the number of U.S. advisors, reaching 1.346 in 1961 and 9.965 by the end of 1962 (Hickey 1982a, 74).

In order to carry out independent investigations, in 1961, Washington sent some research delegations to SVN. For example, the group of Vice President Lyndon B. Johnson (arrived in SVN in May), the delegation of Stanford Research Institute led by Dr. Eugene Staley (came to SVN in June) or the deputation of Maxwell D. Taylor and Walt Whitman Rostow represented for the U.S. Department of Defense (arrived in SVN in October). These surveys resulted in the birth of a new global strategy called "Flexible response."[192] The pilot program of this approach was deployed in Vietnam with an operational plan named Staley-Taylor[193], by which, the U.S. believed to bring the Vietnam War to an end in three phases:

---

190 American military advisors estimated that until 1961 VC regular forces had about 25.000 men, organized into larger formations and employed with increasing frequency (Pentagon Papers 1971, 128–159).
191 See more in: Lê Xuân Nhuận, *Ấp chiến lược (Strategic hamlets)*. Sources: http://sachhiem.net/LICHSU/LEXNHUAN/LeXNhuan03.php. (Accessed 14th October 2016).
192 Flexible Response or Flexible Deterrent Options (FDO) is a U.S. defense strategy in which a wide range of diplomatic, political, economic and military options are applied to prevent an enemy attack. The term flexible response was first used by General Maxwell D. Taylor in his book entitled *The Uncertain Trumpet* (1960). See more *Flexible Response* in Encyclopedia Britannica. Https://www.britannica.com/topic/Flexible-Response. (Accessed 30th March 2018).
193 The project was named after two drafters; economist Eugene Staley came from Stanford Research Institute-Stanford University and General Maxwell D. Taylor.

1. The first step would be conducted from mid-1961 with the purpose of appeasing SVN within 18 months by the national policy of Strategic Hamlet;
2. The second period would start in early 1963, aiming at restoring the economy, strengthening military forces and completing the pacification plan;
3. The third step would be implemented until the end of 1965 to develop the economy, stabilize SVN and finish the war.

In the Pacification Plan, the Strategic Hamlet and Village Defense Programs assumed the central role. Both of those programs were considered the highest effort of the U.S. and the GVN to consolidate rural areas as well as mountainous regions where most of the ethnic minorities resided (FRUS 1991, 99). In the cities, the security was more assured due to the high concentration of police forces; the coastal areas were considered rural and also put within the scope of pacification programs. The Americans armed the Montagnards because they realized tribesmen's capability to fight in jungles. To build up local paramilitary forces, American instructors came to every village located in government-controlled zones where they organized community defense groups in the countryside or civilian indigenous security groups and native special force of every ethnicity. After being trained and armed, those troops were assigned the responsibility to fight back VC guerrillas those who dared to penetrate into the villages, at least until the government troops arrived.

There was a fact that in mountainous and rural areas, regular troops of Republic of Vietnam Military Forces (RVNMF)[194] were relatively dispersed. Also, the restrictions on transport conditions caused difficulties in moving troops and weapons reducing the efficiency of "search and destroy" campaigns. Meanwhile, Communist guerrillas frequently launched propaganda operations with high effectiveness attracting a large number of sympathizers in remote areas. The RVNMF's raids, therefore, often could not obtain significant results because VC guerrillas would scatter quickly into thick forests or be hidden by the villagers. Finally, by resettling mass people in secure hamlets and building local paramilitary forces, the U.S. and the GVN hoped to "Resolve the contradiction between concentrating military force to search and destroy and the stationing of tactic occupying positions, especially in the large expanses of rural areas" (Elliott 2003, 353).

Theoretically, a pacification program, in which strategic hamlets was thought to be the backbone, was the best endeavor to apply counterinsurgency doctrine

---

194 Republic of Vietnam Military Forces (RVNMF) was also known as Army of the RVN (ARVN) or South Vietnamese Army (SVA).

into the battlefield of Vietnam. As asserted in the Pentagon Papers "The objective was political though the means to its realization were a mixture of military, social, psychological, economic and political measures" (Pentagon Papers 1971, 128-159). American tacticians steadfastly believed that by using this method, they could achieve allegiances or "win the hearts and the souls" of all villagers. Until then, as an inevitable result, VC partisans could not mobilize adequate supplies and must be isolated and destroyed gradually. However, historical reality took place later was far different from what the U.S. expected. The more detail of pacification tactics will be discussed thoroughly in the section of the Strategic Hamlet Program.

Concerning RVN military networks

This section aims to present an overview of military systems set up in ethnic minority areas. As a significant part of pacification program, the strengthening of military and paramilitary forces on the highland battlefield attracted the careful attention of both the U.S. and the GVN. All the units of the regular army, as well as militia, self-defense, intelligence, etc., were built, reinforced and arranged densely. For example, within only two years of 1961-1963, the RVNMF in Gia Lai[195] increased sharply from 7.000 to 27.585 soldiers (Executive Committee of Gia Lai Provincial Communist Party 2009, 326-27). Similarly, RVNMF also arranged powerful regular forces in Kontum with the appearance of the 22nd Tactic Zone, the 22nd Infantry Division in the town of Kontum, the 40th Regiments in Tân Cảnh. Besides that, there were 1.091 militants of local military forces, 885 soldiers of the security forces, 300 militia and 1.656 republican youths (Executive Committee of Kon Tum Municipal Communist Party 1998, 95). Based on this strength and firm supports of the U.S., Ngô Đình Diệm's government announced a plan to pacify Kontum within six months, starting on July 29th, 1961. The set out ultimate goals were "Spreading propaganda campaigns; controlling the Highlanders and making them believe in the government, hate the Việt Cộng; maintaining and strengthening security in regions where were relatively stable while building and strengthening security operations in areas of insecurity" (Executive Committee of Kon Tum Provincial Communist Party 2006, 298).

In the town of Buôn Mê Thuột, the GVN placed the 23rd Tactical Zone, the 23rd Division, and the 45th Regiment. And, as reported by the Darlac provincial chief, the ability to recruit security and militia forces there could reach to

---

[195] While the NLF called this province Gia Lai, GVN named it Pleiku.

some 5.000 people[196]. In Tuyên Đức, Saigon army had three security battalions with 1.225 troops, 1.137 militia, 3.120 fighting youths and 834 U.S. personnel including advisors, infantry and artillery units, and commandos. Of these forces, two-thirds were used to support the construction of strategic hamlets, raid the bases of the VC and control villagers (Lan 2014, 42).

Over the provinces of the Mekong River Delta, where the Khmer and a part of the Cham were dwelling, the RVNMF also arranged the regular military and the local self-defense forces, though not as dense as in the Central Highlands.

Thus, in order to expand the government-controlled areas, the GVN simultaneously enhanced people's control apparatus, especially in towns, plantations and along main roads. Besides the regular troops, there was the presence of the forces of militia, security, and commando in minority regions. The administrative strategic and psychological intelligence officers usually penetrated deeply into rural and mountainous areas to get sympathy from ethnic minorities under the covers of medical or social activists. Many specific operational programs aimed at "conquering the hearts and minds" of the peoples were deployed by SVN's government, of course, with the high support of the U.S. Here are some of the most prominent projects.

The Village Defense Program and the Civilian Irregular Defense Group Program

The Village Defense Program (VDP) (Vietnamese: Chương trình Phòng vệ xóm làng) was initiated by the U.S. Special Forces (under the direction of CIA) since late 1961[197] in order to prevent the highland villagers from influences of the Communist propaganda. Another aim of this program was to build a paramilitary force consisting of ethnic minorities, who would fight against the penetration of the Communists over remote areas to increase control of GVN in the Central Highlands. The VDP was a prerequisite for the formation of the Civil Commando Groups operated in the Central Highlands to carry out destructive missions and prevent the entry of People's Army of Vietnam units from North to SVN. February 1962, these civil commando units officially renamed to the

---

[196] The Provincial Chief of Darlac (1962), *Mật điện đến số 62/NA/QV/M, ngày 3 tháng 3 măm 1962 (Secret telegram No. 62/NA/QV/M), dated 3rd March 1962*, the National Archives Center II, Ho Chi Minh City, dossier code PTTg 14810.

[197] The very first project of the VDP was a medical assistance project to the Highlanders in an area surrounding Pleiku conducted by the U.S. Army Special Forces (Kelly 2004, 7) & (Salemink 2002, 7).

Civilian Irregular Defense Group (CIDG) (Vietnamese: Lực lượng dân sự chiến đấu). All activities of recruitment, training, and mobilization thenceforth were undertaken by both CIA and newly-formed Vietnamese Special Forces. Since July 23rd, 1962, all overt paramilitary operations of Special Forces were transferred from CIA to MACV following the National Security Action Memorandum 57th of the U.S. Department of Defense (Hickey 1982a, 80).

Conceptually, CIDG was *"A program developed by the U.S. government in the Vietnam War. The program raised local security forces in the highlands of South Vietnam to protect the villages from Viet Cong influence and intimidation"* (Stewart 2012, ii). According to this conception, the U.S. and the GVN deployed the CIDG program because they considered the dominance of the VC over the Central Highlands a significant concern[198].

It was suggested that this project, to what extent, was a pilot project of the Strategic Hamlet Program in the Central Highland (FRUS 1991, 107). Nevertheless, when comparing these two programs, Francis J. Kelly argued that there was a principal difference. Namely, in the CIDG program the Highlanders would stay in their own villages and receive training, get updated military equipment and defensive tactics to "Protect themselves, their families, possessions from the Việt Cộng" instead of being forced to move to other sites to live in new resettlement centers as in the Strategic Hamlet Program. That is to say, not only the Montagnards were engaged in the CIDG program, but other groups were also involved in this project were the Khmer, the Nùng and the Việt people from the Cao Đài and Hòa Hảo sects (Kelly 2004, 12, 24).

It is worth noting that the ethnic policies of the NLF from 1960 had a significant impact on the Highlanders. In the founding ceremony of 20th December 1960, the NLF announced their political stance of supporting the establishment of autonomous zones for the ethnic minorities in SVN like what the minorities in the North had earlier attained. The manifesto of the NLF also condemned the policy of assimilation, discrimination, and ill-treatment of Ngô Đình Diệm administration towards minorities. This front then sent many cadres to mobilize, propagate and disseminate the theory of equality and national reconciliation, which would be applied when the country united. The national radio station

---

198 A report by the U.S. State Department stated that in 1961 there were about 8.000 to 9.000 organized troops of VC in 30 battalions operating in the South. That did not include "Many thousands of village guards, political cadres, special agents, bearers and the like." See more in: FRUS 1961–1963, vol I, Vietnam 1961, Document 22: *A threat to the Peace, North Vietnam's Effort to Conquer South Vietnam.*

of Hanoi continually broadcast programs dedicating to the minority peoples in various languages such as Rhade, Bahnar, Jarai, Kaho, Khmer, and Cham. As a result, many minority youths were recruited to serve the resistance movement, of whom some were given to training in the North[199]. Some prestigious village elders even were sent to the North to visit the autonomous zones (S. Jones et al. 2002, 20).

Thus, along with the introduction of flexible ethnic strategies, the NLF sought to fully exploit the limitations of the Diệm's Highland Affairs Policies to win the support of the Montagnards. And, there is no doubt that the "Fatal blunders" of Diệm's domination strategies pushed these "People in between" closer to the NLF.

Derived from a perspective that *"The largest of these minorities, the Montagnards, had always been treated as third class peoples by the government which made them prime targets for Communist propaganda and recruiting"*; the U.S. intelligence experts proposed to build up a paramilitary force of minorities in remote areas to take control of the Central Highlands back. Also, according to CIA strategists, *"The Montagnards had no concept of nation or national defense and they would probably fight for family, home and village if the RVNMF would stay off their backs and if the government provide some social and political benefits"* (Piasecki 2009, 2)&(FRUS 1991, 100)&(Harris 2013, 10). For this reason, social welfare projects always played a significant role in the VDP.

The VDP was planned in mid-1961 with efforts of CIA's headquarters in Saigon to shake up their bases over the hinterlands. William Egan Colby, chief of CIA station in Saigon firmly believed that the Montagnards could protect themselves if they were organized and armed; their armed forces, on the other hand, could increase the GVN's resistance ability against the penetration of the VC in remote areas. Accordingly, 400 men of the U.S. Special Forces were sent to SVN in May 1961 to help villagers in defending themselves by equipping them with weapons, means of communications; instructing village defense techniques, establishing and training commando and militia forces of the Montagnards; and improving their living condition as well (FRUS 1991, 485)&(Leahy 1990, 36).

On the GVN side, after listening to Colby's presentation on purpose and significance of the VDP, President Diệm agreed in principle and sent a representative team of Presidential Survey Office (Vietnamese: Sở Liên lạc phủ Tổng thống) headed by Colonel Lê Quang Tung to collaborate with CIA in implementing

---

199 According to a study of Bernard Fall, the Minority School in Hanoi was graduating 120 Highlanders in every nine months. All trained people later returned to infiltrate to the South (Hickey 1982a, 65).

the pilot program at a Rhade village. Ngô Đình Nhu also repeatedly flew over Darlac with Colby to inspect the reality. A report of the Darlac Provincial Chief Nguyễn Văn Bảng, whom the Americans considered an enlightened official, sent to the Minister of Interior, recorded: *"In late October 1961, the delegation of the Presidential Survey Office introduced some American advisers to us to discuss training issues and establishment of a Montagnards commando force"*[200]. Captain Nguyễn Đức Phú, representative of the Presidential Survey Office, Brigadier General Tôn Thất Đính of the II Corps at Pleiku and Colonel Lê Quang Trọng of the 23rd Division at Buôn Mê Thuột were also ordered to cooperate with the Americans. According to Harris, in a meeting between Colby and Nhu in his office in Saigon on 5th October 1961, Nhu *"Formally gave his blessing to the project but within tight limits"*; he also recommended that the VDP should begin with a single village only. With his skeptical nature, Nhu stressed *"Initially Rhadé self-defense forces would be armed only with traditional weapons: crossbows and spears. Firearms would be issued and trained in their use provided only when villagers had put a fence around their village with signs declaring their allegiance to the Saigon government and threatening with death any Communist soldier or cadre attempting to enter"* (Harris 2013, 14).

As a result of the agreement between Nhu and Colby, on 1st October 1961, the VDP officially piloted in Buon Enao, a village of 400 Rhade people, which located near the 21st Road, in the northeast of Darlac just about six kilometers from Buôn Mê Thuột. By mid-December the same year, the Buon Enao Experiment was recognized fulfilled their part of the bargain by an inspection team of the Presidential Survey Office and the self-defense force was officially equipped with firearms including M2 carbines, Springfield rifles and Madsen 9mm submachine guns (Harris 2013, 18). The Darlac Provincial Chief Nguyễn Văn Bảng then was authorized by Nhu to developed the paramilitary forces over additional forty other Rhade villages to within a 15-kilometer radius of the Buon Enao and to coerce local chiefs, landowners to join the military training[201].

As documented in the book *U.S. Army Special Forces 1961–1971*, the outcome of the VDP (since February 1962 the VDP was renamed to the CIDG) in

---

200 The Provincial Chief of Darlac (1962), *Phiếu gửi số 694/NA/CT/I/M ngày 13 tháng 3 năm 1962 (Confirmation card No. 694/NA/CT/I/M), dated 13th March 1962*, the National Archives Center II, Ho Chi Minh City, dossier code Đệ I CH 7663.

201 Regarding the village patriarchs forced to accede to the CIDG, Kelly wrote: "The village chief was required to affirm that everyone in the village would participate in the program and that a sufficient number of people would volunteer for training to provide adequate protection for the village" (Kelly 2004, 28).

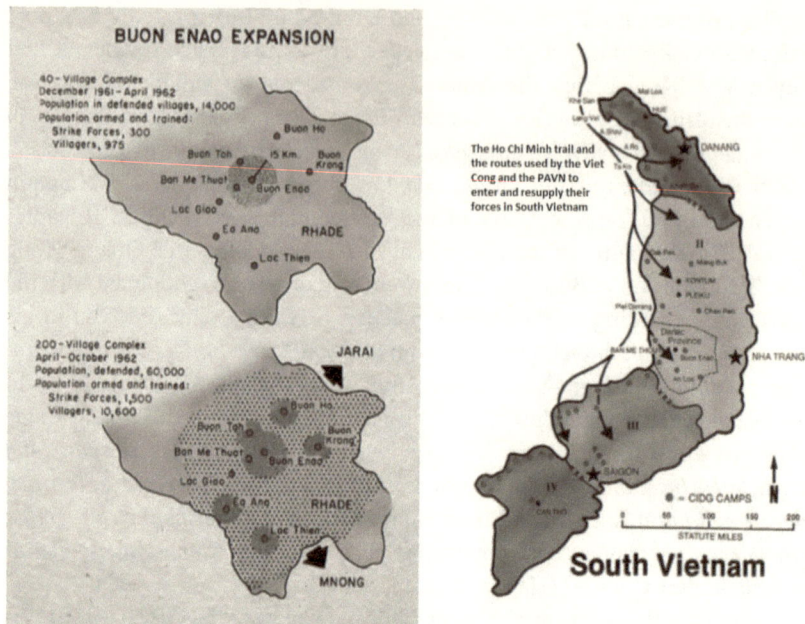

Fig. 7: The Expansion of the CIDG Program between December 1961 and October 1962. Sources: (Kelly 2004, 2, 5), edited by Author.

40 Rhade villages from December 1961 to April 1962 were as follows: 14.000 residents lived in the defensive communities; 300 villagers were armed and trained to be Strike Forces; and 975 local militia (Kelly 2004, 29). The CIDG program then continued to increase, within eight months from April to December 1962 with two more hundred Rhade villages were in "regimented." Of those, the protected population were 60.000; trained Strike Force personnel were 1.500, and village defense militia were 10.600 (Kelly 2004, 29)&(Hickey 1982a, 84).

Since late 1962, based on obtained achievements, the CIDG program was unceasingly expanded over localities of Jarai, M'nong and other smaller ethnic groups. However, in Darlac, the provincial authority did not continue to develop this program independently, but combined, integrated with plans to build the province's strategic hamlets. Perhaps the provincial chief thought that regarding purpose, both programs shared a goal of organizing and training village defenders or hamlet militia to prevent the Việt Cộng's infiltration.

Also in late 1962, the U.S. Army Special Forces, which later were assumed as full operational control of the SVN's Special Forces, was assigned a task of building the RVNMF Special Forces. On the Central Highlands, the U.S. Special Forces assumed a pivotal role in system of civil fighting camps that were established in disputed areas, on the strategic roads, along borders between SVN and Laos, Cambodia such as Sapa, Đức Lập, Bu Prang, Mi Gar (Darlac), Pleime, Kuai, Đức Cơ, Plei Jơrang, Plei Jit, Plei Blang 3 (Pleiku) and so on. Those civil fighting camps undertook a supporting role for pacification projects; expansion government-controlled areas; intrusion prevention and creating a blockade, separating bases and transportation routes of Việt Cộng. Each CIDG camp was assisted by six to twelve American advisors (Kelly 2004, 45–64).

Many training centers for commando and civilian fighting forces were constructed in the heart of highland provinces as Plei Morong, Chud'rong (Pleiku), Enao (Darlac), Dam Pao (Tuyên Đức), Tan Rai (Lâm Đồng), etc. As reported by the Darlac Provincial Chief, beyond the objectives of training supporting forces like the commando and the Strike Forces, these centers also aimed at spreading a hatred campaign against the VC and propaganda of enhancing SVN government prestige. After courses of training, those paramilitary forces were issued weapons and returned to their own villages to perform the anti-communist mission[202]. With the advantage in arms and techniques, these paramilitary units caused many difficulties and losses for the Việt Cộng. A document of the Darlac Provincial Administrative Court disclosed that: *"Operation of the two forces (commando and Strike Forces) caused significant casualties and weapon damage to the enemy; at the same time repulsed our enemy in order to widen the scope of control; regain sovereignty in rural areas."*[203] In a report sent to Washington, CIA also confirmed that these programs were effective to prevent the infiltration of Communists in the northern part of the Central Highlands. Namely, the number of the VC in Kontum fell from 5.000 to 500 over the first three months of 1962 (Hickey 1982a, 78). Regarding this matter, although not explicitly mentioned in evidence of losses, the Dak Lak Provincial Communist Party also acknowledged: *"Since the U.S. directly controlled minority Strike Forces, they increased attacks on bases, scoured in the forest, ambushed the roads; these*

---

202 The Provincial Chief of Darlac (1962), *Phiếu trình số 7215/NA/CT/M, ngày 24 tháng 8 năm 1962 (Report No. 7246/NA/CT/M, dated 8th August 1962)*, the National Archives Center II, Ho Chi Minh City, dossier code Đệ I CH 7274.

203 The Provincial Chief of Darlac (1962), *Phiếu trình số 7215/NA/CT/M, ngày 24 tháng 8 năm 1962 (Report No. 7215/NA/CT/M, dated 24th August 1962)*, the National Archives Center II, Ho Chi Minh City, dossier code Đệ I CH 7274.

forces caused many difficulties and losses for the revolution" (Executive Committee of Dak Lak Provincial Communist Party 2003, 98–99).

In short, the VDP, which aimed at training tactics and equipping weapons for the Montagnards to help in protecting themselves against Việt Cộng's attacks, developed rapidly. Within a year, from late 1961 to late 1962, there were 200 villages trained with 18.000 guns of various types distributed. Nevertheless, after the local self-defense units formally incorporated in the CIDG in February 1962, all operations then were put under the control of CIA, separated from the supervision of the GVN. As previously noted, July 23rd, 1962, the U.S. Department of Defense enacted the 57th National Security Action Memorandum whereby CIA would hand over all paramilitary activity including the CIDG for the MACV.

The formation of civilian commando forces which were armed by the U.S. and gradually got out of the control of the GVN later led to serious consequences. Due to ethnic conflict and the absence of concern, even discrimination of the Saigon administration, many minority commandos fighting for the U.S. Special Forces and the Strike Forces joined the separatist movement of BAJARAKA and FULRO. Realizing this threat, by early 1962 Diệm government made efforts to restore its control over the Highlands by requiring the U.S. to merge the CIDG project into the Strategic Hamlet Program in the Highlands. The GVN also tried to repossess rifles from hands of the Montagnards, but the number of weapons revoked was insignificant[204].

From late 1962, the GVN was unable to provide financially or logistically support to CIDG units. Those forces, thenceforth, were funded by the U.S. Mission until the last self-defense villages were assimilated into the Strategic Hamlet Program that was covered by regular U.S. Vietnamese funds. In April 1963, the Strike Force was turned over to the provincial chiefs and ended concentrating on village defense to participate in more general operations, most prominently boundary surveillance. Since 1970 most of those were turned into Vietnam Army Ranger that better known as the RVNMF Rangers units (Vietnamese: Biệt Động Quân).

---

204 According to Kelly, the recovery of armaments distributed to the Highlanders was tough because they thought that those weapons could be kept permanently to protect themselves and their own villages. Therefore, though the GVN had applied various measures to get back the weapons, for example, exchange guns for farm tools. Finally, only 2.000 rifles were taken back (i.e., just accounting for over 10 percent of the emitted weapons) (Hickey 1982a, 85).

The Land Development Centers and the Agroville Program

Since 1957, in order to isolate Communist guerrillas from the Việt ethnic in the countryside as well as the minorities in mountainous areas, Ngô Đình Diệm administration launched a plan of construction the Land Development Centers (LDC). Of the land development centers, some later were upgraded to the Agrovilles[205]. On 23rd April 1957, under the Decree No. 103-TTP the Commissariat General for Land Development (also known as the General Commission for Agriculture Development) (Vietnamese: Phủ Tổng ủy Dinh điền) was organized as a ministry in the GVN and put directly under the Presidency to operate this project (Thêm 1966, 214).

In addition to political and military goals, the Land Development Centers was considered the critical socio-economic program of the First Republic. By which, Việt people those living in plains of Central Vietnam and migrants from the North were brought to uncultivated regions in the Central Highlands and the Mekong River Delta for economic development and preventing the infiltration of the VC and the People's Army of Vietnam forces. The GVN invested in building schools, clinics, and other infrastructures. In these inhabitants, the residents were encouraged to use new farming methods and advanced farm tools including tractors, fertilizers, pesticides, herbicides and industrial crops. Until July 1960, after more than three years of implementation, there had 189.545 people dwelled in 126 land development centers over 16 provinces of SVN (Hickey 1982a, 18, 63). And according to government figures, in 1963, the number of centers increased to 225 with 52.182 families, and 274.945 individuals were settled[206].

Since 1959, in parallel with the Land Development Centers, the Diệm government deployed building the Rural Community Development Centers (better known as the Agroville Program) (Pentagon Papers 1971, 128–159). As an official announcement, the primary objective of the Agroville Program was to

---

[205] Under the First RVN, the Agrovilles were understood as the standard land development centers or the higher land development centers. When a land development center had decent houses (house had a yard, orchard, livestock stable), parochial office, maternity home, clinic, wells, schools, information agents, pagoda, church, market, bus station, roads, bridges, watercourses for easy transport, would be upgraded to be an Agroville. The facilities as mentioned earlier aimed to ensure not only self-sufficient needs but also advanced to prosperity. See: Lê Xuân Nhuận, *Ấp chiến lược (Strategic hamlets)*. Sources: http://sachhiem.net/LICHSU/ LEXNHUAN/LeXNhuan03.php. (Accessed 25th November 2016).

[206] See: *The Montagnards of South Vietnam*, p.8. In: TTU, VC, VA 2321507006.

"Closely coordinate activities of rural economy into an agricultural system, solidity handicraft industry and support those economic activities to obtain steady progression. Peasants, after the farm work, can also participate in trade; do gardening; breed chickens, ducks and fishes; and do other productive tasks; avoid eating in lazy and idling"[207]. The propaganda campaigns of the government said that the goal of the Agroville Program is to establish defended places, in which residents were protected from the invasive war of VC guerrillas and the People's Army of Vietnam. However, during the course of building, Ngô Đình Diệm, on the contrary, instructed to *"Demolish houses, destroy gardens and fields, grab farmlands and ask for public labor with no compensation to anyone."*[208] As revealed by the Saigon National Revolution Newspaper issued on 18th February 1960, like strategic hamlet model[209], each Agroville was turned into a closed community, strictly controlled by the RVNMF, which *"Separates the mass from sympathetic elements to Communists, banishes Communists to forests then destroys them"* (Giàu 1968, 16). Ngô Đình Diệm and his brother Ngô Đình Nhu had the ambition to erect 80 Agrovilles over SVN to resettle for thousand peasants (Tucker 2011, 12).

Under the designed plan, an Agroville would consist of four main zones, each zone then was further divided into four subsites; subsequently, each subsite continued to be divided into several plots; and finally, the plots were separated by surrounding canals. This layout helped Diệm government controlled Agrovilles easily. In addition to the supervision of the RVNMF, villagers were also tasked to monitor each other. The local authority organized every five families into a Joint Security Contingent (Vietnamese: Hội Liên gia), headed by a patriarch. There was only one shared-gate for such a group of household, and all members must report to the patriarch whenever they went in or out. In those

---

207 *Agrovilles, Cần Thơ (1960)*, dossier code: ĐC.96/KH500, office for geography documents, ĐC 07, Hậu Giang provincial library, p.25.
208 *Công văn số 555-VPM/CT của Tỉnh trưởng Kiến Phong gửi Bộ trưởng Bộ Nội Vụ, ngày 24-2-1960 (Official Dispatch No. 555-VPM/CT of Provincial Chief of Kien Phong submitted to Minister of Internal Affairs, dated 24th February 1960)*, the National Archives Center II, Ho Chi Minh City, dossier code Đệ I CH 6360, p.2.
209 Because of all three programs of "Strategic Hamlet," "Land Development Centers," and "Agroville" were new settlements of migrants, surrounded by barbed wires and trenches and guarded by the militia, from 1962 onwards the people commonly called them the "Strategic Hamlet." Compared to a Strategic Hamlet, a Land Development Center was larger, more populous, with more open houses and better-organized living activities. Agroville, as previously mentioned, was a typical form of Land Development Center.

communities, commodity and food were very tightly controlled. Namely, parochial administrators built public granaries. After harvesting crops, per household, received only enough rice to eat in a month, the rest must be deposited in the repository. In an Agroville, the parochial authority erected what so-called the Board of Expropriation controlled by three officers, who were responsible for demanding peasants to be in charge of corvée. Residents between 18 and 45 years old had to go for corvée in ten days (each year?), by their own means with self-support food. Many had to commute very far; some even must go up to 30 kilometers of the waterway, which took them two to three hours[210].

Theoretically, in Agrovilles, infrastructure such as electricity, roads, schools and health care centers would be built, but financial incentives for peasants were inadequate. Furthermore, because none of the peasants pleased to leave their ancestral homelands, they encountered the policy of coercive migration. According to David Coffey, *"The peasants largely resisted relocation, and many came to view the Diem government as a greater menace than the Viet Cong."* Finally, the over-tight control made *"The Agrovilles more resembled concentration camps than the advertised protected havens"* (Tucker 2011, 12).

As an inevitable result, the Agroville Program was abandoned in late 1960 when the government committed its resources to the Strategic Hamlet Program. By the end of 1960, although Diệm government established 42 Agrovilles over SVN the success of the Agroville Program was mainly just on paper. As a consequence of having too many drawbacks, the program, in fact, was doomed from the beginning. According to the Pentagon Papers, the Agroville Program finally plagued to failure because *"The peasants had many complaints about it ranging from clumsy, dishonest administration to the physical hardship of being too far from their fields and the psychological wrench of being separated from ancestral homes and burial plots"* (Pentagon Papers 1971, 128–159).

The Strategic Hamlet Program

On 3rd February 1962, President Ngô Đình Diệm signed Edict 11/TTP setting a Central Committee to be in charge of strategic hamlets (Thêm 1966, 314). This event marked the launch of one of the most common pacification projects

---

210 *Tờ trình ngày 20-4-1960 của Sở Báo chí về việc phái đoàn báo chí viếng thăm Khu trù mật Vị Thanh ngày 18 và 19 tháng 4 năm 1960 (The report of Press Department on the visit of press delegations to the Vị Thanh Agroville on 18th and 19th April 1960, dated 20th April 1960)*, the National Archives Center II, Ho Chi Minh City, dossier code Đệ I CH 6356, p.4.

deployed in the rural and mountainous areas in SVN named the Strategic Hamlet Program. The Central Committee for strategic hamlets rallied once a week. Political adviser, Ngô Đình Nhu was appointed as Chairman of the Committee; Interior Minister Bùi Văn Lương served as General Secretary; Commissioners were comprising representatives of the Ministries of Defense, Interior, Education, Public Services, Agriculture, etc., and many senior military and civilian officials (C. Đạo 2000, 251).

April 1962, the RVN Parliament declared the Strategic Hamlet Program to be a national policy, against the Communism. In the president's message broadcast on the National Day 26th October 1962, President Diệm stressed: *"The Strategic Hamlet is indeed also and primarily the point of impact of a political and social revolution which will serve as the foundation for our economic revolution"* (Leahy 1990, 1). With the Strategic Hamlet Program, the GVN expected to build some 16.000 protected hamlets and to collect around 10 million rural and mountainous people[211]. Those achievements would bring the pacification program of SVN government to an end within 18 months (Hãn et al. 2000, 180)[212].

Shared the concern about political issues with Diệm, but U.S. presidential adviser Roger Hilsman argued that ensuring security and using guerrilla tactic must be included in Strategic Hamlet Program. According to Hilsman, "Strategic concept" must comply with three core principles: *"That the problem in Vietnam presented by the Viet Cong was political rather than military in its essence; that an effective counterinsurgency plan must provide the people and villages with protection and physical security; and that counter-guerrilla forces must adopt the same tactics as those used by the guerrilla himself"*[213] (Pentagon Papers 1971, 128–159).

---

211 According to a CIA declassified source, until 1960 the population of SVN was 14.1 million. See: *Economic intelligence report: A comparison of the economies of North and South Vietnam*. At: Https://www.cia.gov/library/readingroom/docs/CIA-RDP79R01141A002200070001-8.pdf. (Accessed 12th May 2018).

212 See also: Nguyễn Đắc Xuân, *"Quốc sách Ấp chiến lược" - một sản phẩm chính trị thâm độc của Ngô Đình Nhu tan theo số phận của gia đình họ Ngô* ("The national policy of strategic hamlet"- a political produce of Ngô Đình Nhu, broken together with the fate of Ngô family). See: http://sachhiem.net/NDX/NDX018.php. (Accessed 12th October 2016).

213 Guerrilla warfare is a form of political-military strategy warfare in which a small group of combatants such as armed civilians, paramilitary personnel, or irregulars, use typical military tactics including ambushes, raids, sabotage, small warfare, hit-and-run, and fast-moving to fight against a larger, well-equipped, and less-mobile regular military (Simandan 2017). See also *Guerrilla warfare*, Encyclopaedia Britannica, Sources: https://www.britannica.com/topic/guerrilla–warfare. (Accessed

Thus, both the U.S. and Diệm considered a political and ideological triumph as the primary goal of the Strategic Hamlet Program. According to MACV's military experts, *"All civil-military measures necessary to gain or maintain security and population control and establish an effective presence of the government among people"*[214] (Leahy 1990, 4). Also on this view, the Pentagon's officers considered the Strategic Hamlet Program a way to "Achieve security before winning loyalty" (Pentagon Papers 1971, 128–159).

In November 1961 Robert Thompson, an English military expert on anti-guerrilla, who had served as the Secretary of Defense in Malaysia, was appointed as the Chief of the British Advisory Mission to Vietnam. Bring experiences in controlling the local population in "New Villages,"[215] Thompson became a senior advisor to President Diệm in the Strategic Hamlet Program. To make sure of success, Ngô brothers not only applied Malaysian experiences but also learned from Philippine counterinsurgency experiences (Leahy 1990, 37).

In fact, this was not the first time the authorities used the tactic of collecting rural people into protected villages. In other words, the strategy of erecting fences

---

25th December 2017); *The Theory and Practice of Insurgency and Counterinsurgency*, Sources: http://www.nwc.navy.mil/press/Review/1998/winter/art5-w98.htm. (Accessed 25th December 2017)

    It should be added that the guerrilla warfare tactics were efficiently used by Communist-led forces during the Vietnam War. Principles of guerrilla warfare as "Using weak armed forces to defeat a stronger one" (Vietnamese: Lấy yếu thắng mạnh), "Using smaller armed forces to defeat a larger one" (Vietnamese: Lấy ít địch nhiều), and "Fully utilizing available resources such as the advantages of topography and climate, especially the comprehensive support of the people", etc., were unceasingly developed by the Vietnamese generations in thousands of years of struggle against the powerful Chinese invaders, and in the resistance war against the French and the Japanese in recent history. During the Vietnam War, guerrilla warfare training materials developed by generals Võ Nguyên Giáp and Nguyễn Chí Thanh were thoroughly disseminated to Communist-led forces. The fact reals that while the U.S. military adopted a large armored infantry force of scale, even up to army corps, to conduct "sweeping attacks," the NLF used small, flexible infantry units, armed with rudimentary equipment to counteract. After the Tet Offensive of 1968, the VC continued to maintain guerrilla warfare and the "people's war" on a smaller scale while in the main battlefield the guerrilla forces were replaced by regular troops.

214 The U.S. MACV Special Report No. 01 (Leahy 1990, 4).
215 New villages were settlements formed during the last days of British rule over Malaysia in the mid-1950s. The principal purpose of the new villages was to separate the villagers from the Malayan Races Liberation Army insurgents led by the Malayan Communist Party.

around villages to isolate insurgents from the villagers had nothing new to the Vietnamese[216]. Historical documents showed that under the Nguyễn Dynasty, this method had been successfully used by a mandarin named Nguyễn Tấn in the pacification of the Đá Vách people's uprising in western Quảng Ngãi in 1863[217]. Or in the last years of the First Indochina War, French General Francois Linares also resettled approximately three million of the Việt people in the Agrovilles in the Red River Delta to segregate them from Việt Minh forces[218].

In order to thoroughly prevent contacts between civilians and guerrillas, each strategic hamlet often surrounded by a moat; two layers of fence made of bamboo and barbed wire; the defensive system was also reinforced by bamboo spikes and landmines. Each hamlet had one or more far-sighted watchtowers and an early warning system to detect any secret intrusion. All the hamlets' gates were closed at night, all activities of moving in or out settlements of the civilians were tightly controlled. And, as stated by Nhu, inside these hamlets *"People have to sacrifice the temporary liberty in exchange for the forever freedom."* Every strategic hamlet was administered by its own committee while its security was ensured by local militia force and the coordination of youth units. With self-management and self-defense methods, strategic hamlets were believed to be fortresses which could isolate Communist guerrillas and their military bases to destroy or to force into surrender (FRUS 1991, 99).

After obtaining some achievements in plain-rural areas, since late 1962 the Strategic Hamlet Program was implemented in minority regions in the Central Highlands. The Diệm government chose Buon Enao (Darlac Province) as the pilot project and demanded officers from other districts to come to study and replicate the model of the strategic hamlet. The Strategic Hamlet Program then developed rapidly in the highland provinces. In October 1962, the High Command of 23rd tactic Zone organized a sizable military operation named An Lạc to raid Krông Knô River valley, moving 12.674 minority people from the district of Lak (Darlac

---

216 However, according to Henry Cabot Lodge, Jr., Ngô Đình Nhu regarded himself as the one who invented the tactic of strategic hamlet: "Nhu was extremely talkative. He repeated time and again that it was he who had created the strategic hamlets, that everyone, including the Americans, had said he couldn't do it but that he had done it", Lodge wrote (FRUS 1991b, 423).

217 The term Đá Vách (Vietnamese: Đá Vách) referred to minority ethnic groups those resided in west quảng Ngãi include the Cua, K'tu, Bahnar, Sédang, etc., of those, the most populous was the Hré.

218 See more in: Lê Xuân Nhuận, *Ấp chiến lược (Strategic hamlets)*. Sources: http://sachhiem.net/LICHSU/LEXNHUAN/LeXNhuan03.php. (Accessed 14th October 2016).

Province) to Lạc Dương and Đức Trọng Districts (Lâm Đồng Province). Until late 1963, the U.S. Special Forces and Saigon troops deployed 629 operations to sweep across Gia Lai Province aiming at repealing the VC and gathering people into strategic hamlets. According to the statistics of Special General Commission for Land Development, at that time there were 1.057 strategic hamlets were completed (out of 1.301 ones in the plan of GVN), with 553.462 people protected[219].

In the Central Highlands, at the early stage, strategic hamlets fences erected solely with pine trees and bamboo poles. Later, due to the increase of VC guerrillas' attacks and objection of the villagers, the local authorities reinforced those boundaries sharply, especially in the Việt people zones. Many hamlets even had three layers of barbed wire and wooden stakes fencing with flares and sensor mines mounted on the rails. Among the barrier layers, there were two systems of deep trenches wide from 2m to 5m with large mines and booby traps on the floors. Each strategic hamlet had two to three gates which only opened from 8 a.m. to 5 p.m. When leaving their home or coming back from work, all villagers must display their backpacks to guards to demonstrate that no one brought supplies to the VC as well as smuggled Communist documents into their communities. As an investigation of the NLF cadres, many Montagnard people lived in strategic hamlets thought that the French were better than Diệm. Under the French era, salt and many other materials were sold much cheaper (than in strategic hamlets)[220].

In strategic hamlets of Việt people, local officers regrouped every five to seven families into a Joint Security Contingent (Vietnamese: Hội Liên gia) with its own surrounding fence. The inter-family barrier carried out preventive function. Once VC forces burst through the external defensive system to raid on the hamlet, the Saigon troops would retreat down those inter-family protected sites to fight. Each family or Joint Security Contingent also had its own bunker that was cleverly disguised with a stable or kitchen on the ground. The secret bunker not only provided shelter when VC guerrillas attacked repeatedly but used for a counter-attack in appropriate situations[221].

---

219 Special General Commission for Land Development (1963), *Tình hình tiến triển công tác xây dựng ấp chiến lược tính đến ngày 31 tháng 10 năm 1963 (The process of building strategic hamlets until 31st October 1963)*, the National Archives Center II, Ho Chi Minh City, dossier code PTTg 63.
220 *NLF Report on Ethnic Minorities of South Vietnam*. See details at TTU, VC, VA2321522005.
221 Presidential Office (1955), *Kế hoạch bình định Cao Nguyên (The plan for the Central Highlands pacification)*, Department of Propaganda, Dak Lak Provincial Committee, dossier code 25-D2-10.

The GVN equipped large-scale strategic hamlets like a military base. In the beginning, those hamlets were defended by security forces and later were replaced by the militia. Depending on the scope of the community, each settlement was arranged one to three militiaman squads, who were fully equipped with weapons to guard day and night. Moreover, each settlement was also enhanced by several pacification officers', those who performed operations of psychological warfare, espionage and tracking the residents. Communications systems among the hamlets or between a village and the county were established quick links by phone and radio. Administrative centers and also the military headquarters were usually located in the heart of strategic hamlets to govern all activities of the community.

As previously mentioned, the U.S. and the GVN determined to take control of the Central Highlands at all costs to block the borders between SVN and Laos, Cambodia; to sever the strategic transport route from the North to the South; to encircle and destroy VC forces in the mountains and finally appeased the South. Therefore, along with arranged active military and thoroughly implemented the national policy of strategic hamlets in the Central Highland, the Saigon government also intensively conducted training programs to instruct and equip minority youths, who later were sent to villages to propagate against Việt Cộng.

The Strategic Hamlet Program, in fact, turned villages into military posts. With communities, whose terrains were not convenient for defending, all the villagers were forced to move to more appropriate places. As an inevitable consequence, the people there had to abandon their houses, ancestral graves as well as other oldest cultural institutions as family temples, pagodas, etc. This program, therefore, betrayed the aspirations, benefits and traditional cultures of ethnic minorities as the same as of almost populace in SVN.

It was suggested that the Diệm government should restructure the old villages instead of building entirely new ones because the cost of constructing new resettlements was very high. There was the fact that most of the compensated money and capital invested in infrastructure fell into the pocket of corrupt government officials. This led to the poverty of living condition and the lack of working materials. Gradually, these drawbacks caused enormous discontent among the people. Until the last phase of the Strategic Hamlet Program of late 1963, Diệm government achieved partially goals of isolating a portion of the Highlanders as well as the Việt people in remote and rural areas from Việt Cộng. The remaining purposes such as gaining support from peasants and constructing strategic hamlets as basic economic units to stability and develop the national economy were only on papers.

Commenting on the Strategic Hamlet Program, eighteen years after the coup d'état of 1963, William Colby[222] commented: *"The Strategic Hamlet Program itself was a blunder of Ngô brothers because strategic hamlet is not a traditional component of the authority"*[223]. Randy Roberts, a professor of history, also emphasized the inappropriateness of the Strategic Hamlet Program that: *"What so-called the Strategic Hamlet Program is essentially herded Vietnam peasants from their ancestral villages and locked them in the firm fenced areas, more like prisons than real communities"* (Olson & Roberts 1999, 98).

According to Lê Xuân Nhuận, who served as chief of administrative police in Huế under Diệm regime, the GVN planned to build 20.000 strategic hamlets within two years of 1962 and 1963. Nevertheless, by the end of 1963, only more than 7.000 settlements relatively were completed. Of those, just some 1.500 communities reached to set out standards[224]. Those figures were somewhat consistent with statistics of the Pentagon Papers that mentioned to over 8,5 million people settled in 7.205 strategic hamlets by July 1963 (Osborne 1968, 33). Vietnamese recent historical researchers, however, noted that there only 3.900 hamlets were established, wherein settled approximately 6 million people (Hãn et al. 2000, 187).

Shortly after the coup of 1963, General Dương Văn Minh issued the Ordinance 103/SL/CT on 9th March 1964 to dissolve the strategic hamlets, allowing the residents there to return their old villages (Thêm 1966, 383).

The following illustrations display the common layout of strategic hamlets.

4.3.3 As for the Economic Policy

It is thought that the Land Reform Program (LRP) (Vietnamese: Chương trình cải cách điền địa) was the most critical project which influenced the lives of the minorities significantly. Aimed to revoke the lands, which were distributed to peasants by the Việt Minh during the resistance war against the French, Ngô Đình Diệm issued two Ordinances, No. 02 and the No. 07, on 8th January

---

222 William Colby served as chief of CIA station in Saigon before and during the Vietnam War. He later took the post of Director of CIA from September 1973 to January 1976.
223 Nguyễn Đắc Xuân, *"Quốc sách Ấp chiến lược" - một sản phẩm chính trị thâm độc của Ngô Đình Nhu tan theo số phận của gia đình họ Ngô* ("The national policy of strategic hamlet"- a political produce of Ngô Đình Nhu, broken together with the fate of Ngô family). See: http://sachhiem.net/NDX/NDX018.php. (Accessed 12th October 2016).
224 See: Lê Xuân Nhuận, *Ấp chiến lược (Strategic hamlets)*. Sources: http://sachhiem.net/LICHSU/LEXNHUAN/LeXNhuan03.php. (Accessed 14th October 2016).

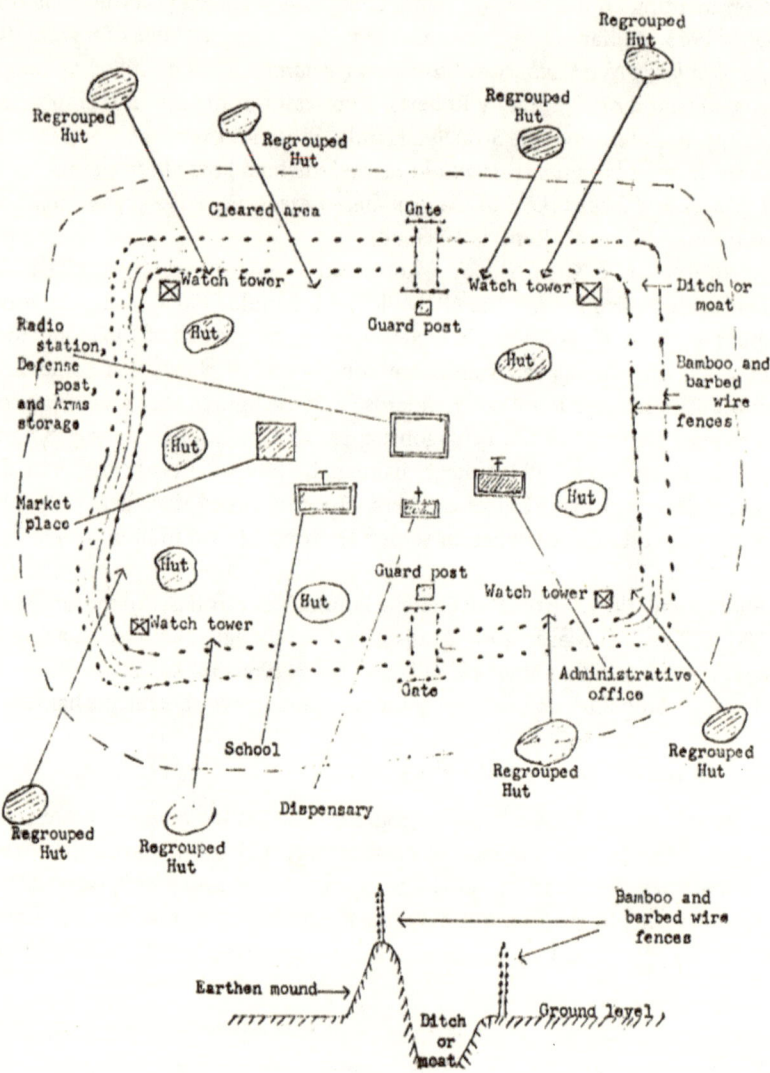

Fig. 8: General Concept of Strategic and Defensed Hamlets. Sources: State Department Strategic Hamlet Study. In: TTU, VC, VA 2130310003.

and 5th February 1955, respectively. Those prescribed the policy of land rent reduction, recovery of abandoned property and ensuring contracts for tenant farmers[225]. The Rule 57, adopted October 22nd, 1956, subsequently fixed the formula of land distribution. According to this provision, each landowner was permitted to hold maximum to 100 hectares. Across SVN, there were a total of 2.033 Vietnamese owners with 425.000 hectares of land to be adjusted under this law. In addition to that, there were 245.000 hectares of 430 French nationality holders were ceded to the government (Thêm 1966, 203).

The government forced landlords who owned more than 100 hectares to sell their excess to landless peasants. The administrators divided poor farmers into four following priority groups: (1) those that had more than two years of the land lease; (2) war veterans; (3) migrants; (4) the unemployed. The compensation for the expropriation of landowners would be given with 10 percent of cash and 90 percent of 12-year bonds. The state also specified the rents should not exceed 25 percent yields. However, this was, actually, a distortion of increasing the land rents because a majority of farmers had been distributed lands by the Việt Minh before Diệm agrarian reform. And, despite government regulations, the land rent, which tenant farmers must pay, was always much higher than the above norm, fluctuated between one-fourth and one-third of crops (Tucker 2011, 621).

Though not a large number of the Vietnamese and French landlords suffered from the Rule 57, it severely damaged the ethnic minorities in the Central Highlands. The slash-and-burn cultivation tradition and living in sparsely populated areas enabled tribal villages to claim ownership for one or more forests with thousands of hectares of lands. The norm of land possession under the Diệm government made the shifting cultivation method cannot be applied as before. Also, compensation levels for Highlanders, whose lands were expropriated, were only in the form of a water buffalo or jar of alcohol. The government imposed these patterns and, of course, "This would not be a lease but a forced sale." According to Hickey, General Lê Văn Kim, the director of the Land Development Program offered his sympathy for the loss of minorities by making payment for lands. The amount of money Kim expended in Darlac Province reached to 30.000 piasters by mid-1957. However, that such payment made Diệm and Nhu, who always said that *"There was no need for negotiation or compensation,"* angry. Consequently, General Kim was dismissed from his current

---

[225] See: *20th century (1955–1959)*. Http://www.bentre.gov.vn/Pages/GioiThieu.aspx?ID= 1956&CategoryId=L%u1ecbch+s%u1eed++V%u0103n+h%u00f3a&InitialTabId=Ri bbon.Read&PageIndex=9 (Accessed 25th December 2017).

position and appointed as the director of the new Military Academy in Đà Lạt, an unrealistic command post (Hickey 1982a, 45).

In the Central Highlands, tens of thousands of hectares owned by the Montagnards were revoked to establish Land Development Centers, plantations, and military bases. The first Article of Decree 513a/ĐT/CCRĐ, issued on 12th February 1958 asserted: *"All the transfer and exchange of lands between the Montagnards and the Việt people, whether large or small acreage, must be preauthorized by the President."* The Official Letter No. 981/BTC/DC, promulgated on 28th January 1959 by the Minister of Finance sent to the Chief of the Special General Commission for Land Development also reaffirmed: *"The Montagnards have no ownership, they only have the right to use their lands, estates; so the previous purchase agreements are invalidated"* (Tiệp 2013b, 36)&(Hickey 1967, 81). The policy of land possession depriving was deployed simultaneously to the grassroots levels. For example, in an administrative conference of the district chiefs and director of departments in Kontum Province that took place on 7th June 1963, the provincial governor stressed: *"On the principles, the transfer, sale or lease of lands between the Việt people and the Highlanders must be approved by the President. Therefore, the Montagnards only have tenure rights"* (Tiệp 2013b, 36).

According to Gabriel Kolko, until 1961 when the Land Reform Program practically ended, the Diệm government retrieved about 650.000 hectares of lands from the Việt and French landlords. Of these, only 244.000 hectares were distributed to peasant households, mainly for Christian migrants coming from the North; war veterans; or new settlers in governmental programs. The redistribution terminated by the end of 1958 (Kolko 1985, 125). Consequently, after the land reform, a lot of reclaimed properties came back to hands of former Việt landowners or to people who could afford to buy among those who support the new government. Although each was officially permitted to own the maximum of 100 hectares, however, greater ownership of a landowning family could be disguised by splitting with its members. In research on the land tenure in Vietnam, Nguyễn Văn Khánh made similar comments to Kolko's ones. According to Khánh, as of the late 1950s in SVN, the agrarian reform touched only one-third of the landlords' estates, 45 percent of cultivation surfaces remained in the hands of large landholders (who owned at least 50 hectares), 42.2 percent acreage still be possessed by small and medium landowners (Khánh 2013, 7). Sharing the viewpoints mentioned above on Diệm's Land Reform Program, Bernard B. Fall argued that regarding nature, the Ordinances 02nd and 07th were not the new policy because *"Most land reform program in 1956 just copying previous reform of Bảo Đại"* (Fall 1965, 310).

Comparing Diệm's agrarian policy and the Communists' one that had been earlier introduced, Spencer C. Tucker pointed out that *"Diem's Land Reform Program was much less generous to the peasants than that of the Communists"* because: (1) it asked tenants to pay for the land they received; (2) it did not promise a thorough resolution of the tenancy problem (landlords were entitled to retain much of their area); (3) and corruption and apathy on the part of officials kept the ordinance from being thoroughly implemented (Tucker 2011, 621).

Together with the Land Reform Program, since 1957, with substantial support of the Americans, the GVN carried out the Highlander Resettlement Program[226] (HRP) (Vietnamese: Chương trình tái định cư người thiểu số ở Tây Nguyên). Deployed under the supervision of U.S. Operations Mission[227], this project was considered a part of the Land Development Program.

According to the governmental plan, the Highlander Resettlement Program was expected to start since March 1957 aiming at relocating 2.500 families with some 12.000 people in 25 villages. New resettlements would be arranged in 3.730 hectares of land belonging to the national domain locating in some areas of Darlac, Bình Định, and Pleiku Provinces. Concerning the implementation cost, the U.S. agreed to spend 1.053.070 USD for the fiscal year 1957 and the counterpart funds of the GVN was 2.288.992 USD that also was taken from the U.S.-financed commercial import program. In addition, to provide arable fields for households, the project was intended to *"Orient the Highlanders towards grouping into communities, and rational exploitation of their lands*[228]*"* (Hickey 1982a, 20).

The land area provided for each model household in model villages was not the same in different localities. This difference might come from dissimilarities of land resources and population size among provinces as well as in the number

---

226 This program was also known as the Domaine de la Couronne du pays Montagnards du Sud (P.M.S.) Land Development Project.
227 An organization which funded U.S. programs during the early American intervention in the Vietnam War.
228 As assessed by agricultural experts came from the U.S., the traditional farming practice of the Highlanders (slash and burn agriculture) was "backward and wasteful." To bring modern farming methods for the Montagnards, the U.S. government funded the GVN opening the National School of Agriculture, Forestry and Animal Husbandry in 1955. This school had the task of training agricultural agents those who would serve in the "Model Villages" to which the Highlanders would be moved in. The curriculums for highland students focused on practical skills including the use of chemical fertilizer, light agricultural machines, and rotation of crops.

of new villages resettled in each territory. For example, in Buôn Mê Thuột, per highland family would receive two hectares (each relocated Việt family was to win five hectares) while in Djiring (Lâm Đồng) each household was planned to get one hectare. In case the Montagnards refused to move into the new villages, provincial chiefs might ban sweeden farming, leaving them no choice but accepted the authorities' offer (Hickey 1982a, 32).

Though the Highlander Resettlement Program had been planned meticulously and propagated widely, it was aborted quickly after President Diệm suffered an assassination attempt at an agricultural fair in Buôn Mê Thuột on 22nd February 1957 (Thêm 1966, 212).

To set up anti-communist defensive lines in positions of military strategy, since 1954, the GVN settled a large number of migrants from the North into the uplands. In the following years, many Việt people from over-populated coastal provinces, southern part, as well as demobilized soldiers were also displaced to establish Land Development Centers and the Agrovilles. Each land development center was firmly organized to turn into an anti-communist bastion while pursuing socioeconomic goals. As announced by the GVN, until 1963 there were such 225 land development centers over SVN territory.

From the beginning of 1962, the Strategic Hamlet Program was also deployed as a national policy. By applying the tactic of *"slapping the water to catch fish,"* (Vietnamese: *tát nước bắt cá)*[229] the Diệm government collected all residents from conflict zones into strategic hamlets constructed along roads or nearby towns. The anti-communist experts assumed that when being isolated from villagers, the VC would lose supplies then would be besieged and destroyed quickly. On the theory, strategic hamlets were considered economic basis units for recovery and development of national economy. However, in the course of the deployment, while concentrating on military matters, the authorities overlooked issues of economic growth and people's life in protected hamlets. Namely, the residents there not only lacked arable land but also suffered from an unfree atmosphere with many disruptions in traditional customs and habits. Because of these reasons, the Highlanders unceasingly sought to escape from new settlements or to struggle against strategic hamlets or tried to return to their old villages without any subsidies or supplies.

The exodus and resettlements also led to the rapid increase in the number and proportion of the Việt people in the Central Highlands. While getting arable

---

229 The name of this tactic was possibly inspired by a slogan of the People's Army of Vietnam: "The army and the people are like fish and water."

lands from the government, the Việt newcomers grabbed more possession of indigenous populations somehow. Swiddens of minorities therefore increasingly shrunk and moved back to the remote, isolated areas, causing a lot of inconvenience for the cultivation of those who were living in resettlement areas. In many localities, the Highlanders complained about the "ill-treatment by the Viet." For example, the Việt soldiers entered villages to steal animals in Pleiku or, in a market Việt people "would pluck fruit and vegetable from Highlanders' back baskets"; illiterate Highlanders were often deceived by the Việt traders because their lack of understanding of the currency's par value; or some civil servants revealed that they were relegated to an inferior status by the Việt officers (Hickey 1982a, 49). This situation, along with problems in cultural and educational policies, contributed to rising in boycott sentiment toward the Việt, opposition to the government, and to the outbreaks of protest movements like BAJARAKA and FULRO (MDEM 1972, 12–13).

Of the ethnic minorities living in plains, the GVN paid more attention to the Chinese because this group had the most dynamic economic life in SVN. The government fully exploited financial tools to force the Chinese into applying for the Vietnamese citizenship. Notably Diệm administration prohibited the aliens (primarily aimed at overseas Chinese) to participate in eleven kinds of work including the trade in fishes and meats; groceries business; charcoal commerce; gasoline, kerosene, petroleum jelly trade; affordable pawn; fabrics, silks, yarns trade; iron, copper scrap trade; rice milling factories; cereals business; transporting goods or passengers by cars, trains, boats; contractors (Act No. 53). According to statistics of the GVN, the Chinese merchants' economic potential accounted for 21 percent of the 11 occupations, which they were banned, while this ethnicity only made up around 2.5 to 5.5 percent of SVN population. The Chinese merchants must select one of three measures including applying for Vietnam citizenship to continue trading; franchising for their wives (officially married) or children (born in Vietnam); cooperating with Vietnamese business partners whose capital accounting for 51 percent and of course, Vietnamese businesspeople would lead the manufacturing and trading activities. If any Chinese merchant did not choose one of above three measures, he/she would be forced repatriation to China or Taiwan before 31st August 1957 (Linh 2012, 114)&(Thêm 1966, 201).

About the enormous wealth of organizations called Bangs, Congregations, or Regional Administrative Groups accumulated by overseas Chinese for almost 150 years in Vietnam. With an estimated value of 500 million piasters, the asset mainly was real estate including apartments for rent, schools, pagodas, hospitals, cemeteries; notably the property of Teochew Congregation in Chợ Lớn (Great

Market) of up to 100 million piasters (equivalent to 300.000 USD at that time). The Diệm regime had set out solutions for this complex and challenging matter in Article 2, Decree 133-NV, which stated that *"Assets of Congregations and Asian Bangs will be controlled by Managing Committees those operated under the chairmanship of local administrative authorities until these assets are entirely disposed of."* Subsequently, Interior Ministry was ordered to disband the Chinese social organizations because whose members had already got Vietnamese citizenship (Linh 2012, 115). Eventually, all property of the Chinese congregations, as well as the administration of their population, officially reverted to the GVN (Schrock et al. 1966, 944).

4.3.4 The Policy of Assimilation and Discrimination of the Minorities

For many countries in Southeast Asia, the integration of much and varied ethnolinguistic was considered as one of the most important goals after the Second World War. In that general context, soon after coming to power, Diệm made an extraordinary effort in the assimilation of ethnic minorities including the Montagnards, the Khmer, the Chinese and the Cham into the Vietnamese language and culture. Derived from the Chauvinism, Diệm concluded that in order to obtain the national integration, traditional ties which performed the linking role among peoples (particularly minority groups), religious sects, clans or villages must be replaced by the loyalty to the state. He also stressed, *"The primitive highland people would have to be civilized,"* and *"The Highlanders were intelligent enough to be assimilated into the Vietnamese type of village life"* (Hickey 1982a, 6, 8). Of course, that only was the official way of thinking. The minorities, in contrary, perceived that these efforts of the central administration merely aimed to destroy their cultural identity to Vietnamize them. In this regard, Đỗ Mậu, who served as military security chief of Diệm administration, argued that the brutal intervention of the GVN to the humanistic lifestyle of ethnic minorities had exacerbated the disharmony between the Kinh and the Montagnards, transforming them into permanent enemies[230].

---

230 See more in: Mậu, H. L. Đ. (2007), *Việt Nam máu lửa quê hương tôi (The bloody war in Vietnam)*, Chapter IX, at http://lmvn.com/truyen/index.php?func=viewpost&id= z4ibpv4gJOaHD7c1POI3IBx WKnxOjQ Dc&ssid=2166. (Accessed 6th April 2017).

Regarding the Montagnards

Under the direction of the central government, all new settlements of the Highlander Resettlement Program must be arranged in valleys, near towns, along the transport routes, in places where the Việt people had been residing or where the Highlanders had previous contacts with the Việt people. This halted the occupant in isolation of minorities and created conditions for them to access and to acquire customs and traditions of the Việt ethnic. On the other hand, Diệm regime moved Montagnards administrative and military officials to work in the coastal provinces of Quảng Trị, Huế, Quảng Nam and Quảng Ngãi to separate them from their home areas of residence. All positions held by highland officials under the administration of the Crown Domain then were replaced by the Việt people. Diệm government also abolished "the cadre Montagnard" a category of public servants with more incentives for the Montagnards. According to Circular No. 1369-BPTT/VP/M issued 9th May 1958, cadres must be recruited based on education and capacity "regardless of the Việt or the Highlanders" (Tiệp 2013b, 37, 41).

To meet the demand for a new appearance of the upland, many places were changed from original names to Vietnamese ones. For example, Cheo Reo was renamed Hậu Bổn, Buôn Mê Thuột had been modified to Lạc Giao, Lak County became Lạc Thiện, Cư Ewi County was changed to Phước An, Pleiku was altered to Lệ Trung, Djiring was changed to Di Linh, and Blao became Bảo Lộc, and so on. Despite President Diệm's purpose of "making those sites civilized and meaningful," the majority of the new names, those made sense in Vietnamese but were entirely unfamiliar with the indigenous languages or cultures, existed only on paper. The local people, in reality, remained to use their old ones.

As for the traditional highland courts, although this conventional judicial system had not been formally abolished, it could not run well since the government stopped paying salaries to the minority judges and put the national laws into effect in the Central Highlands (Chi 2006, 306)&(Hickey 1982a, 46).

Also aimed to achieve the national customs unification, some of the Việt provincial administrators had been applying various methods to alter highland tradition manners. In a little more detail, the Provincial Chief of Darlac forced the Rhade people to wear shirt and trousers instead of loincloths when entering the city, especially while coming to the public authorities. Furthermore, the local government also required Montagnards notables to wear turbans and long shirts like the Việt officials. Similarly, the administration in Pleiku ordered the Jarai refugees not to erect their traditional stilt houses and requested that all new homes should be built on the ground like the Việt style (Tiệp 2013b, 37)&(Hickey 1967, 29).

As for the education, since early 1955, the Directorate of Education for the Southern Highlands was transferred from the secretary general of the Crown Domain to the new administration of Diệm and was put under the Department of Education in October 1956. The national language (Vietnamese) was stipulated as the primary language at the general education levels. Therefore, French and highland languages, which had been taught in schools ever, were annulled (Dĩ 1968, 13). Simultaneously with the effort in decolonization, the curriculum was reformed by replacing subjects such as French history and geography by Vietnamese history and geography. According to Y Toeh Mlo Duon Du, a Rhade intellectual, the authorities even destroyed all the teaching materials in Rhade languages (Hickey 1982a, 9). Since 1955, the supportive policy for highland young people to enroll in National Institute of Administration applied under the Crown Domain was abolished. Consequently, no Montagnard students were enrolling in this training institution during the period from 1958 to 1963. On the other hand, to meet the demand of teacher training to serve the needs of the Highland Affairs, on 18th February 1957 the GVN promulgated Decree 552/GD/ND establishing the Highland Pedagogical School in Buôn Mê Thuột.

There is no doubt that, Diệm government failed to inherit some advancements in ethnic policies applied under the French colonialism and the Crown Domain. Along with the unfair treatment of civil servants and military officers based on their ethnic origin, the GVN did not have an appropriate strategy to educate Việt officials who were appointed to serve in the upland. Namely, the Central Highlands was considered the destination for administrators, those who were being disciplined. To some extent, these cadres often served with the discontent of exiles, increasing the distance between the government and the people. Those mistakes contributed principally to contradictions between the GVN and the Montagnards as well as between the Montagnards and Việt people.

It should be emphasized that, since the French set their first steps on the Central Highlands in 1891 until their withdrawal from Vietnam thereafter the Geneva Agreement, the colonists had repeatedly tried to reform the highland customs, but all encountered strong reaction. Ultimately, the protectorate government had to establish a special status of administration and judiciary, as well as organized the Montagnards military units for the upland. Under the Crown Domain regime of Bảo Đại, the former emperor remained ruling methods of the French, kept maintaining the special regulation for ethnic minorities.

The abolition of the particular status for the Highlanders in 1955 led to severe mistakes in Diệm's Highland Affairs Policies. A survey carried out in the Buôn

Đôn pointed out that the Rhade always regarded the Việt people as outsiders, even colonialists. Similar assessments were also conducted in a 16-page report of Michigan State University Group (of which, 13 pages were taken from interviews with the tribesmen)[231]. Accordingly, the Highlanders blamed that the Việt took their lands, stole cattle, cut down fruit trees, administrative abuses and insufficient in medical care and education chances (Salemink 1999, 191).

In a secret meeting of a group of the Montagnards intellectuals and officials that took place at Buon Ale-A (a Rhade village) in early 1955 to discuss their grievance against Diệm government policies for the future of the Highlanders, one of the core members named Y Thih Eban (a Rhade man) was giving evidence of discrimination by the Việt people and their troops against the minorities, considered it an outrage over his compatriots. Y Thih Eban alleged that: *"Military personnel would enter villages to carry away animals, fruits and garden produce. They even entered houses to steal sleeping mats, blankets and personal belongings. In one incident, when the villagers complained, the soldiers boasted that now that the Vietnamese ruled the Highlanders they could do as they pleased"* (Hickey 1982a, 44). After some more gatherings, that elite group declared to found a secret organization to fight for fundamental rights of the peoples in the Central Highlands named the Front de Libération des Montagnards (FLM) (Vietnamese: Mặt trận Giải phóng Dân tộc Thượng). The delegates selected Y Mot Nie Kdam (Rhade) as president and Y Thih Eban (Rhade) as secretary. In March 1955, the Front de Libération des Montagnards sent a petition to President Ngô Đình Diệm to require the government to respect the Montagnard traditions and customs (Dharma 2012, 28–29).

The front also made a formal request for a flag of the Highlanders as it had been accepted under the Crown Domain. The letter contained a plea for the right of land ownership and the right to equal treatment with the Việt. However, as recorded by Hickey, after flying from Saigon to Buôn Mê Thuột and was welcomed by a group of Rhade people, with a "script" already prepared by Việt officials, Diệm concluded that the reports (of Hickey and Michigan State University Group's experts) were *"inaccurate"*; that *"the highland people loved the Vietnamese and desired to emulate them"* (Hickey 1982a, 50–51). And, of course, the proposal of the anthropologists, as well as request of the Highlanders gradually drifted into the past.

---

231 Manual, Michigan State University Viet-Nam Advisory Group - *A Study of Montagnard Names in Vietnam*. In: TTU, VC, VA 21940102001.

In short, due to lacking attention to the actual circumstance and had been covered by his dishonest administration officials, Diệm underestimated the discontent of ethnic minorities. Therefore, the miscalculations in the ethnic policies of the GVN were not promptly adjusted and increasingly deepened the divide between the Việt and the Montagnards; put the minorities into struggles to defend themselves. Many conflicts occurred continuously against Diệm's Highland Affairs Policies, most notably the BAJARAKA[232].

As for the overseas Chinese

Also in the forced-assimilation policy of ethnic minorities in SVN, Diệm administration implemented a strategy of Vietnamization of overseas Chinese all over the fields such as citizenship, economic, cultural and social. This process was consulted by relevant ministries and was proceed in stages.

First and foremost was the policy of forcing the overseas Chinese to apply for Vietnamese nationality. The Article 16 of Decree 10 (issued on 7th December 1955) stated that any child born in Vietnam, whose parents were Chinese and if one of them also born in Vietnam, automatically qualified Vietnamese residents and had no right to renounce Vietnamese citizenship. Afterward, Decree No. 48 dated 21st August 1956 amended the Vietnam citizenship law that made all overseas Chinese born in SVN Vietnamese citizens, regardless of their family choices. First-generation immigrants born in China, however, were not authorized to apply for Vietnamese citizenship and should ask for residential permits, which were to be renewed periodically, on top of paying residential taxes. Furthermore, on 29th August 1956, the government issued Decree No. 52 required all Vietnamese citizens, irrespective of their ethnic origin, to select Vietnamese names within six months, failing which they had to pay a hefty penalty (up to five million piasters). Most Chinese disliked this provision because it prevented them from the option of returning to their motherland and forced them to adopt citizenship. As a gesture of easing the annoyance of the Hoa people on citizenship matters, the GVN passed Article 58 of the Ordinance No. 58 on 25th October 1956.

---

[232] In 1957, Montagnards intellectuals from various professions including civil servants, teachers, military personnel, etc., established a struggle movement named BAJARAKA, chaired by Mr. Y Bham Enuol (a Rhadé). The movement quickly spread across the Highlands, but until July 1958, its leaders overtly stated methods of non-violent struggle (Dĩ 1968, 14).

Accordingly, *"for the Chinese, those who can be President customized each case accepting exemption conditions for citizenship in Vietnam"* (Khanh 1993, 28–29).

Thus, the GVN institutionalized the strategy to integrate ethnic Chinese into Vietnamese society by the edicts, accompanied by appropriate sanctions. Initially, the process of Vietnamization of the overseas Chinese in southern Vietnam took place quite slow; the majority was waiting for the intervention of the Government of the Republic of China (ROC). According to Joann L. Schrock, until 10th August 1957, up to the ultimate deadline to receive Vietnamese citizenship licenses, less than ten percent of Chinese origin had finished the formalities (Schrock et al. 1966, 932).

Realizing the political solution was insufficient to Vietnamize the overseas Chinese, Diệm regime rapidly supplemented by economic policy. Decree No. 53, passed on 6th September 1956, prohibited all foreigners from engaging in eleven different trades, most of those controlled by the Chinese. The foreign stockholders were obliged to convert their business or transfer their title to Vietnamese citizens within six months to one year, and failure to do so could result in exile or a fine of up to five million piasters (Khanh 1993, 28–29).

By using a combination of economic and citizenship policies, the number of Chinese applied for Vietnamese nationality increasing rapidly. According to statistics from the Chinese Affair Department, as of 31st October 1960, there were 231.160 out of 235.000 over-eighteen-year-old Chinese residents in SVN converted to Vietnamese name. The number of overseas Chinese resided in Vietnam as aliens were only 2.550. It is worth considering that among the ethnic Chinese representatives in southern Vietnam, there had 158 over 227 Secretaries and Deputy Secretaries of Bangs, Congregations, or Regional Administrative Groups adopted Vietnamese nationality. That was an appropriate time for Diệm government to raise the issue "Should social organizations of the Chinese in SVN exist or not?" To answer that question thoroughly, the GVN issued Decree 133-NV on 10th June 1960 dissolving the Chinese Congregations and other overseas Asian Bangs in southern Vietnam. The first Article of this Decree professed: *"Now is the time to abolish Chinese Congregations and other foreign Asian Bangs throughout the territory of Vietnam; simultaneously terminated the positions of Secretaries and Deputy Secretaries of Bangs and Congregations"* (Linh 2012, 115). This ordinance aimed to break the independent existence as well as eliminate the intermediary role of those social organizations between the local government and the ethnic Chinese. Thenceforward, the Chinese community in SVN was under the direct control of the RVN government.

Concerning the Khmer

Like for other ethnic minorities, the GVN also applied the policy of assimilation to the Khmer. However, similar to the Cham in SVN, the Khmer community not only had a small population but performed no leading socio-economic role. Their areas of residence were also not in a strategic region as the homeland of the Montagnards. Therefore, this community attracted less attention from the government. Under the First Republic, the most important strategy was the abolition of the Khmer language in schools and pagodas over the Mekong River Delta. Khmer intellectuals, who opposed this plan, were seen as dissidents. As an inevitable result, many Khmer Krom elites[233] immigrated to Cambodia. Others though still stayed in Vietnam but sent their children to Phnom Penh to continue to get to school.

The forced assimilation policy directly caused the resurgence of the Khmer Krom's ethnonationalism from the late 1960s leading to the founding of the Struggle Front of the Khmer of Kampuchea Krom (KKK) (French: Front de Libération du Cambodia Krom, FLKK) one year later. The movement's members elected Chau Dera as their president, built headquarters in Phnom Penh and set out a plan to attack SVN to reclaim Cochinchina for the Khmer.

4.4 Responses of the Minorities to the Highland Affairs Policies

As mentioned above, after establishing a pro-American government in SVN, authoritarian Prime Minister Ngô Đình Diệm quickly implemented the so-called the policy of nation-building or "integrative revolution" which aimed to assimilate the minority groups into Vietnamese cultural sphere, made them loyal to the GVN. Following the French withdrawal from the plateau formally terminated the Crown Domain on 10th August 1955, Montagnards intellectuals and officers believed Ngô Đình Diệm government would welcome them. But the reality then disappointed the Highlanders; all senior positions in the administration and army over the upland were held by Việt officials those who came from plains. All of the Montagnard military units including the 4th Infantry Division, seven maneuver battalions, and other combat units were placed under the command of RVNMF's officers. The agencies of administration, health, and education were also put under the control of the Offices of Government Delegate located in Buôn Mê Thuột and Đà Lạt.

---

233 Khmer Krom (or Lower Khmer) was a part of ethnic Khmer, those who lived in the Mekong River Delta of Vietnam.

Contrary to Diệm's volition, the forced assimilation measures not only failed in integrating ethnic identities of the tribal groups in Vietnamese culture but strengthen the collective identity of being Highlanders. Also, the policies of ill-treatment, discrimination, the abolition of land ownership and other preferential regulations for minorities in the Central Highlands exacerbated the discontent among the Montagnards. This led to the establishment of an anti-government movement since early 1955. On the other hand, some highland intellectuals, officials, and soldiers were disgruntled at the central government and return to their villages; others remained in the agencies only went to work for the salary. Taking that opportunity, Communist cadres infiltrated into many communities to propagate and lobby the Highlanders against SVN government (Dĩ 1968, 13).

4.4.1 Non-BAJARAKA Political Struggles

Soon after Diệm merged the Crown Domain into the territory of the State of Vietnam, in August 1954, a struggle of highland women took place in the suburb of Buôn Mê Thuột and district town of Cheo Reo. The struggle advocated for a movement for demanding to get their husbands and sons those who had been joining the army back. Hundreds of women gathered at the military posts and district towns to raise the slogan *"Peace came; the government must give the soldiers back to their families."* The fight lasted for several days; some VC cadres were disguised to enter garrisons along with strugglers whom they led directly. The Highlanders also accelerated a movement against forced corvee, against the massive tariff policy forcing Diệm government to repeal unpaid-labor obligation. September 1954, 5.000 demonstrators from the zones 2, 7 and An Khê (Pleiku) rallied around administrative offices and military agencies in An Khê to require food aid, medical treatment and to object the arrest of those who had participated in the struggle. The demonstration made Vice Provincial Chief of Pleiku go to An Khê to promise a solution for the mass' request and to distribute rice, salt among the local people. Three months later, the Highlanders of 20 villages in Dak Bot (Zone 6, Pleiku) struggled against the establishment of Kon Ngot military post. Protesters not only argued with officials but also performed songs and dances to enlist the sympathy of soldiers and civilians. Ultimately, the local authority had to abandon the plan to set up the Kon Ngot bunker. Although the demonstrations mentioned above were on small scales, those proved the Montagnards' capability of political struggle and made the Diệm government unexpected, produce disoriented reactions (B. M. Đạo, Thu, & Lan 2006, 256)&(Lan 2014, 38).

In the year 1955, the struggle of highland people demanded Diệm regime to conduct the general election spreading widely from rural areas to urban centers in various forms and levels. For example, in Đà Lạt, the Municipal Communist Party released secret documents to propagate and explain terms of the Armistice Agreement. Thousands of copies of the material were transmitted to the populace, especially to workers, intellectuals, small business owners and vegetable and flower growers, those who lived in surrounding hamlets of Đà Lạt Town as Nghệ Tĩnh, Hà Đông and Tây Hồ. After that, the protesters gathered representatives of social classes to submit petitions to the Đà Lạt Mayor, required the government to conduct the general election to unify the country, implementation of freedom and democracy. August the same year, Small Business Union of Đà Lạt Market convinced more than 300 business women for a demonstration to cease or stop doing business. This union also sent their representatives to meet with local government leaders to *"Require strictly implementing the terms of the Geneva Accords; demand the U.S not to interfere in SVN."* As a result, the Mayor of Đà Lạt had to send agents to negotiate and promised to reduce the market tax and permit civilians to trade in some areas in the town (Standing Committee of Da Lat Municipal Communist Party 1994, 106–107). Source reveals that merely between the last three months, 1955, hundreds of struggle erupted in Gia Lai Province which attracted a lot of interest of even the elders, soldiers and civil servants (Executive Committee of Gia Lai Provincial Communist Party 2009, 274). In Darlac, there were several struggles, in which some villages cooperated with each other against the suppression of the GVN. Late 1955, more than 800 people flocked to the county seat of Cheo Reo to question Diệm government about the reasons for not organizing the general election. Getting no answer, protesters then refused to disperse as ordered by the local authority. Consequently, 20 leaders of the protest group were arrested (Lan 2014, 39).

Late 1956 and early 1957, the Diệm government conducted a campaign to denounce the VC in the Central Highlands. In the province of Kontum, the local authority organized teams, what so-called citizen services, eradicating malaria. Ostensibly, those people visited every village to help the villagers with medical treatment or to spray insecticides; however, their paramount objective was to trace the Việt Cộng. In many communities, the Highlanders not only refused the medical help of the authority but also used spears, bows, and arrows to resist when working groups entered their home.[234] An operation report conducted by the

---

234 Office of Government Delegate in the Central Highlands (1959), *Báo cáo hoạt động năm 1959 (Operation Report 1959)*, National Archives Center II, Ho Chi Minh City, dossier code Đệ I CH 290.

Office of Government Delegate in the Central Highlands in 1959 disclosed: *"On 16th September 1959, a group of social workers came to eradicate malaria in the district of Dak Sut-Kontum; although the team has explained the benefits of insect spraying, they still be blocked, chased away and beaten by the indigenous people. The villagers also requested to retrieve the Việt Cộng rebels, previously arrested. They (villagers) also threatened that from now on, if we (the local authority) capture one of their people, they would tell the Việt Cộng to arrest 4 of ours"*[235].

Together with political activities, the Montagnards also launched struggles for economic goals; protested the policy of relocating civilians to establish land development centers of Diệm government. Most important was the demonstration took place in the western part of Gia Lai, which rallied more than 40.000 participants from 143 villages. The protesters chanted and carried placards such as *"Stop seizing lands to build land development centers;" "Do not deprive of the compatriots' lands and forests;" "The government levels fields and forests, the Jarai compatriots die of hunger."* The movement made the local authority compensate for damaged villages, and to reduce and slow down the process of land seizing (Executive Committee of Gia Lai Provincial Communist Party 2009, 291).

It is believed that the mistakes in Diệm Highland Affairs Policies also indirectly pushed many Highlanders towards the NLF. Notably, on 19th May 1961, twenty-three Highlander representatives chaired by Y Bih Aleo organized a conference to form the Committee for Autonomy for the People of the Western Plateau (Vietnamese: Ủy Ban Dân tộc tự trị Tây Nguyên) (Hickey 1982a, 66)&(Salemink 2002, 7). Soon after the establishment ceremony, this committee declared its support for the NLF, ensuring the autonomy of ethnic minorities and posed the goal of defending highland cultural traditions against the forced assimilation strategy of the GVN.

In the Mekong River Delta, after founding the Struggle Front of the Khmer of Cambodia Krom in 1961, Chau Dera and his Khmer Krom collaborators moved back to the Bảy Núi (Seven Mountains) (Châu Đốc Province), where this front recruited and trained an armed force of about 1500 fighters. Since having its own armed forces, the requirements which the Struggle Front of the Khmer of Cambodia Krom posed for the GVN were becoming more extreme. From demanding the government accorded better treatment for the Khmer people, they later asked for equality between the Khmer and the Việt ethnic.

---

235 Ibid. Office of Government Delegate in the Central Highlands (1959), *Báo cáo hoạt động năm 1959 (Operation Report 1959)*.

Furthermore, Chau Dera also required Ngô Đình Diệm regime to recognize the Khmer Krom as Cambodian citizens.

During the early period of Diệm presidentship, since the GVN was busy with anti-communist programs, it more or less offered a compromise with the Struggle Front of the Khmer of Cambodia Krom. However, before increasingly outrageous demands of the Khmer, the RVNMF had no choice but made raids on the Bảy Núi base. In late 1963, Chau Dera was detained, the struggle movement of the Khmer then weakened steadily (Hickey 1982a, 61).

Also in 1960 a Front for Liberation of Champa was established and led by Lieutenant-colonel Les Kosem a Cambodian Cham who was serving in the Royal Khmer Army security forces. The movement then later spread across regions where most Cham people lived such as Ninh Thuận, Bình Thuận, Châu Đốc and Tây Ninh Provinces. However, with a small population size (under 40.000 in 1960), it was challenging for the Cham to launch a struggle movement against the GVN without associations with other minority groups. After a period of inefficient operation, early 1964 Cham people in central provinces joined with leaders of the BAJARAKA, those who were released after the overthrown Diệm coup d'état, to form the Front for the Liberation of the South Vietnamese Highlands (also known as the Front for the Liberation of the Champa Highlands - French: Front de Libération des Hauts Plateaux, FLHP).

4.4.2 The BAJARAKA Movement

The BAJARAKA was considered the most significant struggle of the Highlanders under Diệm regime. As mentioned earlier, in March 1955 the Front de Libération des Montagnards sent a petition to the central government manifesting the widespread discontent among the minorities. The letter, however, was ignored by Prime Minister Diệm. Therefore, along with participation in small struggles in their respective localities, in 1957 by reforming the Front de Libération des Montagnards, a group of Montagnard intelligentsia announced the establishment of the BAJARAKA movement[236], which aimed at demanding the government to

---

236 It is worth noting that During the French colonial period, the political consciousness of the Central Highlanders had not developed. They mostly carried out sporadic armed activities against colonialists or joined the Cần Vương Movement - a patriotic movement made by a large group of Vietnamese officials in the French protectorate administration.

change the discriminatory contents in the Highland Affairs Policies[237]. Founders and also leaders of the movement included Y Bham Enuol (a Rhade), Siu Sipp (a Jarai), Y Dhon Adrong (principal of Lạc Thiện elementary school), Y Nuin Hmok (secondary school teacher at Buon Kram and a political commissar), Y Nam Eban (an army officer), Y Bhan Kpor, Y Chon Mlo Duon Du, Nay Luett, Paul Nưr (a Bahnar intellectual) and some of the Cham, Ma, and Stieng representatives (Hickey 1982a, 53).

The first publicity activity of the BAJARAKA was an event which occurred in mid-September 1957 in a Vietnamese school class for the Highlanders. There, Mr. Y Bham Enuol outlined differences between the Montagnards and the Việt people. In conclusion of his speech, Enuol required autonomy on administrative and political for the Central Highlands. In response to the grievance of the minorities, on 3rd July 1957 Decree 302/NV was passed to upgrade the Standing Advisory Office (Vietnamese: Văn phòng Cố vấn Thượng Vụ) to be the Bureau for Highland Affairs (Vietnamese: Nha Công tác Xã hội Miền Thượng) (Dharma 2012, 32). This newly established agency then was put directly under the Presidency and built its headquarters in Huế. Three months later, Decree 1070 TTP/VP was issued in order to expand Bureau for Highland Affairs' sphere of influence to the provinces of Bình Long, Phước Long, Bình Tuy and Bà Rịa-Long Khánh. The mission of this specialized agency was to study and implement the Highland Affairs Policies under the guideline *"For the Montagnards, By the Montagnards."* According to the Ministry of Information (GVN), for the Montagnards means *"Staff, officers at all levels and sector, who are working in ethnic minority regions, have to set the highest goals for each of their work is for the compatriot; for the purpose of improving living standard of the Montagnards, make it on equal terms with living condition of the Việt people".* And, by the Montagnards, means *"(the authorities) must try using Montagnard cadres and compatriots in every task, every position. Whatever works in the upland that Montagnard cadres and people are capable of undertaking, let them do. To do so, the authorities have to educate and train the compatriots, and elevate Montagnard personnel as well"* (Nưr 1966, 113–114). The Bureau for Highland Affairs then appealed to the Highlanders to cooperate with the government in the framework of "nation-building" and "anti-Communism" in the nation's egalitarian spirit (Hickey 1982a, 59).

---

237 See: Po Dharma. *Phong trào thanh niên Chăm tham gia Fulro vào 1968 (The Cham youth movement joined FULRO in 1968).* P. 12. Sources: http://champaka.info/images/ky%20su%20fulro.pdf. (Accessed 25th December 2017).

Though were not promptly, the adjustments in the ethnic policies of the GVN somewhat brought positive changes to economic, political and social lives of the minorities in SVN. For instance, thanks to working groups sent by the government and the substantial support from U.S. Agency for International Development, some advanced cultivation techniques such as the use of machinery, fertilizers, and pesticides were applied widely. Besides that, customs and traditions of the Montagnards were more respected in comparison with the early years of First Republic. Notably, in the propaganda campaign for building "new life," officials merely encouraged the Highlanders to perform Việt cultural activities instead of forcing them to do so[238]. The process of appointment for the Montagnards cadres was also more flexible than the earlier period. Montagnard officials those who were not eligible for qualifications but had "satisfactory manners" and "good reputation" would be remained to appoint. Furthermore, the National Institute of Administration also resumed training intensive courses to cultivate Montagnard public servants. Together with that, many Highlanders students awarded scholarships to study at newly established schools in the Central Highlands. The GVN and the Americans also organized relief teams in the mountainous areas of famine and built some dispensaries in needed places (Tiệp 2013b, 40–41). Of course, as previously analyzed, the humanitarian groups were always tasked to enhance the government's understanding of local people as well as to broadcast anti-Communism propaganda. And, to benefit from humanitarian projects, the village patriarchs and their villagers had to commit to participating in programs of military defense against the infiltration of the VC such as the programs of Highlander Resettlement, VDP, and CIDG.

It is evident that changes in the ethnic strategies already created some improvements in the living condition of the Montagnards, but still did not meet the requirements of BAJARAKA's leaders, especially regarding politics. President Diệm decided not to approve the request for an autonomous status or an own flag for the tribal peoples. The contradictions between the government and the Montagnards practically had been resolved on the surface only. The struggle of the Highlanders, therefore, would not end there.

---

238 For example, local authorities set up delegations to mobilize villagers to improve their poor standards of daily hygienet, stop organizing costly grave-leaving ceremonies, eliminate of harmful habits such as superstition, eradicate malaria, etc. See more in Office of Government Delegate in the Central Highlands (1959), *Báo cáo hoạt động năm 1959 (Operation Report 1959)*, National Archives Center II, Ho Chi Minh City, dossier code Đệ I CH 290.

In May 1958, the BAJARAKA continued to dispatch petitions signed by Y Bham Enuol and 16 other Highlander representatives to diplomatic missions in Saigon of the United Nations and some countries such as the U.S., UK, France, India, and Laos (Dharma 2012, 36). Those letters denounced the racist behaviors of Diệm government for ethnic minorities; recounted the contributions of the mountainous peoples against "the enemy" (the Communism); requested the world powers to intervene in creating an "Autonomous Highland" to maintain the highland collective ethnic identity for the Montagnards. Moreover, the BAJARAKA's representatives even proposed their aspiration for an independent Central Highlands within the French Union or under the direct leadership of the U.S. instead of being put under SVN government. In the petition submitted to the United Nations, they recommended that the hinterland should be merged into the Kingdom of Laos as the French had done in 1893 (Hickey 1982a, 57).

On 30th July 1958, the BAJARAKA Movement sent a four-member delegation to Saigon to meet with the U.S. ambassador. Meanwhile, Y Bham Enuol announced the establishment of "the Central Autonomous Commission," placed its headquarters in Pleiku to take command all local committees which had been founded in Buôn Mê Thuột, Kontum and Di Linh. These committees quickly recruited many Montagnard officers and soldiers who were serving in the RVNMF. The design for the BAJARAKA flag of Y Thih, which had several meanings, was finally chosen. In this pattern, the red circle carried a dualistically meaning: the "red soil of the Highlands" and "the blood shed by the highland people in their struggle for survival"; the green background implemented "the green highland forests"; the four white stars on the upper left corner represented for four highland provinces of Kontum, Pleiku, Darlac and Haut Donnai (Đồng Nai Thượng) (Hickey 1982a, 54). Along with the flag template, an open letter entitled "Aspirations of the struggling Highlanders" was widely publicized. This open letter was a powerful indictment against Diệm regime. It listed and analyzed the discriminatory acts of Việt officials towards the Montagnards in all spheres of politics, administration, military, security, economy, culture, education, etc.

In September 1958 two personnel worked under the command of Paul Nưr were captured in Dak To, northern Kontum. This event aroused the anger of the BAJARAKA's members. On 8th the same month, on behalf of the BAJARAKA movement, Y Bham Enuol wrote a letter to President Diệm to protest the arrest and required the government to solve the crisis in the Highlands. Multiple copies of the grievance were also sent to National Assembly and highland provincial chiefs. That gesture made the Saigon government react sharply. As a consequence, hundreds of BAJARAKA's members, those who were considered dangerous, were arrested. Most of Montagnard leaders including Y Bham Enuol,

Y Dhon Adrong, Y Dhe Adrong, Y Nuin Hmok, Y Wick Buon Ya, Y Het Kpor, Y Tluop Kpor, Y Senh Nie, Y Bun Sor, Y Yu Eban, Y Thih Eban, Touneh Yoh, Siu Sipp, Paul Nưr, Nay Luett, etc., then were put in jails. Remaining members of BAJARAKA attempted to hold several rallies in Kontum, Pleiku, Buôn Mê Thuột, but all were suppressed (Dharma 2012, 37-38).

To prevent the indigenous peoples from sparking off a general uprising, the GVN requested local authorities to confiscate the traditional weapons such as bows, spears, knives, etc. Reputed Montagnards officers and civil servants working in the Central Highlands were transferred to the Central coastal plains and the Mekong River Delta. Montagnard military officers were also requested to take Việt names (S. Jones et al. 2002, 21)&(Dharma 2012, 39). The repressive measures of Diệm government already prevented public struggles, but those could not extinguish the discontent flame in minority regions. That spark was still simmering and exploded within the FULRO movement under the Military Junta of 1964.

It should also be added that in the period from 1956 to 1962, American advisors and anthropologists were present throughout the Central Highlands. Based on field studies, experts repeatedly warned the Saigon government about drawbacks in the ethnic policies, but their recommendations brought no significant change. Even interventions of the Pentagon and the U.S. Embassy in Saigon, those required the GVN to expand democracy and strengthening the policy of equality for ethnic minorities, could not convert Diệm's chauvinism stance too. Those disagreements made the relations between Saigon and Washington increasingly gloomy. Responses of Ngô brothers showed that they were always skeptical and did not want the Americans intervening in internal affairs of Saigon government. It was believed that Diệm's agreement with the American ambassador, Frederick Nolting on releasing Y Thih Eban and his fellow prisoners including Nay Luett, Touneh Yoh, Siu Sipp and Y Ju Eban from Huế prison on 18th August 1962 merely aimed at maintaining of aid sources and a harmonious relationship with the U.S.

Late 1963, the Americans had found themselves no longer able to control the Ngô Clan. As a result, the group of disaffected generals was soon green-lighted to conduct a military coup to overthrow Diệm brothers (Hãn, Đệ, & Thư 2000, 192). After the coup d'état, the "short-sighted" Highland Affairs Policies of the First Republic was almost abolished by the next SVN political regimes.

V The Policies of the Second Republic toward Ethnic Minorities in the Central Highlands (1964–1975)

Like late President Diệm, the GVN successive leaders evermore considered the Central Highlands a strategic area. With the intensification of the Vietnam War in the early 1960s, the Central Highlands then became one of the main battlefields, among other things because the North Vietnamese Army and the Việt Cộng were able to lead a guerrilla war in the jungle terrain there. Aimed at isolating the liberation war zones, and cutting off the vital supplies from the North throughout the Hồ Chí Minh Trail, the Americans and the GVN attempted to gain control of the hinterlands. Therefore, along with deployment of powerful military forces in the II Tactical Zone, the U.S. and the GVN endlessly applied various methods to seek for the minorities' allegiance.

In order to meet the aspiration of the minorities, Premier Nguyễn Khánh announced the policies of his government towards the minorities with three primary principles of "equality," "respect," and "special support," those later became "ethnic harmony" and "co-development in a united nation" under Nguyễn Cao Kỳ leadership. Since its establishment in late 1967, the Second Republic then continued adopting and developing the highland affairs strategies framed in the Military Junta and the Central Executive Committee. The relative stability the South created a better foundation for further progress in the ethnic policies towards the minorities. During this period, the deployment of many socioeconomic programs contributed significantly to the improvement of the livelihoods and farming techniques of ethnic minorities. Besides, the government cultural and educational projects also brought many positive effects such as restoration of customary law courts, the opportunity to pursue the national education system for ethnic children, etc. The governmental agency, which was responsible for the minority affairs, was also continually upgraded to the Ministry for Development of Ethnic Minorities as the wishes of the minorities.

Besides achievements, the ethnic strategies of the U.S. and the Second Republic also contained some inadequacies and limitations those brought various unwanted changes in the minority regions leading to the outbreak of struggle movements, typically the FULRO.

5.1 The Ethnic Policies of the Military Junta 1964–1967

5.1.1 Historical Background

As previously presented, realizing it seemed to be impossible to settle disputes with Diệm brothers, American President Kennedy backed the Revolutionary Military Council (RMC) led by General Dương Văn Minh (commonly known as Big Minh), conducting the military coup on 1st November 1963. The death of President Ngô Đình Diệm and his younger brother, chief political adviser Ngô Đình Nhu put an end to the First Republic of Vietnam. The RMC then took over the control of the administration. Generals Dương Văn Minh, Lê Văn Kim, Trần Văn Đôn, and Tôn Thất Đính became heads of the new-born junta. The Council then appointed Nguyễn Ngọc Thơ, who had served as vice president under Diệm regime, as prime minister on November 4th (Engelbert 2014, 94).

For about two years later (until General Nguyễn Cao Kỳ established the war cabinet on 19th June 1965) there was the replacement of five other governments in SVN[239] (Hãn et al. 2000, 198–199). Excepting for the Nguyễn Khánh administration[240] which existed nearly nine months (between February 28th and November 2nd, 1964), none of the four remaining civilian governments could last up to half a year[241]. Finally, after the failure of all civilian politics, the power

---

[239] During this two years, there were entirely ten coups and counter-coups conducted by military generals in SVN (Hãn et al. 2000, 199).

[240] Though participating in the coup overthrew Diệm regime, Nguyễn Khánh had not been sufficiently trusted by RMC members. Anyway, after the coup d'état, Khánh was promoted from brigadier general to lieutenant general and was appointed the commander of the Corps I stationing in Huế. Disgruntled with that award, Khánh, with the firm support of General Trần Thiện Khiêm who was serving as Corps III Commander and also Governor of Saigon, conducted a coup on January 30th, 1964, that he called a re-adjustment. Khánh later deposed key generals of the November 1st, 1963, coup including Trần Văn Đôn, Lê Văn Kim, and Mai Hữu Xuân; naming himself Chairman of the Revolutionary Military Council and Commander of the Army. On February 28th, 1964, he removed the government of Nguyễn Ngọc Thơ and became prime minister. While the "old Generals" were condemned neutral and pro-French, Khánh was supported by some American politicians and regarded as a new hope of the RVN (Ahern 1998, 17–18).

[241] In particular, Nguyễn Ngọc Thơ's cabinet was established on 5th November 1963 and dissolved on 28th February 1964; Trần Văn Hương's government lasted from November 4th, 1964, to January 26th, 1965; Nguyễn Xuân Oánh's cabinet remained during the period since the demise of Prime Minister Trần Văn Hương until February 15th, 1965; Phan Huy Quát's administration lasted from 16th February 1965 to 11th June 1965.

was transferred back to the military resulting in the birth of Nguyễn Cao Kỳ government on 19th June 1965 (Hãn et al. 2000, 199)[242].

Ruling for short periods, in the wartime, while always facing political pressure from various sides including Buddhism, Catholicism, political parties and military[243], those cabinets could not wholeheartedly shape advanced socio-economic policies (Donnell & Joiner 1967, 53, 56)&(Hàm 1993, 61). However, not like many other aspects, the ethnic strategies during this period had been looked carefully by the central government. It cannot be said that adjustments in the ethnic policies made by Generals Khánh and Kỳ were only products of the situation to deal with the rising ethno-nationalism in SVN. Like late President Diệm, the GVN leaders always viewed the Central Highlands as a strategic area. The pacification of this land had a vital meaning to the fate of SVN. Therefore, except governments, those existed for very short periods the policies towards ethnic minorities were always considered one of Saigon's top concerns.

On the U.S. side, after adopting Ambassador Henry Cabot Lodge Jr. and CIA officer of in Saigon Lucien Emile Conein green-lighted the military generals to overthrow President Diệm, the Americans realized the coup d'état did not provide the stability that they had been seeking. The deterioration of the political situation in SVN made the U.S. get rather confused in choosing a better substitute (Pentagon Papers 1972, 106–157).

Not only playing the role of building the First Republic, but the Americans also involved in most of the other political upheavals took place in SVN. According to CIA declassified documents, after Diệm's death, at first, Ambassador Henry Cabot Lodge forbade CIA to contact the RMC to "maintain the independence" of the GVN before international opinion. But a few months later, witnessed the incompetence of generals in restoring country order, Lodge again allowed CIA to work in close collaboration with the new junta to "monitor and adjust personnel." That was why CIA could resume its significant role in the political transformation in Saigon like as under President Diệm (Ahern 1998, 10).

Since the NLF born in late 1960, the conflict in Vietnam increasingly caused unfavorable for the Americans. Facing the risk of a complete failure in the "Special War,"[244] from mid-1965, Pentagon moved to implementing

---

242 Ibid. Đỗ Mậu (2007), *Việt Nam máu lửa quê hương tôi (The bloody war in Vietnam)*, Chapter XVIII.
243 While still in power, Nguyễn Khánh ever stated: "Army is the father of the nation." Ibid. Đỗ Mậu (2007).
244 According to Lê Mậu Hãn, *Special War* (Vietnamese: Chiến lược Chiến tranh đặc biệt) was a modern American invasion war, in which South Vietnamese military forces

the "Limited War."[245] With this new strategy, the U.S. massively dispatched American expeditionary and its allied forces, together with weapons and warfare equipment into SVN battlefield; at the same time, they deployed air and naval forces attacking key cities in the North. In the "Limited War," the U.S. troops played a significant role and were increasingly enhanced in quantity and equipment (H. C. Minh 1996, 228)[246]. After arriving in Vietnam, the American Expeditionary along with allied forces those who came from South Korea, Austrailia, New Zealand, Thailand, Philippines, etc. launched a strategic offensive in the two dry seasons of 1965–1966 and 1966–1967. Applying the so-called Search and Destroy tactic, the American-led allied forces, and Saigon army attempted to defeat the NLF troops, as well as their sympathizers to put an end to the war[247].

As previously mentioned, as a strategic area the thick forests in the Central Highlands also offered Việt Cộng guerrilla forces ideal hideouts. To isolate the liberation war zones, and to cut off the vital supplies from the North throughout the Hồ Chí Minh Trail, the Americans must seek to gain control of the hinterlands. Therefore, along with deployment of powerful military forces in the II Tactical Zone, American military advisers, as well as of CIA personnel also endlessly applied many methods to obtain the minorities' allegiance.

After the coup of 1963, the U.S. committed to cooperating with the new administration in maintaining the socioeconomic programs which had been implementing previously. Foreseeing that *"The Montagnards in both cities and hamlets would like to rid Highlands of Vietnamese settlers and government,"* the

---

under American advisors and modern American equipment were used to fight against Vietnamese people (Hăn et al. 2000, 179).

245 Ibid. *Limited War* (Vietnamese: Chiến lược Chiến tranh cục bộ) was another modern American invasion war carried by American, South Vietnamese and their partners' troops wherein American troops performed the most vital role (Hăn et al. 2000, 201).

246 By the end of 1964, the U.S. and allied forces in the South had some 26.000 men; until late 1965, this figure increased to 200.000; and reached 537.000 by the end of 1967. Besides, 70.000 U.S. troops based in Guam, Philippines, Thailand and the Seventh Fleet always ready to fight (Hăn et al. 2000, 200–201).

247 Aiming at "Breaking the Việt Cộng's spine," during four months of the dry season 1965–1966, with forces of 720.000 including 220.000 expeditionary troops, the U.S. opened 450 operations in NLF bases. During the dry season 1966–1967, with a force of more than 980.000 soldiers, of which 440.000 Expeditionary troops, the number of "search and destroy" operations expanded to 895 (Hăn et al. 2000, 204).

Americans developed a win-win relationship with the Montagnards[248]. The U.S., on the one hand, implemented socioeconomic development programs; they pressured the new administration to release BAJARAKA leaders imprisoned by the Diệm regime to "win the hearts and minds" of the Montagnards. Simultaneously, they procured the consent of some minority leaders to deploy powerful military forces to pacify "the holy land of Việt Cộng." MACV, U.S. Operations Mission and U.S. Embassy officials were ordered to liaise regularly with Highlander leaders to take advantage of them (FRUS 1992, 1300–1301). Ironically, peasants in the South *often welcomed American help but sympathized with the Viet Cong* (Karnow 1984, 323).

5.1.2 The Ethnic Strategies of the Military Junta 1964–1967

In a variety of ways, policies form a society's appearance. In return, feedbacks from the people also contribute significantly to enhance administration system of that community. In SVN, the government fell into hands of military generals after a deep crisis. Within that context, Prime Minister Nguyễn Khánh and his successor, Nguyễn Cao Kỳ[249], showed considerable efforts to get rid of the critical situation, deal with NLF's growth and control the rising ethno-nationalist movement in the minority groups[250]. The administrative reforms, therefore, consisted of some improvements in the minority strategies, which partially satisfied demands of the ethnic minorities.

In overall, the ethnic policies during this period were considered contributing a significant rise in the correlation between the central government and

---

248 According to the U.S. Embassy in Saigon, the final target of struggles carried out by the Montagnards against the GVN was autonomy, so they would not stop until reaching their goal (FRUS 1992, 1300).
249 The remaining cabinets in this period lasted for only a few months and quickly being replaced before fully arranged personnel apparatus or reviewed policy system.
250 On September 20th, 1964, some combative teams of Highland Special Forces Commandos and Civilian Irregular Defense Group (CIDG) revolted and attacked Highland Special Force camps of Saigon army in Buon Sa Pra and Bu Prang. The insurgents then tied the Special Forces commander to the flagpole, killed 35 Vietnamese soldiers and threw their bodies into the latrine. The High Committee of Highlands Liberation Front (French: Front de Libération des Hauts Plateaux, FLHP) also announced a manifesto demanding the Việt people to give the territories which were "stolen" from the Highlanders, the Cham and the Khmer Krom back. Rebel leaders also threatened to attack Buôn Mê Thuột and gave an ultimatum asking the Việt people to leave the Highlands (Hickey 1982, 99–103)&(Tiệp 2013a, 80).

the minority groups. Though the new policy could not meet all the minorities' expectations, to some extent, it gained several remarkable achievements, most important was to soften the struggle of FULRO and to pave the way for this armed force to cooperate with the GVN.

Coming to power while the struggles of the minorities were intensifying, Nguyễn Khánh made substantial efforts to improve the Highland Affairs Policies formed by Diệm. In March 1964, soon after became Premier, Nguyễn Khánh, under pressure from the U.S., released leaders of BAJARAKA movement those were arrested and jailed by Diệm government[251] (FRUS 1992, 1022). In order to create a breakthrough in the relationship between the Saigon and the minority groups, on 28th April 1964, Khánh signed official letters inviting 59 highland representatives to Saigon to discuss their people's outstanding needs and desires. This gesture of goodwill was seen as unprecedented under the First Republic[252].

The meeting between the prime minister and the highland representatives then took place on 9th May. Among the guests invited to the capital, they were many former leaders of the BAJARAKA such as Y Bham Enuol, Paul Nứr, Nay Nuett, etc. Five days before that formal meeting, Premier Khánh signed a decree to upgrade the Bureau for Highland Affairs (Vietnamese: Nha Công tác Xã hội Miền Thượng) to the Directorate of Highland Affairs (Vietnamese: Nha Đặc trách Thượng Vụ) and put it under the Ministry of Defense[253]. The central office of the

---

251 After being freed from prison, some of former BAJARAKA members became leaders of the FULRO movement like Y Bham Enuol and Y Ju Eban, otherwise many others were appointed as government officials such asPau Nứr became Commissioner for Highland Affairs in the central government, Nay Nuett also worked for Highland Affairs, Touneh Yoh served as Deputy District Chief of Đơn Dương District (Tuyên Đức Province), etc.

252 Eight years after being kicked out of the Saigon government apparatus, in a talk at Cornell University on 6th December 1973, Khánh affirmed he understands the Highlanders better than most Saigon leaders. And, his background had been accumulated since he was a commander of the Mobile Group II in highland operation in 1954 and during the period he served as commanding officer of the II Corps. Therefore, after becoming prime minister, Khánh already did his best to "*Give the Highlanders an opportunity to assume some responsibility in the administration*" (Hickey 1982, 94).

253 After the coup in 1963, the presidential office which directly managed the Bureau for Highland Affairs no longer existed. Also, the unstable political situation prompted this agency not to operate effectively according to its assigned function. Therefore, the restructure the Bureau for Highland Affairs into the Directorate of Highland Affairs that then was put under the Ministry of Defense marking the return of a specialized agency dealing with issues of ethnic minorities.

Directorate of Highland Affairs then was relocated from Huế to Saigon where Lt. Col. Nguyễn Phi Phụng, an official of the Central Intelligence Organization, was appointed as its chief (Hickey 1982a, 94–95)&(Dharma 2012, 56).

As for the tribal groups, those who mostly resided in the Central Highlands where was arranged as II Tactical Zone of the RVNMF. The II Corps Command stood to host a Montagnard Congress in Pleiku on 26th August 1964 that attracted 55 delegates to attend. Like the meeting held in Saigon three months ago, this gathering also aimed at gathering wants and needs of ethnic minorities to form the basis of an appropriate policy for the Highlanders (Tiệp 2013a, 80). Also, General Nguyễn Hữu Có, the commander of the II Corps, organized a standing committee to receive aspirations of highland leaders. Except for Lieutenant Nguyễn Văn Nghiêm, all remaining members of that committee were representatives of the tribal groups including Captain Touprong Ya Ba, Captain Y Pem Knuol, Y Chon Mlo Duon Du, and Siu Plung. The formal meeting of the committee then took place at a new club of RVNMF officers in Pleiku named Phoenix (Vietnamese: Phượng Hoàng). There, the majority of the delegates who came from the tribal groups elected Y Bham Enuol as their spokesman. In the meeting, Enuol requested the government to reinstate the statute particulier like under former Emperor Bảo Đại regime. Namely, the GVN should recognize Highlanders' land ownership, restore customary law courts and re-open a specialized secondary school for the Montagnards students like the Collège Sabatier (Hickey 1982a, 99)&(FRUS 1992, 1023).

Concerning the U.S. military forces deployed in the Central Highlands. July 1965, the 1st Brigade of 1st Cavalry Division arrived in Tân Tạo military base to survey the area and prepare to send troops into An Khê, a strategic location on Route 19 that held the eastern gate of the Highlands. At the same time, hundreds of American military advisors and technical specialists were dispatched to Corps II and 22nd Division of RVNMF. Since January 1966, a series of search and destroy campaigns were deployed in highland provinces. For example, Operation Matador in Kontum and Pleiku did by the 1st Brigade of 1st Cavalry Division; some others were conducted by 3d Brigade, 25th Infantry Division in Pleiku and Buôn Mê Thuột. In some villages, residents accused the U.S. forces of attacking them instead of raiding the Việt Cộng. From March onwards, the 3d Brigade of 25th Infantry Division took the mission to move along Route 14 to search for VC guerrillas. In April, the 1st Air Cavalry Division opened Operation Lincoln in Pleiku. Two months later, the 1st Brigade of the 101st Airborne Division cooperated with RVNMF launched Operation Hawthorne in Kontum, etc. Also during this period the border defense and surveillance program was intensified. Some 23 new camps along the boundary lines between Laotian, Cambodian and

RVN were established. Also, the Mobile Strike Force was born on the basis of the restructuring of Mobile Guerrilla Force. This force specialized in conducting helicopter strikes in areas controlled by the VC over the Highlands. Also, as of late 1966, the Americans recruited and trained some 34.800 tribesmen of CIDG forces (Hickey 1982a, 156–157).

About Saigon military forces that stationed in the Central Highlands, by mid-1965 RVNMF launched the 22nd Division along with armored, air and artillery units in Kontum. As a critical province in the northern part of the Central Highlands, Pleiku was chosen to set up headquarters of the II Corps. In Darlac, there was the 23rd Division Command, Regiment 45th, two reinforced artillery battalions, two armored brigades. Besides that, there were 20 outfits of the security forces those stationed in residences and three districts of Buôn Hồ, Lạc Thiện, and Phước An. The Trường Sơn Special Forces here consisted of 31 platoons. Of these forces, while most personnel were tribesmen, the commanders were American officers. Late of 1965, there were some 16 security companies in Tuyên Đức, 47 militia platoons, 86 youth fighting squads, 36 Trường Sơn Special Force teams, 350 members of rural pacification staff and 3.341 trained civilians of CIDG forces. In addition, there also were thousands of cadets, who were training at schools of National Military, Political Warfare, Police and Command and General Staff College, who were ready to serve pacification campaigns (Lan 2014, 68–69).

With the superiority of military forces and equipment, the U.S. Forces and RVNMF set up numerous armed camps along strategic routes, border lines, and populated areas and in "new life hamlets" to prevent the influences of Việt Cộng. The powerful defensive tactic was combined with the promotion of military operations to occupy NLF-controlled zones, destroy Communist forces and regain the initiative on the battlefield Highlands. Search and destroy operations were massively deployed, especially along the borderlines between SVN and Laos, Cambodia to destroy NLF fundamental forces and to raid the North-South strategic corridor.

Merely in Darlac, there were 130 search-and-destroy operations conducted within the last six months of 1965. The number of such activities in Pleiku was 959 in the year 1966. At the same time, U.S. and RVNMF bolstered air strikes continuously into adjacent areas where they supposed to have liberation forces. Besides, the U.S Air Force conducted a large-scale of toxic chemical spraying named Ranch Hand[254] lasting from 1962 to 1971. Together with the aim of

---

254 Within nine years of Operation Ranch Hand the U.S. Air Force sprayed about 19 million gallons of defoliants over 20 percent tropical forest and 36 percent mangrove forest in southern Vietnam (Thắng 2008).

destroying forested zones over SVN, this program also sought to damage crops, livestock, forcing the local people to move into new life hamlets. Forces engaged in military operations were often assigned tasks quite clearly, while American troops "searched and destroyed," RVNMF promoted "pacification" (Lan 2014, 69)&(Thắng 2008).

The most prominent achievements of Nguyễn Khánh government in implementing the minority strategies were to hold the Pleiku Conference successfully on October 17th, 1964. The Congress brought 11 delegations with four deputy province chiefs and 64 other deputies representing the Montagnards and Cham in the South Central Coast and Central Highlands (Nứ 1966, 123). The conference was considered a golden opportunity for representatives came from the Central Highlands and coastal plain provinces including Kontum, Pleiku, Darlac, Phú Bổn, Tuyên Đức, Tuyên Đức, Phú Yên, Khánh Hòa, Quảng Ngãi, Bình Định and Ninh Thuận to present their hopes and demands of their people. This also was to give the Saigon a chance to explain the governmental ethnic policies clearly.

After three days of free discussion, the delegates submitted to the GVN an aspiration of the minorities consisting of seven following contents:

1. Politics, culture:
    - Request the government to issue special policies to protect and support the Montagnards. Because both Highlanders and Lowlanders are citizens of RVN, they should be treated in the same manner;
    - The Highlanders are less civilized than the Lowlanders, so the government should reserve certain privileges to permit them to catch up with national progress;
    - Respect the customs, manners, habits, and culture of the Montagnards; reserve for the Montagnards some seats in parliament, the provincial and local people's councils;
    - Request the government to convene a national convention of ethnic minorities to gather their aspirations and submit them to the government for consideration.
2. Administration:
    - Upgrade the Directorate for Highland Affairs to a Special Commission for Highland Affairs in the central government which should be directed by Highlanders;
    - Request cancellation of Decree 513a/ĐT/CCRĐ (issued on 12th February 1958) and Official Letter No. 981/BTC/DC (promulgated on 28th January 1959) because they severely restricted the land ownership rights of the

Montagnards; enact a particular statute for obtaining land title and simplify the procedures for recognizing land ownership;
- Request treated equitably between Việt and Montagnards civil servants from central to local levels;
- Restoration name of indigenous places such as Tuyên Đức, Phú Bổn, Tuyên Đức, Lâm Đồng, etc., that called previously by the local people.

3. Military:
- Request formalize CIDG force, naming it the Montagnards Military Force (Vietnamese: Liên đoàn Thượng Quân) with between 25.000 and 50.000 troops; command should be given to the Highlander officers, Lowland officers should only control units that are consisting entirely of Việt soldiers;
- Requests commanders of CIDG force attending officer courses and non-commissioned officer (NCO) courses, depending on the ability of each;
- Young Highlanders with high school diplomas should be approved to take courses in military academies; open officer cadet school for young Highlanders;
- Request allow the display of a flag of the Montagnards; the task of pacification the Central Highlands should be given to the Montagnard military units, those were trained, guided and equipped by RVNMF.

4. Economy:
- Request the government to sponsor fertilizers, seeds, farming utensils such as bulldozers, tractors and farm animals to develop agriculture;
- Train more professional staff in cultivation, livestock to guide Highlanders.

5. Education:
- Request open more elementary, secondary, and technical and vocational schools; build dormitories for Montagnard students;
- Montagnard students should be taught their mother tongues along with the national language to the end of the primary level;
- Request assist Montagnard students in exams and give them a privilege to enroll in colleges and universities; grant scholarships for outstanding Montagnard students to study abroad.

6. Social welfare:
- The government should organize free medical programs for the poor people;
- Build more hospitals, infirmaries, aid stations, maternity homes, medicine cabinets and train more public health workers at all levels, especially nurses and midwives.

7. Judiciary:
   - Request re-establish customary law courts, the regulation texts that adjust organizational structure of traditional law courts should be issued by the Ministry of Justice, by consultation with tribal groups (Nứr 1966, 125–130)&(Hickey 1967, 115–120).

It is thought that this is the first time in the history of the RVN the minorities submitted a detailed petition letter, expressing their outstanding needs and desires, as well as welfare they expected to receive from the GVN (Tiệp 2013a, 81). In addition to proposing wants and requirements in raising the living standard of the minorities, the request also referred to long-term demands as training human resources for socio-economic development; resolving the long-standing disharmony between the Lowlanders and the Highlanders; on the role of the Highlanders in electing to prevent the appointment as well as to remove corrupt men; requesting return of highland administrators, those who had been transferred to the lowlands since 1958 by the Diệm administration, etc.

Getting aspirations of the minorities, Prime Minister Khánh quickly responded by announcing the new government ethnic strategies towards the Montagnards with three primary principles: (1) the Việt and the Montagnards would be treated uniformly; (2) the state guaranteed to respect the custom, traditional culture of the Montagnards; (3) the government would give minority compatriots privileges to help them have the same living standards with the Việt people. Those fundamental principles were described by a specific action plan with a spirit of comprehensive reform; making policies in line with the aspirations and particular conditions of each locality, as follows:

1. Politics: The Highlanders are free to choose their representatives to participate in the parliamentary, provincial and communal councils. The government will consider abilities of each nominee to appoint at central or local positions.
2. Military: In addition to a fair and reasonable choice of the Highlanders in the process of training as well as appointment, an officer cadet school will be set up in the Highlands.
3. Economy: Respect land ownership of the Montagnards. Remove the documents determining ownership of the land of mountaineers, issued in 1958, 1959 by the old regime; improve farming, animal husbandry and build roads on the plateau.
4. Education, culture: Build schools, dormitories; grant scholarships for Montagnard students; at the primary level, the mother tongue of the compatriots will be taught in parallel with the Vietnamese.

5. Health, social welfare: Open more clinics, maternity homes, mobile medical services and especially relief when needed.
6. Reinstate the highland customary law courts (Tiệp 2013a, 80–81).

In overall, the Khánh government approved most of the demands of highland representatives. The new policies applied not only to the Montagnards in particular but also to the Northern minority migrants, Chams, and Cambodians of the Mekong River Delta. However, the prime minister resolutely rejected two requests of receiving foreign aid directly and establishing an independent highland military force. Foreign aid would be managed by a Special Commission for Highland Affairs under the central government supervision. And, the requirement for a separate flag of the Highlanders also was partially accepted by allowing a highland pennant to be flown with the national flag. In this regard, the Department of State was quite subtle in its assessment: although the sincere fulfillment of promises of General Khánh at the conference would not fundamentally change relationships between the Việt people and the Montagnards, it undoubtedly did much to win more enthusiastic response from at least a part of Montagnards (FRUS 1992, 1300).

Then, in December 1964, Deputy Director for Highland Affairs Ngô Văn Hùng held a meeting with 14 representatives of the main ethnic groups in the Central Highlands including Jarai, Bahnar, Rhade, Sédang, Mnong, and Churu to discuss the land registration. At the conference, the delegates outlined some of the shortcomings that caused frustration for the Highlanders including:

1. In many localities, local governments expropriated private land to set up Land Development Centers to relocate migrants from northern Vietnam and coastal plains.
2. In other areas, the Lowlanders have taken advantage of the minorities' ignorance to make profits in land transfer agreements.
3. Minorities with land requisitioned by local authorities were promised compensation in the form of property, but these promises were never carried out.
4. Many Highlanders whose property were sequestered by public works such as roads, hydropower dams (Danhim) received less compensation than the Việt people in the same circumstances.

The participants recommended that these drawbacks should be remedied soon. They also agreed on land registration measures. Accordingly, the authorities need to ensure fairness in the right to exploit and use land between the Montagnards and the Việt people. Due to their "underdeveloped economy," the Montagnards should be exempted from land-use tax for particular periods.

Finally, the delegates recommended that Land Registration Committees should be set up at all province, district and village levels with specific rules about the structure and function for each. In each of those assemblies, beyond the head and his deputy to represent local government, representatives of Land Reform Service, it must include a corresponding number of deputies representing the Highlanders and the Lowlanders (Hickey 1967, 36–37).

Inheriting the advances in Khánh's ethnic policies, the war government of General Nguyễn Cao Kỳ then also devoted particular attention to ethnic minorities. In the statement, dated 2nd August 1965, Premier Kỳ affirmed that he would continue to implement the contents that the Nguyễn Khánh government had committed in the Kontum Conference in October of 1964. According to the statements of the state, the central task of ethnic strategies in this period was to implement the motto *"Ethnic harmony, co-development in a united nation."* In particular, *"Ethnic harmony means all ethnic groups in the country have duties to each other, essential is fair treatment, brotherhood making solidarity that no power can divide or suppress"*; *"Ethnic co-development means the government will give more privileges to support the Montagnards to have the same Lowlanders' living standards"* (Tiệp 2013a, 82).

Speaking at the ceremony in Buôn Mê Thuột to accept the surrender of the Montagnard FULRO, Prime Minister Kỳ argued that during the wartime, the responsibility of building national unity and ethnic harmony needed to be placed on top. In the meantime, there were too many political parties and trends in the system of politics in SVN. Therefore, creating and defending a solidarity country became the most important assignment. *"This country is the common nation of our people, irrespective of the Kinh (Viet) or the Montagnards. The Kinh or the Montagnards all have the same obligations and rights. Those duties and entitlements require us to keep our solidarity"*; *"United we stand, divided we fall."*[255]

In addition to the demands made by representatives of the FULRO movement, in this period, non-FULRO representatives from the Jarai, Bahnar, Rengao, Sédang, and Halang also submitted to General Vĩnh Lộc, Commander of the II Corps a list of Highlanders' aspirations. At a talk held on 7th October 1965 in Kontum, Paul Nứr, Deputy Province Chief for Highland Affairs presented hopes and needs of the Highlanders. Like the points discussed in the Pleiku Conference of October 1964, the contents of this petition also consisted of the land claims, improving living standards, a military unit recruited and led by the Highlanders,

---

[255] Instructive of Prime Minister Nguyễn Cao Kỳ, dated 15th September 1965 (Thêm 1989, 147)&(Tiệp 2013a, 82).

a more significant chance to participate the local and central administrations and preserving the traditional law courts, the teaching of minority languages and a flag for the Highlands.

While negotiations were still ongoing, on 17th December 1965, extremists of FULRO revolted attacking some military bases of RVNMF at Lạc Thiện District, Phú Bổn Province, causing the death of many of both Việt and Montagnard peoples. The reason for the uprising was later determined to be due to promised programs made by the Prime Minister Khánh did not satisfy the rebel forces (FRUS 1992, 1301). Soon after the rebellion, of many captured Highlanders, three FULRO leaders were executed in Kontum (Hickey 1967, 40). This riot made the negotiation process between representatives of the government and the Highlanders fall into a deadlock.

Contacts between the government and FULRO only were resumed in May 1966. Because of disadvantages brought back by the riot, FULRO representatives scaled down their aspirations to four main points including a special status, a highland pennant in the national flag, a highland military force and establishing a Commission for Highland Affairs in Buôn Mê Thuột. As a concession, the war cabinet of General Kỳ accepted to create a Commission for Highland Affairs to replace the Directorate for Highland Affairs and appointed Paul Nưr as chief of the new institution (Donnell & Joiner 1967, 59)&(Hickey 1967, 41). To take action in reply, FULRO representatives committed to bringing 500 armed personnel to cooperate with the government within one month (Dĩ 1968, 34)&(Hickey 1982a, 153). On 8th August the same year, General Kỳ signed a decree to set up the Delegation Special Office of FULRO (DSO FULRO) (French: Délégation Spéciale et Officielle) in Buon Ale A (Buôn Mê Thuột), marking the birth of the FULRO's official representative office in Vietnam (Dĩ 1968)&(Dharma 2012, 84).

The message Khánh sent to the Montagnards in the October Conference 1964 then was institutionalized by Decree No. 006/65 dated 22nd July 1965 and Circular No. 9593 QP dated 7th September 1966, signed by Chairman of the National Leadership Committee Nguyễn Văn Thiệu. These documents regulated and guided the reorganization of the highland law court system.

Prior to the Constitutional Assembly election held on 11th September 1966, on July 22nd, 1966, Premier Kỳ signed a law to allow FULRO members, those who returned to cooperate with the government before August 15th of the same year, to run for the election. As a result, two FULRO representatives named Y Wik Buon Ya (Rhade), and Ksor Rot (Jarai) were elected. Besides, there were two non-FULRO candidates as Nay Blim (Jarai), and Đinh Văn Rổi (Hre) also won the election (Hickey 1982a, 153–154).

In mid-October 1966, a Montagnards-Việt Solidarity Conference was convened in Kontum chaired by General Vĩnh Lộc, Command of the II Corps. The Convention was to celebrate the second anniversary of the Pleiku Conference of 1964 and to welcome 800 FULRO members, who pledge to return to serve the government. Here, one more time, Y Dhe Adrong, chief of the representative of FULRO made a speech expressing the aspiration of a "Bill of Rights" for the Highlanders. In which, he emphasized three following prominent requests:

1. The right to own their land;
2. The right to access education for their people;
3. The right to speak and learn their own languages in schools (Hickey 1967, 44).

Although the ethnic strategies of the Military Junta still contained some weaknesses and also had not been entirely framed and fully implemented, its principles considered core premise for the development of the ethnic policies of the Second RVN.

5.2 The Policies of the Second Republic toward the Minorities (1967–1975)

5.2.1 The Americans and the Birth of the Second Republic

Appointed as U.S. Ambassador in Saigon since July 14th, 1964 to replace Henry Cabot Lodge Jr., who returned to the U.S. for the presidential campaign, General Maxwell D. Taylor quickly felt frustrated by the unstable political situation. He supposed nothing else but the disputes between the junta's senior officers were derailing the war effort (Karnow 1984, 399). In an informal meeting organized by General William Westmoreland, commander of U.S. forces in SVN, Taylor asked for an end to the constant changes in Saigon leadership. Although affirmed that the situation was tense, General Khánh and his men assured the Ambassador of stability (Moyar & Carland 2006, 344). According to Karnow, Westmoreland also cautioned that long-lasted instability could turn American politicians and mass against the GVN, as they would deem it would be useless to support such a regime (Karnow 1984, 398).

General Nguyễn Khánh, who the CIA headquarters in Saigon had considered as an irreplaceable South Vietnamese leader, had no more capacity than General Minh in unifying entire SVN army forces for a new counterinsurgency campaign. SVN under his government leadership even became more chaotic. The coup d'états[256] broke out consecutively made Khánh increasingly dependent on

---

256 September 13th, 1964, the General Dương Văn Đức and Lâm Văn Phát sent troops to Saigon to bargain with the government. Less than half a year later, on February 19th,

the "Young Turks"[257] in maintaining the social order. Inconsistencies among generals increased after Khánh unveiled the decision on dissolving the High National Council[258] because the board disagreed with the forced retirement policy of the Young Turks applied for "old generals" including Dương Văn Minh[259] (Ahern Jr 1998, 29).

With the aggravation of the discord between Premier Khánh and U.S. Ambassador Taylor, the Young Turks turned to support American intention of removing General Khánh to maintain U.S. military and economic aid (Ahern Jr 1998, 29)&(Karnow 1984, 399). As an inevitable consequence, General Khánh must resign as army chief after being offered to serve as a roving ambassador of RVN since February 24th, 1965. General Nguyễn Văn Thiệu later replaced Khánh in his post of the Armed Forces Council's chairman (FRUS 1992, 1014–1023)&(Ahern Jr 1998, 33). After Khánh regime, merely in a half of year, SVN's political arena repeatedly witnessed replacements of three civilian cabinets of Trần Văn Hương, Nguyễn Xuân Oánh, and Phan Huy Quát.

In parallel with taking constant efforts to reorganize Saigon government personnel, the U.S. escalated into a full-scale war to seek a decisive victory. After one year as ambassador in Saigon, Maxwell Taylor did not please President Johnson due to his tense relations with South Vietnamese generals and his opposition to the U.S. military policy in Vietnam. On July 8th, 1965 Taylor resigned as ambassador, and former Ambassador Henry Cabot Lodge returned to Saigon to replace him. This change of American personnel is considered the first step to Americanize the Vietnam War.

1965, another military coup led by Colonel Phạm ngọc Thảo and General Lâm Văn Phát broke out. Rebels almost caught Premier Khánh and refused to withdraw until Kỳ threatened large-scale air strikes.

257 Young Turks is a term used by the Americans to refer to a gathering of young army generals led by chief of the SVN Air Force Nguyễn Cao Kỳ, commander of IV Corps Nguyễn Văn Thiệu and I Corps commander Nguyễn Chánh Thi.

258 The High National Council (Vietnamese: Thượng Hội Đồng Quốc Gia) was founded on 8th September 1964 was a civilian legislative gathering convened by the Military Revolutionary Council led by the three Generals Dương Văn Minh, Nguyễn Khánh and Trần Thiện Khiêm. In essence, this council is a civilian coat worn by the military government during the military administration of the RVN (Engelbert 2014, 105). See also *Chronology 1 November 1963–3 August 1967*. In: TTU, VNC, VA 0720814005.

259 As mentioned earlier, the Young Turks hated a group of experienced officers who had been in high power positions but were now in powerless posts and wanted to sideline them completely.

The political crisis only subsided when the country's leadership was again transferred to the Armed Forces Council[260] where Generals Nguyễn Văn Thiệu and Nguyễn Cao Kỳ ultimately emerged as new flamboyant representatives of the Young Turks (Ahern 1998, 19, 21). Soon after Prime Minister Phan Huy Quát announced his resignation and "returned the administration to the military" after less than four months in office, the Armed Forces Council convened its members to discuss the takeover of power. In the meeting, all participants agreed to form two special commissions: the National Leadership Committee (Vietnamese: Ủy ban Lãnh đạo Quốc Gia) chaired by General Nguyễn Văn Thiệu (equivalent to Chief of State); and Central Executive Committee (Vietnamese: Ủy ban Hành pháp Trung ương) led by General Nguyễn Cao Kỳ (equivalent to Prime Minister) (Karnow 1984, 422)&(Ahern Jr 1998, 35). These two provisional political institutions assumed the leadership of SVN through November 1967, since the creation of the Second Republic of SVN.

On May 1st, 1967, Ambassador Ellsworth Bunker who was well known for being a hawk on the wars in Vietnam and Southeast Asia arrived in Saigon to replace Lodge. The arrival of Bunker and his approach of presidential elections in SVN was considered as "beginning a new CIA effort to influence Vietnamese politics" (Ahern Jr 1998, 48). Bunker quickly intervened in the election that CIA prepared since February 1967 by asking Kỳ set up a national unity front to create a mass base for the military ticket (of Thiệu and Kỳ) (Ahern Jr 1998, 52).

In the panorama of the election, although received instructions from Washington to back the slate of Generals Thiệu and Kỳ[261], CIA should *"pretend to be neutral and use its influence to create a democratic election"* (Ahern Jr 1998, 53). Furthermore, to ensure the victory of Thiệu and Kỳ, CIA simultaneously agreed with Loan's[262] proposal of using national police to "lobby" for them in areas

---

260 Armed Forces Council was an institution consisting of 50 RVNMF key generals, found by General Nguyễn Khánh on December 18th, 1964. This council declared itself dissolved on June 14th, 1965 to cede national administration to National Leadership Committee and Central Executive Committee.

261 In the presidential elections in 1967, in addition to the ticket of Nguyễn Văn Thiệu and Nguyễn Cao Kỳ there also had nine other slates of Trương Đình Du, Trần Văn Chiêu; Phan Khắc Sửu, Phan Quang Đán; Trần Văn Hương, Mai Thọ Truyền; Hà Thúc Ký, Nguyễn Văn Định; Nguyễn Hòa Hiệp, Nguyễn Thế Truyền; Vũ Hồng Khanh, Dương Trung Đường; Hoàng Cơ Bình, Lưu Quang Khình; Phạm Huy Cơ, Lý Quốc Sinh; Trần Văn Lý, Huỳnh Công Đương.

262 General Nguyễn Ngọc Loan was a trusted subordinate of Kỳ, at that time Loan was serving as Director of National Police.

where they had less advantage than other candidates (Ahern Jr 1998, 54–56). In the presidential election that took place on 3rd September 1967, the Thiệu-Kỳ ticket gained the triumph with 34.8 percent of the votes[263]; a modest result compared to the military candidates' dominance (Thêm 1989c, 196–197)&(Nohlen, Grotz, & Hartmann 2001, 331).

Along with efforts to intervene in the administration building process, CIA also began to prepare for the forthcoming parliamentary poll that was scheduled to take place in December 1967. Declassified documents of the U.S. intelligence agency revealed that the U.S. State Department agreed to pay $ 3.000 to each pro-U.S. member of Congress, though Ambassador Bunker only proposed an expense of $ 1.500 (Ahern Jr 1998, 58).

Thus, with the U.S. great assistance in various aspects, the military slate represented by Thiệu and Kỳ won the last victory in 1967 presidential election. On October 2nd the same year, the Constituent Assembly validated the election results, recognizing President Nguyễn Văn Thiệu and Vice President Nguyễn Cao Kỳ, marking the birth of the Second Republic of SVN (Thêm 1989c, 222). There is no doubt that the method of setting up the First Republic then was reapplied in the process of creating the Second Republic administration. Because of grasping the Saigon political arena, CIA headquarters and Ambassador Bunker had exact steps. They selected not only suitable candidates but also applied appropriate intervention measures, including frauds to help the "selected persons" win the "democratic election." After the vote, the U.S. only needed to adopt the pro-American dictatorship president to control both the executive and the legislative to implement its long-term interests in SVN and Southeast Asia. During almost ten years existence of the Second Republic, the U.S. indefinitely maintained the "carrot and stick approach" to press Thiệu government into implementing its military and socioeconomic programs; executing the role of an "anti-communist outpost." Whenever Thiệu became stubborn, the bosses of the White Houses seemed not to hesitate to send him a message of "change of personnel"[264] as an

---

263 The following positions in the race to the Independence Palace belonged to the slates of Trương Đình Du and Trần Văn Chiêu with 17.2 percent; Phan Khắc Sửu and Phan Quang Đán with 10.8 percent; Trần Văn Hương and Mai Thọ Truyền with 10 percent of the votes, respectively (Thêm 1989c, 196–197)&(Nohlen et al. 2001, 331).
264 In the professional language of U.S.-RVN relations, the term "adjust personnel" or "personnel change" is a lightweight statement, meaning a coup. In 1963, when preparation for the overthrow of Ngô Đình Diệm was under way, Kennedy, in an interview with Walter Cronkite on CBS television, mentioned the need to "change personnel" that was the "green light" from the highest level to the coup generals (Hưng 2009, 34).

early warning: what happened to Diệm absolutely could repeat with Thiệu (N. T. Hưng 2009, 34).

5.2.2 The Ethnic Policies of the Second Republic 1967–1975

It can be instantly ascertained that the ethnic policies of the Second Republic was a continuation of the highland affairs strategy under the Military Junta, especially of the National Leadership Committee and Central Executive Committee. On the surface, until mid-1967, the power struggle within the Saigon administration gradually receded; South Vietnamese society gradually came into order. This was the principal foundation to make further progress in the ethnic strategies in order to "win the hearts and minds" of the minorities (MDEM 1972, 11).

However, after two years escalating into a full-scale war, the U.S. and its alliance, the GVN, could not win a decisive military victory as they expected. Meanwhile, the anti-war movement intensified not only in Vietnam but all over the world. In the meantime, NFL's strategic supplies from Hanoi had been expanding along the borders between Vietnam and remaining Indochina countries. The influence of the Communism on ethnic minorities through routes of access from Hồ Chí Minh Trail to the Central Highlands also dramatically enhanced.

Derived from a perception that the Communist forces could expand many corridors to penetrate from national borders into the inland and descended to the coast because they had been doing better than the GVN in gaining the sympathy of the minorities there, the SVN government, therefore, posed the task of taking control of the Central Highlands at any cost to encourage the Montagnards to join its anti-Communist mission; pulling all the separatists or Communist enemies. The minorities, those accounted for 15 percent of the total population of RVN, if being organized and guided well, would turn into a powerful force in SVN national community[265] (Tiệp 2013a, 83).

Therefore, American military advisers and RVNMF's strategists determined a proper implementation of the ethnic policies, at that time, was the key to denying food and shelter to the Communists. New technologies such as toxic chemical deforestation[266], Rome

---

265 See more in: *Hoạt động của Hội đồng sắc tộc, quyển II, trang 72–73 (Activities of the Council for Ethnic Minorities, Volume II, pp. 72–73).*
266 Those included several types of defoliants such as Agent Orange, Agent White, Agent Blue, Agent Purple, Agent Pink, etc. All these chemicals were colorless, but they were named after the color bands on the drums in which each category of chemicals was stored. Each container deposited 55 gallons. Some of which contributed to Vietnam's

plow[267], destructive bombs[268], etc., could not be maximized their destroying power unless the GVN gained the allegiance of indigenous minorities (Young 2009, 4)&(Westing 1972, 322–327).

In order to win the support of the minorities, the Americans continued to carry out the military and socioeconomic programs that had been launching since 1965. The long-term strategy of the U.S. embassy and CIA headquarters in Saigon was to satisfy the stated aspirations of the minorities, helped them improve their living conditions while not undermining their traditional cultural values and ethnic identity. Based on the greater availability of cash, technology, and experience in economic management, American experts proposed many measures to improve farming techniques, marketing methods to rise in demand for consumer goods, together with developing the organization of transport, etc. The improvement of cultivation techniques was considered as the precondition for the transition from traditional subsistence crops into cash crops. Solutions to enlarge knowledge for Vietnamese officers who worked in the minority areas were also proposed to rid themselves of many popular misconceptions about the indigenous peoples and cultures. Along with that, the radio programs and exhibits should be widely implemented to make Vietnamese people, in general, to become familiar with the culture, cultivation methods, handicraft products and performing arts of ethnic minorities. Last but not least, the expansion of access

---

ecosystem change from a once-pristine habitat to an almost apocalyptic after the war. Especially a highly toxic chemical Dioxin can destroy forests, cause exposed people and animals to give birth to offspring with many defects as well as diseases such as lung cancer, blood cancer, diabetes type 2, etc., which can be inherited from parents to children (Young 2009, 4). The majority of 6.397.000 pounds of toxic chemicals expended from 1962 to the end of 1969 were sprayed in the Central Highlands, causing great losses of life and food sources to the Montagnards. See more in: *U.S Food Destruction Program in South Vietnam*; and *The Effects of Herbicides in South Vietnam*, TTU, VC, VA2250202039; and TTU, VC, VA2250208009.

267 Rome plows were large, armored, specially modified bulldozers used in SVN by the U.S. Military during the Vietnam War. This machine was made by the Rome Plow Company of Cedartown, Georgia. It was simple in design with an eleven-foot wide, two and a half ton blade attached to a 20-ton tractor, but caused massive destruction. A fleet of 150 tractors could remove up to 1,000 acres of land per day (Westing 1972, 322–327).

268 The most frightening was napalm. Its adhesive material was dispersed onto plants and ignited quickly. It burned as strong as gasoline and destroyed all nearby vegetation in a while (Tucker 2011, 788–789).

to the education system from primary to university to train future minority elite was also a priority (Hickey 1967, xviii-xix).

On the GVN side, during the course of building and gradually improving the ethnic policies, the Thiệu government generated many important documents related to this matter. First and foremost the system of equality among peoples regardless of majority or minority was not only set out in the authorities' statements or decrees but also recognized in Articles 2, 24, 97, 97 of the 1967 Constitution. In particular, Article 2 of the Constitution stated: *"The State advocates the equality among citizens regardless of gender, religion, ethnicity, political party. Minority peoples are primarily supported to keep pace with the general evolution of the nation"*; Article 24 asserted: *"The State recognizes the existence of ethnic minorities in the Vietnamese community. The State respects customs and habits of ethnic minorities and law will soon be enacted to regulate special rights to support ethnic minorities"*; Articles 98, 98 of the Constitution proposed the establishment of a Council for Ethnic Minorities with the task of advising the government on matters relating to ethnic minorities[269].

With the above-presented terms, the 1967 Constitution legitimized the issue of supporting ethnic minorities with the notion that all Kinh (Việt) and Montagnards were citizens of RVN. Minority peoples had full rights as the Kinh; however, because of being in "backward condition", they needed to be given extraordinary supportive measures. In addition, based on the requirement that only minorities had sufficient grounds to address their own issues, therefore, an advisory council should be established to assist the government in matters relating to ethnic peoples (MDEM 1972, 15).

Soon after, on 20th April 1967, General Kỳ, Chairman of the Central Executive Committee announced the government's statement of guidelines and policies regarding national unity. Three principles of this system were People's benefit, harmonious society, people's mutual advance (Vietnamese: Dân tộc, dân hòa, và dân tiến) (Thêm 1989c, 87). Simultaneously, to pave the way for the policy of national unity coming to life and also to meet collective aspirations of the minorities, the GVN urgently prepared to issue a draft law specifying a peculiar regulation for ethnic minorities. In subsequent, an ethnic minority

---

269 *Hiến pháp Việt Nam Cộng hòa 1967 (năm 1967) của Quốc hội Lập hiến Việt Nam Cộng hòa (The Constitution of the Republic of Vietnam (1967) promulgated by the Constitutional Congress of the Republic of Vietnam)*. In: VNTTX: Văn kiện căn bản tổ chức công quyền Việt Nam, tập I Sài Gòn 1974, tr. 31–42 (VNYTX: Fundamental Documents issued by Vietnamese Governmental Institutions, Volume I, Saigon 1974, pp. 31–42).

conference was convened on June 25–26, 1967 in Pleiku with the participation of 170 representatives. Of whom, 120 delegates were representing the Region II tactics, 14 representatives of Region I tactics, 15 representatives of Region III tactics, ten representatives of FULRO, eight representatives of the congressional delegation, three representatives of the Military Council (MDEM 1972, 15)&(Tiệp 2013a, 84). After two days of discussion, the convention agreed to submit to the government a petition, a request, and a manifesto. The general spirit of the appeals was to propose the rule should soon enact a law setting out a special status of ethnic minorities consisting following fundamental principles:

1. People's benefit, harmonious society, people's mutual advance in the National Unity;
2. Real solidarity among peoples;
3. Special support to help ethnic minorities to catch up with national progress;
4. Respect and protect customs and habits of ethnic minorities.

The conference also recommended that the government should pay considerable attention to issues related to life as the rights and duties of the minority people such as the development of minority affair institution; the spheres of administration, politics, military, economy, culture, education, judiciary (Tiệp 2013a, 84).

Two months after the nation-wide ethnic minority conference, on August 29th, 1967, the Chairman of National Leadership Committee Nguyễn Văn Thiệu signed Decree No. 033/67 on the issuance of a particular regulation to support minorities to keep up with the national progress with the following fundamental contents:

1. Politics (Article 1):
   - The GVN acknowledges the existence of ethnic minorities and intends to thoroughly implement the particular support policies that the government has committed to this community;
   - The Ethnic Development Program will be elevated to national policy, listed in the Pacification Program and other national development plans.
2. Administration (Articles 2, 3, 4):
   - Establish the Ministry for Development of Ethnic Minorities (MDEM) (Vietnamese: Bộ Phát triển sắc tộc) in charge of issues related to ethnic minorities and the implementation of ethnic strategies;
   - Establish the Council for Ethnic Minorities to advise the government on matters related to ethnicity;

- Minority civil servants will be offered favorable measures in the process of recruitment, promotion, domestic and foreign training programs; be appointed to positions that are appropriate to their abilities; be provided with means corresponding to the positions;
- Administrative candidates receive additional points in the recruitment tests and entrance examinations for training courses. Depending upon the needs and recommendations of the ethnic minority agencies, the government will organize specialized training programs for minority staff and commanders in the sectors of administration, judiciary and education.
3. Military (Article 4):
    - Temporarily postpone for military service to young Highlanders those who have not joined the army yet;
    - Establish local forces consisted of the minority people. Officers and non-commissioned officers are assigned command duties corresponding to their abilities;
    - Youth volunteers, who attend training courses for officers and non-commissioned officers, are accepted at lower qualifications compared with the general regulations.
4. Economy (Articles 5, 6):
    - Recognize land ownership of the Montagnards by issuing Decree No. 034/67 of 29th August 1967;
    - Establish the agency for agricultural investigation and development which is responsible for supporting the people in the improvement of trade, technology, animal husbandry, cultivation, etc., depending on specific needs of each locality. 5. Social Welfare (Article 6):
    - Set up new clinics, maternity homes, drug stores; organize mobile medical teams, as well as broaden existed medical facilities and medical support services to strengthen the capacity of healthcare for people; at the same time, promote hygiene education and health care for ethnic minorities;
    - The government will open training schools at all levels to train health workers, who are minority people, those who will be in charge of taking care of their own compatriots' health;
    - In cases of natural disasters, fires, etc., depending upon demands, the agency in charge of ethnic minorities should plan efficient assistance programs to help victims in restoring their normal lives;
    - The agencies in charge of ethnic minorities should establish by themselves or advocate charity organizations opening more new orphanages.

5. Education, culture (Article 7):
   - Compose Montagnard languages textbooks; teach indigenous languages in parallel with the Vietnamese language program at primary school; focus on customs and practices of local peoples;
   - The government advocates the establishment of more elementary and secondary schools widens dormitories and grants scholarships for minority students studying at home and abroad;
   - Apply policies of priority and support for minority students in entrance and graduation exams in specialized schools. Depending on the level of education, minority students are given a privilege in entrance and graduation exams;
   - The government entrusts the Council for Ethnic Minorities with a research project to establish a museum of anthropology to protect and promote the ancient civilizations of ethnic minorities; to install the Institute of Ethnography to assist the government in making plans for the improvement of minority livelihood.
6. Judiciary (Article 8):
   - The customary law courts at the commune, district, province levels re-established under Decree 006/65 dated 22nd July 1965 will be maintained. Based on proposals of the Council for Ethnic Minorities, the government will set up more traditional law courts in the missing areas;
   - The unwritten rules of the ethnic minorities will be collected and preserved[270].

It can be said that the Decree 033/67 conveyed the primary content of the Second Republic's ethnic policies. With ten articles expressing the spirit of supporting the minorities in the fields of administration, politics, judiciary, economy, social welfare, education and culture, the decree was an agreement between the national unity policy outlined in the 1967 Constitution and the aspirations of ethnic minorities.

There is an interesting question that should be posed why the GVN agreed to allow minority young men to temporarily postpone participating in military service (Article 4) in wartime? To understand this seemingly absurd concession of

---

270 Sắc luật 033/67: Ban hành quy chế riêng biệt cho đồng bào thiểu số (Decree 033/67: Issuance of a special regulation for ethnic minorities). Vietnam Official Gazette 1967, p. 4935. Library of Social Sciences in Ho Chi Minh City. Documents of the puppet government on ethnic policies from 1954–1975.

the GVN, we need to look into its particular historical context. Prior to the issuance of Decree 033/67, the relationship between the GVN and FULRO remained intense, even led to several armed conflicts. Under that circumstance, skills of fighting in the rainforests of Montagnard soldiers, those who had been training by the Americans in the CIDG program and commando training courses, became a double-edged sword. Minority militants and commandos could efficiently fight against the penetration of VC guerrillas into isolated villages, but they could also be a significant threat to the GVN when the FULRO separatist forces successfully recruited them. This was also the reason why GVN leaders repeatedly criticized the U.S. policies of broad intervention in the Central Highlands after FULRO rebels attacked several RVNMF barracks in highland provinces.

In agricultural societies, one of the most permanent concerns is the matter of land ownership. In the Articles 5, 6 of the 033/67 special regulation, the government claimed to recognize and respect the Montagnards' land title. At the same time, depending on the specific circumstances and needs of each locality, the government would explicitly support programs to assist ethnic minorities in improving farming techniques, developing the cottage industry, tiny business, etc.; and expanding roads in the Highlands to facilitate the needs of travel and trade. The map below shows segments of arterial roads 14 which connected three over four main cities in the Central Highlands and Đà Nẵng, a most critical seaport in Central Vietnam, were under construction in 1966.

Considered as a kind of "Bill of rights," the particular regulation opened up an excellent opportunity to help the Minorities to come up with the national progress (Giang & Ánh 1974, 199)&(MDEM 1972, 15, 18).

Regarding the implementation of contents of the Decree 033/67, as mentioned earlier, ministries and specialized agencies were tasked to work in close collaboration with bureaus in charge of ethnic minority affairs. Mainly responsible for the implementation of the particular regulation was Chairman of the Central Executive Committee and chief of the Special Commission for Highland Affairs which later promoted to the MDEM. Programs and plans must be carefully studied before promulgation. For a specific application, measures and timetable for implementing needed to be built based on the actual situation of each locality and the qualifications of the separately ethnic group (Giang & Ánh 1974, 201).

In order to concretize the Montagnards' ownership on fixed cultivation lands recorded in the Decree 033/67, also on August 29th, 1967, GVN continued to issue the Decree 034/67. According to this decree-law, the process of giving the land title for the Montagnards would consist of two main phases: endorsing ownership towards fixed farming areas of each family (Article 1) and granting land tenure towards shifting cultivation properties to highland compatriots

(Article 2). After completing necessary administrative procedures, certificates of land ownership and land tenure would be issued free of charge by professional working groups to households in their villages (Article 3)[271].

A remarkable step forward in the ethnic policies of this period was in the election of September 3rd, 1967, two FULRO representatives were Ksor Rớt (Jarai), and Tôn Ái Liêng (Cham) elected to the 60-member Upper House. One month later, on October 22nd, six Southern Highlanders and two Northern minority migrants were elected to the 137-seat of Low House (Thêm 1989c, 221)&(Hickey 1971, 8)&(Dharma 2012, 113). Most importantly, on November 9th the same year, for the first time the MDEM was established within the government of Prime Minister Nguyễn Văn Lộc and functioned equivalently to other ministries. Mr. Paul Nứr, a Bahnar, who was serving as chief of the Special Commission for Highland Affairs, was appointed as the first ever minister. Mr. Đoàn Chí Khoan (a Tay), Châu Văn Mỗ (a Cham) and Y Chon Mlo Duon Du (a Rhade) were chosen as deputy minister, superintendent, and secretary general, respectively. The MDEM was organized from central to local government with 25 departments and 65 branches. One month after being established, the ministry was authorized by the National Assembly of SVN to prepare a draft law on the Ethnic Minorities Council (Thụy 2010, 39)&(Thêm 1989c, 254).

The escalation of the war in the dry seasons of 1967 and 1968, however, made the implementation of the GVN's ethnic policies significantly impeded. The land surveying program merely resumed since the Minister of Land Reform and Agriculture issued Decree No. 76/SL/CCĐĐ on July 15th, 1969 (Thêm 1989b, 232). According to this Decree, there would be two committees established to carry out the related works: the Land Surveying Team in each village and the Provincial Administrative Commission. These two agencies consisted of representatives of the Land Department, Department for Ethnic Development, local officials, three witnesses, one polan (the representative for land ownership of the matrilineal family in the traditional highland society, if applicable), two landowners who knew perfectly the ground situation in the village. Later that year the Minister of Land Reform and Agriculture issued Decree No. 788-CCĐĐNN/HCTC3 of November 28th, 1969, limiting the maximum area of rotational land that would be granted ownership to each Montagnard family. Accordingly,

---

271 Sắc luật 034/67: xác nhận quyền sở hữu của đồng bào Thượng trên đất đai đã định canh (Decree 034/67: confirm the Montagnards' ownership of their sedentary agricultural lands). Vietnam Official Gazette 1967, p. 4938. Library of Social Sciences in Ho Chi Minh City. Documents of the puppet government on ethnic policies from 1954–1975.

each Montagnard household should be entitled to a maximum of 10 hectares of rotational land. The authority to issue land title belonged to the Provincial Administrative Commission; the responsibility for implementation associated with the Land Surveying Team (Article 1) (Tiệp 2013a, 86-87)&(Hickey 1982a, 203).

The GVN also sought to install main living areas *"to ensure and adequately settle land ownership and stabilize living spaces within the unique cultural and social space of ethnic minorities."* On November 9th, 1970, Prime Minister Trần Thiện Khiêm signed Decree No. 138-SL/Th.T/PC2 fixing additional measures to enforce Decrees 033/67 and 034/67 of 29th August 1967[272]. Under the new law, apart from the residential area and farmland, each village would be allocated an amount of the public land that was more or less depending on the number of households in the community. The allotted land deemed a common property of the community which would be equally distributed to each family. Concerning hamlets, where main living areas had been established, the authorities must compile a file relating to land surveying activities including a map, inventory and land register, specifying the boundary and parcel number of the public property that had been designated to each household. Administrative documents related to land allocation, such as the decision to set up committees, announcements, listings, etc., all must be translated into local languages for compatriots to understand. The specialized government agencies should issue documents guiding the methods and progress of particular land allocation process in localities to unify the direction of implementation.

In order to promote the implementation of land surveying for the Highlanders, on 29th

September 1971, the MDEM continued to issue Decree No. 230-ST/NĐ, establishing at each central and local agency under this ministry a committee of land surveying for Montagnard compatriots. The council had three following functions: (1) Studying and preparing learning materials related to works of land surveying for Montagnard compatriots; (2) Organizing training courses for staff from central to local levels to guide, disseminate and explain about the land surveying program and the establishment of main residential areas for Montagnard

---

[272] Sắc luật 138-SL/Th.T/PC2: ấn định các biện pháp bổ túc để thi hành các Sắc luật 033/67 và 034/67 ngày 29 tháng Tám năm 1967 (Decree 138-SL/Th.T/PC2: fixing additional measures to enforce Decrees 033/67 and 034/67 of 29th August 1967). Vietnam Official Gazette 1970, p. 8009. Library of Social Sciences in Ho Chi Minh City. Documents of the puppet government on ethnic policies from 1954-1975.

compatriots; (3) Inspecting and supervising the implementation of land surveying and setting up the main living areas for the Montagnards[273].

In general, it can be said that the recognition of ownership of sedentary agricultural lands for the Montagnards, basically, met merely the needs of leaders, the wealthy or upper class in the ethnic minority society over the Central Highlands. This policy simultaneously validated the ownership of Việt plantation owners in the Highlands, who mostly were civil servants and officers in the GVN and RVNMF. In other words, Decree 034/67 did not bring significant benefits to the majority of Montagnard compatriots who were poor people with little or no agricultural land.

It is worth considering that almost ethnic minorities in the Central Highlands held the tradition of having multiple nuclear families dwelling together under collective ownership in longhouses. The new regulation on land ownership, however, only considered every extended family, that consisting of several nuclear families, as one household. Therefore, in order to avoid being confiscated the cultivated soils, nuclear families in each longhouse must disperse into small homes leading to the breakdown of the Montagnards' traditional way of life.

To a certain extent, the implementation of Decree 138-SL/Th.T/PC2 contributed to creating relatively stable conditions in the context of wartime for the Highlanders to practice their own cultural habits in main living areas and preventing the risk of land disputes between the Montagnards to Việt people and foreigners. However, in terms of strategic goals, similar to the Highlander Resettlement Program model under Diệm regime, these main living areas aimed at strictly controlling the economic and political lives of the Highlanders, eliminating sources of supply in place and shelters of VC guerrillas and North Vietnamese liberation army (Thụy 2010, 39)&(Vân 2003, 92–93).

To enlist the cooperation of Montagnard intellectuals, those who tended to be moderate in political activities, the GVN founded the Movement of Uniting Ethnicities in the Central Highlands, headquartered at Buon Ale-A. The launch of this solidarity movement was solemnly celebrated at Buôn Mê Thuột on April 22nd, 1969. Except for the position of honorary president was given to

---

[273] *Nghị định số 230-ST/NĐ thành lập tại các cơ quan trung ương và địa phương thuộc bộ Phát triển Sắc tộc một ủy ban mệnh danh là Ủy ban tác động kiến điểm cho đồng bào Thượng (Decree 230-ST/NĐ establishing a land surveying commission for Montagnard compatriots at central and local agencies under the Ministry for Development of Ethnic Minorities)*. Vietnam Official Gazette 1971, p. 7198. Library of Social Sciences in Ho Chi Minh City. Documents of the puppet government on ethnic policies from 1954–1975.

President Nguyễn Văn Thiệu, all remaining members of the Executive Board were Highlanders including official president Y Bling, three vice-presidents of Y Dhat Nie Kdam, Ya Duk, Hbi and general secretary Y Kuot Ayun. The Advisory Board also consisted of three prominent Montagnard elite including Paul Nứr, Y Chon Mlo Duon Du, and Y Blieng Hmok. The solidarity movement, in fact, was an agency whose function was to select standard Highlanders for government organizations of SVN. And, its very first task was to nominate candidates for the Ethnic Minorities Council, an institution established by Decree No. 014/69 of 14th October 1969 (Thêm 1989b, 316).

According to the charter of operation, the Ethnic Minorities Council would consist of 48 full members and 12 alternates. Of whom the SVN's President should appoint 16 official members and four alternates, the remaining members including 32 formal and eight alternates would be elected by localities. The leadership of the Ethnic Minorities Council was the Standing Office that composed of the President held by RVN's the Vice-President (a Việt man), one vice president, one secretary general, and two deputy secretaries-general, all were minorities. Like many other committees for ethnic minorities, it also found several specialized subcommittees to study the separate issues of Montagnards. In principle, the Ethnic Minorities Council was responsible for making proposals to the government, sending representatives to congressional hearings and defending interests of minorities. However, in practice, this Council had no influence on the government and was purely a consultative body[274].

During the latest years of the Vietnam War, together with the withdrawal of U.S. troops, the gradual reduction in aid made the GVN lose resources to implement its ethnic policies. Although facing many difficulties, the Second Republic government tried to hold the national conference for ethnic minorities in 1971, 1973 and 1975. On 10th September 1971, a meeting took place in Pleiku on occasion of the 4th anniversary of the promulgation of the particular regulation to support ethnic minorities and recognize land title for the Montagnards. Nearly two years later, a congress was held on February 8th, 1973, after the signing of the Paris Accord. Finally, in March 1975 a congress took place in Đà Lạt aimed at consulting with reputable and intellectual elders about issues relating to ethnicity; popularizing results of the implementation of the ethnic policies as well as listening and addressing questions of the minorities.

---

274 Ibid. Nguyễn Văn Huy. *Cộng đồng người Thượng trên cao nguyên miền Trung (The Montagnard community in the Central Highlands).*

As a last effort in developing the ethnic policies, in 1974 the Ethnic Minorities Council announced the Project of Ethnic Policies to create a legal basis for the implementation of ethnic strategies in the short and long term. The project consisted of ten chapters covering fundamental principles of political, administrative, military, economic, social, cultural, educational, health and judicial spheres, was a summary of the Second Republic's ethnic systems that had been forming and applying since the Committees of National Leadership and Central Executive was born in mid-1965.

5.3 Achievements and Limitations of the Second Republic's Ethnic Policies

5.3.1 Remarkable Results

On administrative management

The greatest wish in the process of integrating into the nation of both FULRO and non-FULRO Montagnards was getting more representatives in the upper positions of the central administration. Under the Premier Khánh, to meet the demand of the Montagnards, the Bureau for Highland Affairs established from Diệm era was promoted to the Directorate of Highland Affairs under the Ministry of Defense and later was placed directly under the Premier's office. This change was considered a Premier Khánh's message to express the government's goodwill towards the minorities before the Pleiku Conference of October 1964.

However, after a half-year operation of the Directorate, some highland leaders concluded the institution only served liaison function, and its head, Colonel Ya Ba, had no real authority in deploying programs for the Montagnards. Therefore, in a meeting held in Saigon in March 1965, the highland delegates continued to request that the directorate should be raised to a Special Commission for Highland Affairs.

After several negotiations between FULRO and the GVN, the application was accepted by Prime Minister Kỳ on February 21st, 1966. Accordingly, the Special Commission for Highland Affairs was established, and Paul Nưr was appointed as chief. The commission with clearly defined functions, responsibilities, and prerogatives satisfied the demands of the Highlanders. The operation of the new institution divided into three categories including unilateral, coordinated, motivating activities. Those fields covered entirely primary concerns of the Montagnards including giving them a well-defined position in the national frameworks; covering socio-economic development programs. Paul Nưr sent his commissioners to 23 provinces where Highlanders were residing. Due to be selected and trained well, most dispatched personnel met their assigned tasks, performed efficiently intermediary role between central government and local people.

Soon later, the birth of the MDEM on November 9th, 1967 which, of course, was headed by a Montagnard Minister marked a breakthrough in the process of perfecting the administrative management of ethnic affairs. Subsequently, the establishment of the Ethnic Minorities Council on 14th October 1969 also showed the GVN's goodwill of wanting to listen to and receiving reflections from representatives of the minorities.

As a large part of the ethnic minority community and also resided in a strategic region, the Montagnards, therefore, held up to 90 percent of important positions in the minority affairs agencies. According to Nguyễn Văn Huy, positions in the South Vietnamese government system at all levels held by minorities including one minister, one deputy minister, one general secretary, one general manager of work, one staff member, one director, three assistant directors, one chief inspector, four investigators in the administrative sector, one province chief, 10 deputy province chiefs, eight county leaders, 30 deputy county leaders, 26 directors of the Provincial Department for Development of Ethnic Minorities, 24 department deputy directors, nine petty officials, 58 subdivision leaders, four judges, four court clerks, 74 assessors at provincial and town courts, 270 assessors at commune courts, 106 primary and secondary principals, 10 school inspectors, seven school supervisors and three dorm managers. As regulated by Decree No. 007/71 the fixed-number of seats for the Montagnards in the Lower House, and Upper House was six and two, respectively. 25 out of 49 provincial and town councilors in the Highlands were the Montagnards, most of them were Jarai and Rhade people[275].

As for economy

During this period the U.S. and the GVN continued to implement some programs for Highlanders' economic development aiming at elevating their tribal economic level. Some projects sought to develop agricultural production making the minorities produce not only enough food for local consumption but also cash crops.

---

275 Ibid. Nguyễn Văn Huy. *Cộng đồng người Thượng trên cao nguyên miền Trung (The Montagnard community in the Central Highlands).*

Fact showed that the optimal solution to encourage farming production was to give the minorities land ownership. As previously mentioned, under his regime, Diệm issued Decrees 513a/ĐT/CCRĐ and 981/BTC/DC on land tenure. According to these documents, all land in the Central Highlands belonged to public possession; without the permission of the presidential office, all activity relating to buy and sell or transfer of property would be considered illegal. This meant the Highlanders had only the right to cultivate instead of owning property as in previous periods. These rules were entirely contradictory for traditional land tenure system in the Highlands[276], even to the land policy of the French colonization[277]. The problem worsened since the Diệm government started establishing Land Development Centres to settle migrant lowlanders and deploying the Highlander Resettlement Program moving the Montagnards into resettlement locations, "where they would be civilized" in the years 1957, 1958.

In the Pleiku Conference of 1964, General Khánh declared to abolish Diệm's decrees relating to the confiscation of lands which had been occupying by the Montagnards, though the rule of unused areas in Highlands as public land would be maintained. In Decree No. 26-DD/DB/KS/TT, dated 19th May 1964, the government announced it would organize public land survey missions to provide a scientific basis for granting land title to the Montagnards. This meant until the land title issued, the occupation of public land still be illegal; occupiers had no right to transfer, buy and sell; the public property also could be appropriated by the state whenever in needed after reaching a compensation agreement. However, overall, Khánh government's land policy still was more progressive than that of the Diệm regime.

For production activities of the Highlanders, the government and American humanitarian organizations continued to implement programs such as improving techniques already being used; training agricultural extension staff to

---

276 Before the French successfully set up its colonialism in the Central Highlands, each Montagnard family usually possessed about 10 or more plots of land. The ownership was recognized and protected by customary law. The property owner cultivated of each plot within 3 to 4 years then abandoned and let natural vegetation to regrow while moving to another one. After the last plot of land became infertile, the grower then returned to the first one. This method called shifting cultivation (or slash and burn cultivation or fire-fallow agriculture because of involving cutting and burning of plants or forests), which far differed from nomadic or semi-nomadic farming as many used to mistake.

277 Under French colonial rule, land ownership of the Montagnards was limited only in areas of the French plantations.

guide farmers cultivating appropriate plants and animals; equipping knowledge about disease control; supporting seeds and fertilizers for farmers; supporting to train artisans, etc.

On social welfare

It cannot be denied that, to some degree, U.S. military and volunteer organizations such as CORDS, USAID, USOM, etc., built many infrastructures and physical facilities to improve the people's knowledge and living standards in the Central Highlands[278]. At the settlement centers with the help of the Americans, Montagnard children more or less approached new civilized lifestyle. Catholic churches set up numerous charitable foundations to provide health care and support for the disadvantaged in minority areas. During the escalating fighting years, Catholic clergy also opened classes and relief camps to assist the Montagnard people in Pleiku and Kontum. The Protestant pastors built many churches and infirmaries in provinces of Buôn Mê Thuột, Tuyên Đức, and Lâm Đồng[279].

Regarding the judiciary

According to Lê Đình Chi, during this period the GVN reinstated customary law courts of the Montagnards in seven provinces of Tuyên Đức, Lâm Đồng, Tuyên Đức, Darlac, Phú Bổn, Pleiku and Kontum (Chi 2006, 306). As it was presented in the Decree No. 006/65 and Circular No. 9593 QP, *"The current customary court (1966) will be distinctly different from that under French colonization"*. Explicitly, there would be no special tribunal; judges as well as assessors were all elected by the populace. Traditional courts would have jurisdiction for civilian as well as criminal in case all parties were Montagnards (Article 2). However, for acts of treason, troublemaking, violating national security, murder, committed by the Montagnards would be judged by state courts according to jurisdiction (Article 3) (Lan 2014, 67).

The new customary law court was organized in three levels of the village, district, and province. At the lowest level, chief of the administration would hold the role of judge, assisted by two Montagnard assessors. According to regulations, in early December every year, in all villages, residents would prepare a list of

---

278 *Programs of Technical Assistance in South Vietnam.* In: TTU, VC, VA 1780709052.
279 Ibid. Nguyễn Văn Huy. *Cộng đồng người Thượng trên cao nguyên miền Trung (The Montagnard community in the Central Highlands).*

twelve notables those who were elected earlier. The district chief would, from that list, appointed two assessors and two deputy assessors for the village court.

With the lower level, the district governor presided the traditional law court. The magistrate would also be assisted by two highland assessors and a translator if in need. Like at the village level, reviewers would also be assigned based on a record of those who had been selected by the local populace.

At the province level, differed from the grassroots ones, the customary court was not organized independently but placed in the state court as the Highland Affairs Section. The presiding judge and his two deputy assessors also would be elected from a list of reputed Montagnards previously chosen by local citizens (Hickey 1967, 69–71).

About education

The primary school played a pioneering role in equipping citizens with the fundamental knowledge which contributed significantly to the realization of socio-economic development goals. The long-lasted wars together with consequences of the policy of discrimination under the First Republic hampered expansion of education system for the minorities. However, thanks to efforts of the governments of Nguyễn Khánh and Nguyễn Cao Kỳ, as of 1967, there were 143 primary schools in the Highlands with 425 teachers and 14.494 students; 22 Cham schools in provinces of Ninh Thuận and Bình Thuận with 74 teachers and 3.293 students; 59 Khmer schools (also called Pali pagodas) with 85 teachers and 4.663 students (Hickey 1967, 51). Overall this was significant progress compared to the previous periods.

The training of teachers was also gradually expanded during this time. According to data on minority candidates and students at the Normal Highland School in Buôn Mê Thuột, in 1965 there were 153 candidates of ethnic groups Rhade, Jarai, Sédang, Mnong, K'ho speaking, Cham, and Northern Highlanders took the entrance examination, of those 53 passed. The government planned to build two normal schools in Sơn Hà District (Quảng Ngãi Province) and Lạc Dương District (Tuyên Đức Province) to train additional primary teachers for remote areas in northern and southern parts of the Central Highlands.

Besides, thanks to the preferential policy of the government[280], highland students would get a bonus of ten extra points per hundred in secondary school

---

280 The U.S. assisted SVN by providing funds for school construction, textbooks, and teacher training. See: Health Data Publications, No. 5 (Revised), January 1966 – *The Republic of Viet-Nam (South Viet-Nam) - Department of Health Data, Division of Preventive Medicine*. P. 6. In: TTU, VC, VA 16090119001.

entrance exams and a 20 percent bonus on their first and second baccalaureate exams. The Ministry of Education also opened "seventh level" classes to help minority students supplement their knowledge of math and Vietnamese to enter secondary schools. In response to aspirations of the Highlanders, the number of scholarships for the minority students was doubled, too, from 150 to 300 (Hickey 1967, 54–55).

Statistics of the Special Commission for Highland Affairs showed that from 1964 to 1966 there were 584 minority students attended specialized training programs, of those, 115 students graduated. Although the number of students increased rapidly compared to the previous period, the distribution was very different between groups of disciplines. Specifically, nearly 50 percent of students concentrated in the military field (283 students); over 30 percent (181 students) studied in technical and vocational training courses. Some disciplines had very few minority students enrolled such as Medical and Pharmacy with only three students; technology with seven students, administration with 34 students; cultivation, forestry and animal husbandry was a sector needed a large number of trained cadres, but only 30 students attended (Hickey 1967, 57).

A remarkable achievement in this period was the accomplishment of minority linguistic studies as well as primers for indigenous children written in alphabets. With the help of language experts of Summer Institute of Linguistics and financial assistance from the American Agency for International Development, until 1967 many linguistic studies on languages of the Brou, Pacoh, Katu, Cua, Jeh, Halang, Sédang, Bahnar, Mnong Rlam, Northern Roglai, Stieng, Chrau, Cham and some ethnic minorities migrating from the North like Mường, White Tai and Tho were carried out. Primers prepared with alphabets were first devised and printed in the Bahnar, Pacoh, Brou, Chrau, Northern Roglai, Stieng, Sédang, Cham, Tho and White languages. From 1962 to 1967, Summer Institute of Linguistics had released 85.150 printed copies, of these, 59.700 copies distributed (Hickey 1967, 52–53).

Up until 1975, 65.943 Montagnard students were attending primary and secondary schools; 142 college students, of whom 18 graduated; 1.483 technical college students, of whom 745 graduated; many minority in-service cadres and students were sent abroad for professional training. Also, in 1965 the Directorate of Highland Affairs established the Trường Sơn Training Center in Pleiku, contributing to the training of more than 15.000 officers in charge of ethnic affairs. By October 1970, the Trường Sơn Training Center renamed the Montagnard Staff Training Center; every year trained about 270 Montagnard administrative personnel for hamlets and rural construction teams. From 1970 to 1975, more than 50 outstanding Montagnard cadets were sent to Saigon to attend executive staff training courses at the National Institute of Administration[281].

5.3.2 Some Limitations

Besides positive points mentioned above, the ethnic policies of the Military Junta (1963-1967) and the Second Republic (1967-1975) also contained some flaws that led to negative impacts on the lives of ethnic minorities.

As complained by FULRO leaders, thought the Directorate for Highland Affairs had been upgraded to the Special Commission for Highland Affairs, it was in malfunctioned; its responsibility was "too poor and ill-defined". Also, there were exceedingly many Việt officials serving in directing positions such as Tôn Thất Cứ, Nguyễn Văn Nghiêm, Nguyễn Văn Phiến and Tôn Thất Tú. These all limitations made the commission unable to meet the demands of the Montagnards.

During the implementation of programs of agricultural reform, improve living conditions, medical care, and education, and so on, civil service officers also assumed the role of secret agents. To cover up their real purpose, those officials often organized into teams of crop survey, youth social workers and rural health care workers. While propaganda they cleverly encouraged residents to denounce the Việt Cộng, Communist sympathizers, and dissidents. These activities contributed to creating a tense atmosphere and mutual distrust among people in the minority community.

Under the auspices of the Americans and the GVN, FULRO acted against not only the VC but also the Montagnards those who opposed to them, especially against the presence of the Việt people in the Highlands. These actions caused cracks in the Highlanders' internal solidarity and raised the tension between them and the Lowlanders.

As mentioned above, in the course of conducting "search and destroy" and other pacification operations, the U.S. and RVN Air Forces not only bombed repeatedly but also carried out numerous toxic chemical spraying missions over areas where many civilians lived. The weapons, especially chemical weapons sprayed in the form of dense fog were utterly incapable of avoiding innocent people. Consequently, these military operations caused many casualties and ruined various crops of civilians. Furthermore, the toxic agents ravaged the environment creating severe ecological imbalances for decades, leaving a lot of

---

281 Ibid. Nguyễn Văn Huy. *Cộng đồng người Thượng trên cao nguyên miền Trung (The Montagnard community in the Central Highlands).*

physical and psychological damage to indigenous peoples as well as those who were present in areas sprayed with chemicals.

By recognizing land ownership in the Central Highlands, the GVN simultaneously legalized the land ownership for plantation owners in areas where they were cultivating. There was the fact that most of the estate owners at that time were currently serving in the GVN and RVNMF. And, as a result of the policy of reducing farmland of each family issued by the Diệm administration, tribal peoples, especially poor people had only a few lands for farming. Therefore, for the Montagnards, the meaning of reassertion of land ownership significantly limited compared to what was presented during the state propaganda campaigns.

Last but not least, the deployment of the Limited War strategy led to the presence of a vast number of expeditionary troops of the U.S. and its allies in ethnic minority regions causing disturbances for local people's lives. Many external cultural elements, which were unsuited to the indigenous tradition, heavily contributed to the decline of the ethnic minorities' cultural identity.

In short, though in unfavorable circumstances, it can be said that since October 1964 the GVN made remarkable efforts in policy making for ethnic minorities in SVN. Learning from mistakes under the First Republic, Prime Minister Khánh quickly abolished decrees of discrimination and racial assimilation issued before 1963; built up new ethnic policies with principles of equality, consensus and supporting minorities. Subsequently, Premier Kỳ and his successors continued to promote the positive aspects of their predecessor's ethnic strategies. On that basis, Saigon gradually cooled the struggles of minorities and the disharmony between the Lowlanders and the Highlanders as well. To some extent, the ethnic policies during this period contributed to remarkable socio-economic achievements for the ethnic minorities in SVN. However, although inherited many accomplishments as well as lessons from the previous times, the Second Republic's ninority strategies also manifested some severe limitations leading to the outbreak of the struggles of ethnic minorities.

5.4 The Reaction of the Minorities to the Second Republic's Ethnic Policies

5.4.1 Political Struggles under the Influence of the NLF

In early January 1964, the Highland Autonomy Movement led its 150 delegates to attend the Second Congress of the NLF in Tây Ninh Province. Here, NLF's President Nguyễn Hữu Thọ issued a call for a negotiated settlement after the U.S. withdrawal from SVN (Hickey 1982a, 93). On June 6, 1968, the NLF together with the Alliance of Nation, Democracy and Peace in Vietnam which represented all social classes, political parties, unions nominating the Provisional Revolutionary Government of the Republic of South Vietnam (Vietnamese: Chính phủ Cách mạng lâm thời Cộng hòa miền Nam Việt Nam) and the Government Advisory Council. Mr. Y Bih Aleo, chairman of the Highland Autonomy Movement, representing the Central Highlands ethnicities was chosen as a member of the Advisory Council of the Government (Dharma 2012, 44).

Realizing the war was ending, in March 1975, when North Vietnam Liberation Army attacked the Central Highlands, some FULRO teams here agreed with the NLF not to warn the GVN (S. Jones et al. 2002, 25).

5.4.2 The FULRO Movement

After the successful military coup in 1963, most of BAJARAKA's leaders remained in jails were released. Furthermore, in order to reduce the political pressure and the conflict between the Montagnards and the Việt, as well as to undertake the policy of "Using the Highlanders to rule the Highlanders," the Saigon authorities appointed many leaders of this movement to the main posts in highland provinces. For example, Y Bham Enuol was named as deputy province chief of Darlac; Paul Nưr became deputy province chief of Kontum, etc. (Hickey 1982a, 91, 94)&(S. Jones et al. 2002, 22–23)&(Dharma 2012, 50, 54).

In March 1964, again supported by the Americans, BAJARAKA leaders joined forces with other non-BAJARAKA leaders and the Cham people in the Central Coast to establish the Front for the Liberation of the South Vietnamese Highlands, also known as the Front for the Liberation of the Champa Highlands (French: Front de Libération des Hauts Plateaux, FLHP) (Vietnamese: Mặt trận Giải phóng Cao Nguyên). However, since its inception, this front self-divided into two factions with opposing strategy. The moderate wing represented by Y Bham Enuol while the faction advocated violence led by Y Dhon Adrong. During the March and April 1964 attacked by the Saigon army, the rioters of FLHP had to run into Cambodia to establish a base in Mondulkiri Province, which located 15 km from the international border between the two countries. At this station, they continued to send people back to the Central Highlands to recruit youth for the FLHP against the RVN.

In preparation for a 55-participants Congress of minority groups, scheduled to take place in Pleiku on 26th August 1964, May 5th, the GVN invited 64 Montagnard notables to the preparatory meeting in Saigon. Fear of being excluded from negotiations, the rioters prepared an armed uprising commanded by Captain Y Nam Eban. On 19th September 1964, about 3000 Montagnard combatants in five Special Forces camps and CIDG groups revolted. The rebels quickly captured five military posts of RVNAF in Tuyên Đức and Darlac namely Buon Sar Pa, Buon Mi Ga, Bu Prang, Bandon and Buôn Briêng killed 35 South Vietnamese soldiers, captured the chief of Đức Lập district, occupied Buôn Mê Thuột radio station and called on people to join the insurgency to establish an independent state, against the "expansionist Vietnamese" following a "systematic genocidal policy" (Hickey 1982a, 101)&(S. Jones et al. 2002, 23)&(Dharma 2012, 59–60, 82).

Extraordinarily shocked and angry, the next day Brigadier General Vĩnh Lộc, Commander Area II Tactical, commanded the 23rd Infantry Division and several battalions of tanks and commandos encircling the radio station and occupied fortifications. But, soon, Vĩnh Lộc received the recommendation of Beachner, the third Counselor of the U.S. Embassy in the Highlands, to stop firing for negotiation. The negotiation between the GVN and FULRO, of course, in the presence of U.S. Embassy officials, eventually reached the following agreements: (1) recognizing Y Bham Enuol as the FLHP's official chair[282]; (2) the Montagnards who led the December 19th attacks[283] would be neither prosecuted nor pursued while withdrawing into Cambodia. As a mature chance for a long conspiracy, the negotiation, in which the Americans presided over, was the "midwife" ensuring the emergence of a new political force in line with their intention and arrangement (S. Jones et al. 2002, 23).

Also on September 20th, 1964, Front Unifié pour la Libération des Races Opprimées-FULRO, (Vietnamese: Mặt trận thống nhất đấu tranh của các sắc tộc bị áp bức), (English: the United Front for the Liberation of Oppressed Races) proclaimed its founding in Cambodia. In order to facilitate for controlling of struggle movement in each particular area, FULRO organized itself into three components, including (1) Front de Libération du Champa-FLC, also known as FULRO Cham (Vietnamese: Mặt trận Giải phóng Champa) led by Les Kosem (Po Nagar), a Khmer Cham; (2) Front de Libération du Cambodia Krom-FLKK or FULRO Khmer (Vietnamese: Mặt trận Giải phóng xứ Campuchia Krom miền Tây Nam Việt Nam) chaired by Chau Dera; (3) Front de Libération des Hauts Plateaux-FLHP or FULRO Montagnards (Vietnamese: Mặt trận Giải phóng Cao Nguyên) headed by Y Bham Enuol. FULRO also announced their three-striped

---

282 However, right in the afternoon of 20th September 1964, Y Bham Enuol fled to Cambodia after leaving a petition to the GVN claiming autonomy on the plateau.
283 Those in included Y Dhơn Adrong, Y Senh Nie, Y Nuin Hmok and Y Nam Eban.

rectangular flag: the blue stripe symbolizing the sea, the red line was the symbol of struggle and green band represented mountain and forest. On the red line, three white stars were representing FULRO's three fronts: the Champa, the Montagnard, and the Cambodian Krom[284] (Dharma 2012, 49).

In principle, FULRO had three governing bodies including the Supreme Council chaired by Chau Dera; the Sponsorship Council presided over by Les Kosem, and the Central Executive Committee headed by Y Bham. However, in reality, Y Bham Enuol and Chau Dera had no actual influences, all powers were in Les Kosem's hands because of his weapons and military forces (Hickey 1982a, 100). The FULRO Montagnards led by Y Bham Enuol then continued to be divided into two portions like the BAJARAKA earlier. While the moderate groups directed by Y Bham Enuol persistently making the U.S. give pressure to the GVN for FULRO Montagnards to be officially operational in Vietnam, the armed group headed by Y Dhơn Adrong insisted on using violence to establish an independent country for the Montagnards in the Highlands.

To show up their strength, from 29th July to 2nd August 1965, Y Dhơn Adrong sent 200 combatants to attack and occupy Buon Brieng garrison and took 181 men of the CIDG forces upon retreat. Later Lieutenant Colonel Y Djao Nie led a FULRO Montagnards regiment to a station in Buon Buor, a village located on Route 14 in Darlac Province, to restrain Y Bham Enuol when he was in Buôn Mê Thuột and called on FULRO Montagnards soldiers to return to the GVN. This move generated a new tense circumstance. In Saigon, Premier Khánh repeatedly blamed the U.S. overt and covert programs of training and equipping for the Montagnards was the direct cause of the ongoing crisis in the Central Highlands. At that time, because of wanting to focus all its efforts on the destruction of Việt Cộng's secret bases in the Central Highlands, the U.S. urged the Saigon government to negotiate with the FULRO forces to find a way of living together and cooperating against the intrusion of Communist troops. Carrying out the Pentagon's requirements, Westmoreland dispatched General Ben Sternberg to Buôn Mê Thuột to negotiate with General Nguyễn Hữu Có, commander of II Corps and General Hoàng Xuân Lãm, 23d Division's commander, on a mediation solution. On 23rd September General Richard DePuy was also being sent to Buôn Mê Thuột to defuse the crisis (Hickey 1982a, 103, 105)&(Dharma 2012, 63).

---

284 See Po Dharma, *Phong trào thanh niên Chăm tham gia Fulro vào 1968 (The Cham youth movement joined FULRO in 1968)*, P. 12. Sources: http://champaka.info/images/ky%20su%20fulro.pdf. (Accessed 25th December 2017).

As a result of the tripartite talks among the Americans, the Saigon government and the FULRO representatives, the GVN succeeding approved most of the needs and demands of the Montagnards set out in the Pleiku Conference of October 1964. The fundamental aspirations adopted by the government including recognizing the land ownership, re-establishing traditional highland courts, teaching native languages at primary schools, recruiting educated Montagnards into government agencies, implementing more practical programs to assist the highland community and upgrading the Directorate for Highland Affairs to a Special Commission for Highland Affairs. Of course, the requirements for autonomy, receiving direct foreign aid and an establishment of a Montagnard army were all rejected.

As a result of the joint statement between the Kinh (Việt) and the Montagnards of early August 1965, a ceremony in which 500 FULRO combatants were handing over their weapons to the government, was held at Buon Buor on 15 September of the same year.

The process of reconciliation between GVN and FULRO was going smoothly, from December 12th to 18th, 1965, the extremist FULRO group again attacked Phú Thiện station killing 32 people and injuring 26 others; occupied Krong Pach station then killed all Việt soldiers who were posting there; broke into the administrative building of Tuyên Đức sub-district, killing all Việt workers there and flying the FULRO flag. When Brigadier General Vĩnh Lộc, Commander of the II Tactical Region, was commanding an onslaught on the seized areas, capturing and chasing the remnants of FULRO, he again received recommendations from U.S. Embassy asking for mercy and letting revolt's leaders run to Cambodia. Get information about rebellion in Vietnam, Y Bham Enuol sent his people to arrest the extremists such as Nay Ry, R'Com Re, Ksor Bleo and Ksor Boh at the border and brought to Camp le Rolland (S. Jones et al. 2002, 24). February 12th, 1966, the Military Court of the II Tactical Region brought rebel soldiers to the trial. Of the arrested FULRO's members, four were sentenced to death, fifteen life imprisonment and many others were sentenced to hard labor (Dharma 2012, 96)&(Dĩ 1968, 25).

Though not openly opposed to the FULRO Montagnards leadership of Y Bham Enuol, Les Kossem installed confidant Cham people in senior positions nearby Enuol to curb his strategy of negotiating with the GVN (Hickey 1982a). On September 20th, 1966, Les Kosem sent troops besieging Camp le Rolland to force Y Bham Enuol to surrender the territory of FULRO Montagnards to FULRO Cham but failed[285].

---

285 Ibid. Nguyễn Văn Huy. *Cộng đồng người Thượng trên cao nguyên miền Trung (The Montagnard community in the Central Highlands).*

Early June 1967, Y Bham Enuol led a delegation to Buôn Mê Thuột to negotiate and demanded that the South Vietnamese government quickly issue a special regulation for the Montagnards. As a result, the GVN agreed to hold a congress of ethnic minorities throughout SVN on June 25th and 26th, 1967, to gather their primary needs and demands. The petition, request, and declaration made at the conference were approved by General Nguyễn Cao Kỳ, chairman of the Central Executive Committee and committed to implementation. Then, at the end of August the same year, another national ethnic conference was held in Buôn Mê Thuột under the chairmanship of Generals Nguyễn Văn Thiệu and Nguyễn Cao Kỳ. This congress led to the adoption of Decree 033/67 on the promulgation of a particular regulation for ethnic minorities and Decree 034/67 on the recognition of land ownership for the Montagnards.

In August 1968, Y Bham Enuol led a 28-person delegation from Camp le Rolland to Buôn Mê Thuột to meet with representatives of the MDEM. At the gathering, Y Bham Enuol demanded the GVN to implement preferential policies for the minorities already announced. Later that year, the final negotiations between Y Bham Enuol[286], president of the FULRO Montagnards and the Secretary of the Prime Minister brought to an agreement on the immediate and thorough implementation of the contents of Decree 033/67. Accordingly, the MDEM was established and commissioned by the National Assembly to draft a law on Ethnic Minorities Council.

The final agreement between Paul Nưr, representing the GVN and Y Dhe Adrong (the deputy of Y Bham Enuol), representing FULRO, was signed at Buôn Mê Thuột on February 1st, 1969, under the chairmanship of the President Nguyễn Văn Thiệu and Prime Minister Trần Văn Hương. In his speech to close the ceremony, Y Dhe Adrong announced that FULRO was formally dismissed and replaced with a Montagnard political party, the Ethnic Minorities Solidarity Movement, which advocated peaceful cooperated with the GVN[287]. After the signing ceremony, according to Roy C. Russell, about 13.000 FULRO soldiers and their families were rallied to the GVN in 1969[288]. However, some FULRO leaders of the Montagnards and Cham were not satisfied with terms of the deal.

---

286 Because Y Bham Enuol consistently advocated dealing conflicting issues between Lowlanders and Highlanders peacefully, on December 30th, 1968, he was arrested by Les Kosem at Camp le Rolland and taken to Phnom Penh for detention. In 1975, when the Khmer Rouge occupied Phnom Penh, Y Bham Enuol and his family ran into the French embassy but were still executed there.
287 Russell, *"Their Time Has Come,"* Typhoon magazine, October 1969.
288 Ibid. Russell, *"Their Time Has Come."*

These forces continued to operate resistance until their last 407 combatants in Mondolkiri base surrendered and handed over arms to the United Nations Transitional Authority in Cambodia (UNTAC) in Cambodia in 1992 (S. Jones et al. 2002, 27).

VI Conclusion

As it is presented above, there were profound transformations of several forms of government of the Central Highlands, a strategically important region for the whole of Southeast Asia, from pre-colonial over colonial to post-colonial epoch in the context of decolonization, national state formation, and cold-war. Over this contested space, several actors went into terrible battles to take control. That is the competition among Vietnamese, Siam, Khmer, Laotian imperial dynasties during the medieval period; among French colonial, the Việt Minh, and Japanese before the Geneva Conference of 1954; among the U.S/GVN, the VC/DRV, and the tribal peoples themselves during the Second Indochina War. Each of these players attempted to seek its most appropriate methods to legitimize and develop its power in the Highlands. In this research, that alteration of the rule has been interpreted not only based on some popular theories on legitimate domination but also national and indigenous perspectives.

During pre-colonial era, the Vietnamese feudal regimes considered the Central Highlands as remote and isolated area and took the limited interest in this region. The relation between the Vietnamese emperors and the chiefs of the tribal alliance was primarily maintained in the form of the East Asian system of inter-state ties by vassalage. All connectivities between the indigenous peoples and the Vietnamese were discouraged, even restricted by the state law.

The attitude towards the Central Highlands changed dramatically when the western colonial power discovered the Highlands' resources and in particular understood the high strategic role of the Highlands. There is no doubt that the missionaries, traders, adventurers, researchers, and later were the French soldiers, military officers and civil administrators contributed significantly to bring knowledge of this mysterious land to the western world. In the early colonial times, after setting up the protectorate and military controlling system in the Central Highlands, the French rulers gradually put the Montagnards there under pressure to accept corvée and taxation. Since the French Expeditionary Force principally pacified the Central Highlands in the early twentieth century, most military-administrative posts were transformed into civil-administrations. In general, the French domination strategies for the ethnic minorities were considered more flexible than what formulated in the context of decolonization and nation formation after the Geneva Conference of 1954. As masters of strategies of "divide and conquer," and "using the native people to rule the natives," the French colonizers offered a large part of local chiefs and military officials the mandates of authority. The Montagnard battalions were also formed, trained, and equipped by the French to help the colonial authorities pacify the Highlands. With this policy, the French not only abused partially respected local chiefs but also created suspicion and division among ethnic minorities.

Under the motto of "Highland land to the Montagnards" which was firstly proposed by Darlac provincial chief Sabatier in 1912 and later was set as a pattern for other highland provinces, the French limited the migration of Việt people to the Highlands. This method of controlling aimed at a dual goal: on the one hand, the French protected the Montagnards against the Việt people; on the other, they separated the Lowlander from the Highlanders to prevent the formulation of a national state sentiment.

Also by maintaining the customary law and the highland judicial system, the colonists made the indigenous believe their traditional culture was being respected. Still the same way, the French Indochina government wisely promoted French citizens avoiding establishing plantations in Montagnard-claimed areas to "express the respect to the traditional land title." In Franco-Montagnard schools, local languages were taught parallel to French at primary level[289].

After the Second World War, in the emergence of decolonization trend in Vietnam, the French High Commissioner in Indochina, d'Argenlieu issued a decree to declare the establishment of a particular administrative zone in mid-1946 aiming at restoring French influence over the high plateau. This plan marked the beginning of a period during which the Highlands would be a pawn in French political strategy. Three years later, as a result of Elysée Accords, the Central Highlands was converted into a "Crown Domain," in which Bảo Đại obtained both the Chief of State and a nominal Emperor. A "special status" was granted to the Crown Domain giving the highland people the "eminent rights" to develop following their own customs. That provision defined the role of provincial and district advisers, as well as, positions of the headmen of cantons and villages. Simultaneously, it devoted attention to the issue of economy, health, and education. Finally, the Montagnards merely had been given the mission to join the army that stationed in the Highlands to protect their own territories.

It can be said that the trend of decolonization after the Second World War was an inevitable one. Despite last efforts of France in maintaining its colonial power in the Highlands (as well as over the Indochina in general), until the end of the first Indochina War of 1954, most objectives of the socio-economic

---

[289] Similarly, the French also kept maintaining the pattern of "School in pagoda" and Chinese schools in these two minority communities.

development program for the Montagnards had not been fully achieved. And, it is not hard to realize the racially prejudiced view of policymakers in the French-led administration of Bảo Đại when they determined the prominent role of Vietnamese migrants in helping the Montagnards fight off their backwardness and superstition.

After replacing France's position in Indochina since 1954, the U.S. strategists continued considering the Central Highlands a particular significant zone. It was the gate that blocked the infiltration of the Communist army through the Hồ Chí Minh Trail to the South, an anti-Communist outpost erected in Southeast Asia by the Americans during the Cold War based on Domino Doctrine. The presence of Communist guerrillas there, therefore, raised much anxiety for American advisors who were training the South Vietnamese Army. Since 1956, some first Military Assistance Advisory Group (MAAG) missions were sent to the Highlands to observe the situation and to build anti-guerrilla training camps, in which young tribesmen were recruited and trained. During the period from 1956 to 1963, American experts and military advisors were being throughout the hinterlands. The disagreement over the use of the Montagnards against the Communists caused many disputes between the CIA and the U.S. Embassy.

The CIA advocated that the Montagnards should be armed and trained to exploit their fighting skills in the rainforests thoroughly. According to this method, American military advisors entered minority communities to organize self-defense units, in which villagers were supplied with personal firearms, leading to the creation of CIDG and Special Force teams of all tribal groups. Although the goal of destroying the VC guerrilla's bases in the thick jungles as well as cutting off their strategic supplied network through the Hồ Chí Minh Trail's routers was not achieved, the operation of these forces caused massive damage to the North Vietnamese liberation army and the NLF.

Mid-1965, the Vietnam War escalated since the U.S. adopted the Limited War strategy. In July 1965 the U.S. deployed the American Expeditionary Force including the 1st Brigade of 1st Cavalry Division, 3d Brigade, 25th Infantry Division, the 1st Brigade of the 101st Airborne Division, the Mobile Strike Force to conduct search-and-destroy operations throughout areas controlled by the VC across the Highlands.

The U.S. Embassy, meanwhile, called for long-term cooperation of the Montagnards to improve living standards. To do that, they focused on projects for economic, cultural, social welfare, health and religious development. The Protestant pastors quickly found a solid foothold because they often brought immediate material benefits for the Montagnards while preaching about salvation. Many social activists and experts from the United States Operations

Mission (USOM), United States Agency for International Development (USAID), the Summer Institute of Linguistics (SIL), volunteer organizations, etc., came to instruct advanced methods in preventing and treating diseases; to guide cultivators sustainable agriculture techniques; to help poor people building houses; to create alphabet by Latinizing the local dialects.

To "win the hearts and the minds" of the ethnic minorities, thereby conquering strategic goals in the Central Highlands of Vietnam and South East Asia in general, the Americans not only directly implemented such programs but also sought to engage in the process of developing the ethnic policies of the GVN. That profound intervention made the South Vietnamese leaders worry that the U.S. might publicly support an autonomous Central Highlands as the French had created in 1950.

Although the RVN was a U.S-built entity, sometimes between Washington and Saigon did not reach consensus on some issues including the implementation of the ethnic strategies for the minorities. True to a well-known saying of Winston Churchill *"There are no eternal friends or eternal enemies, only eternal interests."* The allied relations between the U.S. and RVN were insufficiently robust to overwhelm intentions of each side. General Nguyễn Khánh overtly and repeatedly blamed the American intervention on the ethnic minority issues for the crisis in the Central Highlands. According to Khánh, the Americans' training and equipping the Montagnard paramilitary force was the direct cause leading to riots of some FULRO groups. Consequently, the Americans advocated the Young Turks removing Nguyễn Khánh from his position and sending him into exile as a roving ambassador of the RVN. Also, senior U.S. officials in Vietnam previously pressured Diệm government to release detained leaders of the BAJARAKA movement or later asked Thiệu administration to compromise with the FULRO's extremist faction (Dharma 2012, 62–63).

Derived from the difference in views, contents of the ethnic systems for the minorities of the First Republic and the Second Republic contained fundamental differences. The progressive spirits of "For the Montagnards" and "By the Montagnards," in the Diệm policies, however, quickly turned into the strategy for forced assimilation due to his chauvinist thinking and under his framework of nation-building. The promulgation of some decree-laws[290] on the highland issues

---

290 Such as Decree No. 21 (enacted 11th March 1955), officially merged the Crown Domain into the Central Part of the State of Vietnam and terminated privileges of the French and Emperor Bảo Đại in the Central Highlands; Decree 513a/ĐT/CCRĐ (issued on 12th February 1958) drew up a rule that all the transfer and exchange of lands between the Montagnards and the Việt people must be preauthorized by the President; Official

was thought to be extraordinarily bureaucratic and did not respect the objectivity of the economy as well as of sociocultural factors in the minorities' lives.

Also, the government-designed programs, which aimed to achieve broad goals among the spheres of military, politics, economy, culture[291] were implemented in the shortage of human resources, materials, experiences in organizing and managing and the lack of detailed survey on the specific conditions of each locality.

It can be concluded that the Highland Affairs Policies of Diệm regime always took the national interest as central objective while underestimating and paying little attention to the benefits of ethnic minorities. These shortcomings made the implementation of the strategies towards the minorities ineffective; deepened conflicts between the Lowlanders and the Highlanders, between the authorities and the ethnic minorities; and pushed many local leaders into collaborating with the NLF.

Recognizing terrible mistakes in Diệm's Highland Affairs Policies, Premier Nguyễn Khánh promptly abolished the contents which severely threatened economic interests as well as cultural values of the ethnic minorities. Khánh government also released leaders of BAJARAKA movement those were arrested and jailed by Diệm regime; invited highland representatives to the capital Saigon to discourse their people's outstanding needs and desires; convened the Montagnard Congress in Pleiku on 26th August 1964; organized a committee to receive aspirations of highland leaders which consisted of representatives from almost tribal groups.

The most prominent achievements of Nguyễn Khánh government in implementing the ethnic policies were to hold a national conference of the ethnic minorities in Pleiku on October 17th, 1964 successfully. After three days of open debate, the minorities submitted a detailed petition letter, expressing their outstanding needs and desires, as well as welfare they expected to receive from the GVN. To meet the aspiration of the minorities, Premier Nguyễn Khánh announced the policies towards the Montagnards with three primary principles of equality, respect, and exceptional support. Those fundamental principles were

---

Letter No. 981/BTC/DC (promulgated on 28th January 1959) deprived the land ownership of Montagnards and invalidated their all previous purchase agreements; Decree No. 52 (issued on 29th August 1956) required all Vietnamese citizens, irrespective of their ethnic origin, to select Vietnamese names within six months; Decree No. 53 (passed on 6th September 1956) prohibited all foreigners from engaging in eleven different trades, etc.

291 Including the Land Reform Program, Land Development Program, Highlander Resettlement Program, Strategic Hamlet Program.

described by a specific action plan with a spirit of comprehensive reform; making policies in line with the aspirations and particular conditions of each locality.

Since early 1965, inheriting the advances in Khánh's ethnic policies, the war government of General Nguyễn Cao Kỳ then also devoted particular attention to ethnic minorities. The motto of *"Ethnic harmony, co-development in a united nation"* was officially given in statements of SVN's prime minister. To implement good ethnic strategies initiated by General Khánh, mid-1965 Chairman of the National Leadership Committee Nguyễn Văn Thiệu signed Decree No. 006/65 and Circular No. 9593 QP regulating and guiding the reorganization of the highland law court system.

It can be instantly ascertained that the ethnic policies of the Second Republic were a continuity of the Highland Affairs Policies under the Military Junta, especially of the National Leadership Committee and Central Executive Committee. The new strategy of the Second Republic for the minorities was built on three principles of *"people's benefit," "harmonious society,"* and *"people's mutual advance."*[292] These adjustments and additions made the ethnic strategies increasingly active, leading to political stability in ethnic minority areas, especially in the Central Highlands.

The deployment of many socioeconomic programs contributed significantly to the improvement of the livelihoods and farming techniques of ethnic minorities. Besides, the government cultural and educational development projects also brought many positive effects such as restoration of customary law courts, the opportunity to pursue the national education system for ethnic children, etc. Some schools, in which local languages, Vietnamese and English were taught simultaneously, were established in Buôn Mê Thuột, Pleiku, Kontum, and Đà Lạt. Ethnic minority students at all levels enjoyed a variety of incentives in entrance exams, scholarships, and accommodations in dormitories. Students graduated from universities, and vocational schools would be offered favorable conditions in finding appropriate jobs.

It is worth noting that the Military Junta and the Second Republic showed respect and concern for the aspirations of the minorities by organizing the national Congress of ethnic minorities that had never been done by the First

---

292 The 1967 Constitution stated that the State advocated the equality among citizens regardless of gender, religion, ethnicity, political party; the minority peoples would be supported to keep pace with the general evolution of the nation; their customs and habits should be respected, and a law will soon be enacted to regulate exclusive rights to support ethnic minorities (Article 2, 24).

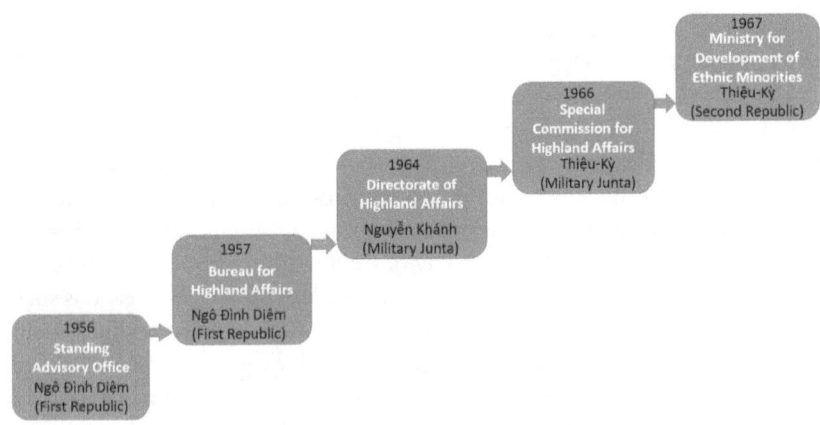

Fig. 9: The Reform of the Governmental Highland Affairs Agency. Sources: Author.

Republic. The petitions submitted by the delegates attending such Congresses were used as a basis to issue, adjust and supplement policies documents promptly[293].

The governmental agency, which was responsible for the minority affairs, was also continually upgraded to meet the wishes of the minorities. After General Khánh came to power, the Bureau for Highland Affairs under Diệm regime was elevated to the Directorate of Highland Affairs within the Ministry of Defense and then was placed directly under the Premier's office. Not long after that, Prime Minister Nguyễn Cao Kỳ reformed the Directorate of Highland Affairs to be the Special Commission for Highland Affairs in early 1966. This institution finally became the Ministry for Development of Ethnic Minorities (MDEM) within the Nguyễn Văn Lộc government late 1967. The whole process of the minority affair agency's improvement is presented in Fig. 9.

Although the reforms pursued by the Military Junta and the Second Republic could not bring back the "eminent rights," which the Montagnards had enjoyed under the Crown Domain of Emperor Bảo Đại, that progress showed a marked improvement over the Diệm administration's ethnic policies.

---

293 For example, Decree 033/67 on the issuance of a particular regulation for ethnic minorities and Decree 034/67 on confirming the Montagnards' ownership for their sedentary agricultural lands were the results of the nation-wide ethnic minority conference convened on June 25 and 26, 1967.

Besides achievements, the ethnic systems of the U.S. and the Second Republic also contained some inadequacies such as the overemphasis on political and military objectives; Việt officials were overwhelming in the agencies in charge of minority affairs; the land reform policy did not indeed benefit the majority of poor indigenous farmers; the establishment of main living areas and new life hamlets, as well as the appearance of too many outsiders (Việt people and U.S. Expeditionary Troops) in the minority zones, brought various unwanted changes in indigenous traditional economic activities, cultural values, and intensified the conflict between the Highlanders and the Lowlanders; destructive weapons such as Rome Plow, the Napalm bomb and toxic chemicals utilized in the "search and destroy" operations caused numerous casualties for the minorities and severe environmental damage. These limitations were significant causes leading to the outbreak of struggle movements of the minorities, typically BAJARAKA and FULRO.

Finally, we should not forget that since the early years of the 1960s, the relationship between two communist countries the Soviet Union and China became increasingly tense surrounding the issue of the method of applying Marxism-Leninism and territorial boundaries, which even led to an armed conflict in 1969. In that circumstance, the visit of U.S. President Nixon to China in mid-February 1972 was a significant event marking the transformation in international relations and U.S. foreign policy in Asia. In particular, the handshakes between the leaders of the U.S. and China put an end to the American concern about the expansion of the Communism in Asia. Since then, the deployment of Containment Policy in Southeast Asia was no longer necessary for the U.S., and the role of an anti-communist outpost of SVN, therefore, fall off. This transformation, coupled with the failure of the U.S. in the Limited War, accelerated the process of "de-Americanization" of the war and negotiation of an agreement on ending the war and restoring peace in Vietnam that initialed in late 1968. As a result, the Paris Peace Accords was signed on 27th January 1973 leading to the sharp decline in both U.S. military and economic assistance[294] for SVN. The government-organized programs deployed in the minority regions "to help ethnic minorities have the same living standards as the Việt people" were also gradually reduced and halted in the last years of the Vietnam War.

---

294 The U.S. economic aid to the RVN reached its peak in 1966 at $ 793.9 million but decreed dramatically to $ 651.1 million in 1968 and $ 240.9 million in 1975, respectively (Dacy 1986, 200).

Conclusion

It can be said that the process of decolonization and national state building, which coincided with the Cold War between the Soviet Union, China, and the U.S., is a significant feature of global modern history. After one and a half decade since 1945, over thirty Asian and African states obtained autonomy or complete independence from their European colonizers. For instance, India gained the independence from the UK in 1947, Burma, Malaysia and then Singapore became independent in 1948 and 1950; the Indonesian led by Sukarno defeated Dutch attempts of reoccupation and won the independence in 1949; similarly, liberation movement in Africa also boomed vigorously, with seventeen former colonies received their independence from European colonial rule, the year 1960 was called "Year of Africa".

In fact, although the struggles for independence in ex-colonies were affected at varying degrees from the bipolarism of the Cold War, there was no single process of decolonization. In some countries, independence accompanied territorial unity while in other ones the newly independent nation was divided between ideological and religious differences. In some areas, independence or autonomy was gained peacefully and orderly while in many others, those were achieved only after a protracted revolution. A few newly independent countries took stable politics almost instantly; dictators or military juntas administered others for years or endured long civil wars.

In the context of decolonization and national state formation under the cold war politics, the situation of Vietnam was a unique case. In addition to some common characteristics those occurred in other newly independent nations as the ideological conflicts between the pro-Communist and anti-Communist factions or the religious-based liberation movements like in most Southeast Asian countries, etc., the process of nation-building in Vietnam contained some different characteristics. First, communist North, those who made the unification of the country by the end of the Second Indochina War of 1975, occupied the national idea as it was in reality not a communist but a nationalist movement. Second, at least until the Nixon-Mao agreements of 1972, the Chinese communist influence in Vietnam was much more than in other Asian countries.

All in all, one can say that the Central Highlands was essentially a plaything for outside interests in the period under review. Powers sought from the outside access and control of this strategically important region. Mainly the Highlands were strategic interests, not the interests of the local population. However, the policy of domination fluctuated between oppression and more indirect control. These followed the logic of colonialism, nation-state formation, and the Cold War. In fact, the Highlands were significantly changed by 1975. With the revival of Vietnam, a new era began that would require other categories of analysis.

Bibliography

Unpublished Sources
+ Vietnamese National Archives Center II, IV.
+ Library of Social Sciences in Ho Chi Minh City.
+ Foreign Relations of the United States (FRUS).
+ Declassified files of the Central Intelligence Agency (CIA).
+ Texas Tech University, Vietnam Center, Virtual Archive (TTU, VC, VA).

Published Sources

Ahern Jr, T. L. (1998). *CIA and the Generals: Covert Support to Military Government in South Vietnam*. Washington, DC: Center for the Study of Intelligence, CIA.

Ahern, T. L. (2000). *CIA and the House of Ngo: Covert Action in South Vietnam, 1954–1963*. Washington, DC: Center for the Study of Intelligence.

Asselin, P. (2007). Hiệp định Giơnevơ 1954 về Việt Nam và Hiệp định Paris 1973: Ngoại giao và thành tựu của cách mạng Việt Nam (The 1954 Geneva Agreement on Vietnam and the 1973 Paris Agreement: diplomacy and the triumph of the Vietnamese Revolution). *VNU Journal of Science: Social Sciences and Humanities, 23*, 87–98.

Ba, H. T., Hanh, D. B., & Cuong, B. T. (2002). *Indigenous Peoples/Ethnic Minorities and Poverty Reduction Viet Nam*. Manila, Philippines: Environment and Social Safeguard Division, Regional and Sustainable Development Department, Asian Development Bank.

Baten, J. (Ed.). (2016). *A History of the Global Economy*. Cambridge University Press.

Báu, P. T. (2008). Nhìn lại hai cuộc cải cách giáo dục (1906 và 1917) ở Việt Nam đầu thế kỷ XX (Looking in retrospect upon the two educational reforms (1906 and 1917) in the early twentieth century in Vietnam). *Journal of Historical Studies, 5*, 11–20.

Biên, P. X., Xuân, L., An, P., & Dốp, P. V. (1989). *Người Chăm ở Thuận Hải (The Cham in Thuan Hai)*. Thuan Hai: Thuan Hai Department of Culture and Information.

Borhi, L. (1999). Rollback, liberation, containment, or inaction? US Policy and Eastern Europe in the 1950s. *Journal of Cold War Studies, 1*(3), 67–110.

Brownell, W. (1963). *The American Mandarin: A Study of the Life of Diem and of the Origins of the American Involvements.* Ithaca, New York: Cornell University.

Catton, P. E. (2002). *Diem's Final Failure: Prelude to America's War in Vietnam.* University Press of Kansas.

Chapman, J. M. (2006). Staging democracy: South Vietnam's 1955 referendum to depose Bảo Đại. *Diplomatic History (Oxford Journals), 30*(4), 671–703.

Chi, L. Đ. (2006). *Người Thượng Miền Nam Việt Nam (The Montagnard People of South Vietnam).* Gardena: Van Moi Publishing House.

Chi, N. K., & Chi, N. Đ. (2011). *Người Ba-Na ở Kontum (The Bahnar People in Kontum).* Hanoi: Knowledge Publishing House.

Chiến, P. N. (2015). *Những khía cạnh học thuật trong vấn đề xác định thành phần dân tộc tại Việt Nam (The Academic Aspect of the Ethnic Groups Identification Issue in Vietnam).* Department of Anthropology, University of Social Sciences and Humanities – Vietnam National University Ho Chi Minh City.

Colby, W. E., & McCargar, J. (1989). *Lost Victory: A Firsthand Account of America's Sixteen-Year Involvement in Vietnam.* McGraw-Hill/Contemporary.

Condominas, G. (1994). *We Have Eaten the Forest: The Story of a Montagnard Village in the Central Highlands of Vietnam.* Kodansha International.

Congressional Research Service. (1984). *The US Government and the Vietnam War: Executive and Legislative Roles and Relationships, Part I: 1945–1961* (Vol. 1). Washington: U.S. Government Printing Office.

Cooney, J. (1985). *The American Pope: The Life and Times of Francis Cardinal Spellman.* New York: A Dell Book.

Cung, N. n. Đ. c., & Tấn, N. n. (1998). *Lịch sử vùng cao qua Vũ man tạp lục thư (History of the Highland Through Vu man tap luc thu).* Philadelphia: Nhật Lệ Publishing House.

Dacy, D. C. (1986). *Foreign Aid, War, and Economic Development: South Vietnam, 1955–1975:* Cambridge University Press.

Dak Lak People's Committee & Provincial Party Committee. (2015). *Địa chí Đắk Lắk (History, Land, Social Culture, and Economic Development of Đắk Lắk Province).* Hanoi: Social Sciences Publishing House.

Dambo. (2001). *Miền đất huyền ảo (Les Populations Montagnards du Sud-Indochinois).* Nguyên Ngọc Translated. Converted to e-book by Nguyễn Kim Vỹ. Hanoi: Writers Association Publishing House.

Đặng, B. V. (1981). *Đại cương về các dân tộc Ê-đê, M'-nông ở Đắk Lắk (Outline of the Ede and the Mnong Ethnic Groups in Dak Lak Province).* Hanoi: Social Sciences Publishing House.

Đạo, B. M., Thu, T. H., & Lan, B. B. (2006). *Dân Tộc Ba Na Ở Việt Nam (The Bahnar in Vietnam)*. Hanoi: Social Sciences Publishing House.

Đạo, C. (2000). *Việt Nam Niên biểu 1939–1975 (Vietnam Chronology 1939–1975), Volume I-C: 1955–1963*. Houston, TX: Culture Publishing House.

Devillers, P. (1962). The struggle for the unification of Vietnam. *The China Quarterly, 9*, 2–23.

Devillers, P. (1988). *Paris-Saigon-Hanoi: les archives de la guerre, 1944–1947* (Vol. 101). Editions Gallimard.

Devillers, P., & Lacouture, J. (1969). *End of a War; Indochina, 1954*. New York: Praeger.

Dharma, P. (2012). *Từ FLM đến Fulro: Cuộc đấu tranh của dân tộc thiểu số miền nam Đông Dương 1955–1975 (From FLM to Fulro: The Struggle of Ethnic Minorities of Southern Indochina 1955–1975)*. IOC-Champa.

Dĩ, N. T. (1968). *Tìm hiểu Phong trào tranh đấu F.U.L.R.O (A Research on the F.U.L.R.O Movement)*. Saigon: Ministry for Development of Ethnic Minorities.

Dĩ, N. T. (1970). *Hội đồng các sắc tộc - Một tân định chế dân chủ của nền đệ nhị Cộng hòa Việt Nam (Ethnic Minorities Council-A New Democratic Institution of the Second Republic of Vietnam)*. Saigon: Ministry for Development of Ethnic Minorities.

Dĩ, N. T. (1972). *Đồng bào các sắc tộc thiểu số Việt Nam (Nguồn gốc và Phong tục) (Ethnic Minorities of Vietnam (Origins and Customs)*. Saigon: Ministry for Development of Ethnic Minorities.

Donnell, J. C., & Joiner, C. A. (1967). South Vietnam: "Struggle" politics and the bigger war. *Asian Survey, 1*(January), 53–68.

Dournes, J. (2013). *Pơ tao, một lý thuyết về quyền lực của người Gia Rai ở Đông Dương (Pötao, une théorie du pouvoir chez les Jörais indochinois), Nguyen Ngoc Translated*. Hanoi: Knowledge Publishing House.

Đôn, L. Q. (1972). *Phủ Biên Tạp Lục (Frontier Chronicles), Translated by Lê Xuân Giáo*. Saigon: Bookcases of Ancient Scripts-Translation Committee.

Dung, N. N. (2008). *Sự thiết lập nền "Tự do dân chủ" của Mỹ ở miền Nam Việt Nam (1954–1973) (The establishment a "Liberal democracy" of America in South Vietnam (1954–1973)*. Hanoi: Proceedings of the 3rd International Conference on Vietnamese Studies, Subcommittee of Vietnam Modern History.

Dutton, G. E. (2004) *Rethinking the Tây Sơn Era (Nghĩ lại về thời Tây Sơn)*. Ho Chi Minh City: Presentation at the 2nd Vietnam International Symposium.

Dutton, G. E. (2006). *The Tay Son Uprising: Society and Rebellion in Eighteenth-Century Vietnam*. University of Hawaii Press.

Đường, M. (1983). *Vấn đề dân tộc ở Lâm Đồng (Ethnic Issues in Lam Dong)*. Lam Dong: Lam Dong Provincial Department of Culture.

Elliott, D. (2003). *The Vietnamese War: Revolution and Social Change in the Mekong Delta, 1930–1975*. New York: M.E Sharpe.

Engelbert, T. 2014. *Vom Chaos zum Inferno. Die Übergangszeit von der Ersten zur Zweiten Republik Vietnam (1963–1967)*. Hamburg: Hamburger Südostasienstudien, University of Hamburg.

Engelbert, T., Anh, N. Đ. M., Kolotov, V., Brocheux, P., Nghiệp, C. Q., & Đạt, C. Q. (2015). *Ethnic and Religious Politics in Vietnam*. Hamburg: Hamburger Südostasienstudien, University of Hamburg.

Executive Committee of Dak Lak Provincial Communist Party. (2003). *Lịch sử Đảng bộ tỉnh Đắk Lắk (1954–1975), Tập 2, (History of Dak Lak Provincial Communist Party (1954–1975), Volume 2)*. Hanoi: National Political Publishing House.

Executive Committee of Gia Lai Provincial Communist Party. (2009). *Lịch sử Đảng bộ tỉnh Gia Lai (1954–2005) (History of Gia Lai Provincial Communist Party (1954–2005)*. Hanoi: National Political Publishing House.

Executive Committee of Kon Tum Municipal Communist Party. (1998). *Lịch sử Đảng bộ thị xã Kon Tum, Tập 1 (1930–1975) (History of Kon Tum Municipal Communist Party, Volume 1 (1930–1975)*. Đà Nẵng: Đà Nẵng Publishing House.

Executive Committee of Kon Tum Provincial Communist Party. (2006). *Lịch sử Đảng bộ tỉnh Kon Tum, Tập 1 (1930–1975) (History of Kontum Provincial Communist Party, Volume 1 (1930–1975)*. Đà Nẵng: Đà Nẵng Publishing House.

Fall, B. B. (1965). *The Two Vietnams: A Political and Mmilitary Analysis*. New York: Pall Mall Press.

Fellowes-Gordon, I. (1971). *The Battle for Naw Seng's Kingdom*. London: Leo Cooper.

Frankum, R. B. (2007). *Operation Passage to Freedom: The United States Navy in Vietnam, 1954–1955*. Texas Tech University Press.

Frus. (1988). *Foreign Relations of the United States, 1961–1963, Volume I, Vietnam 1961*. (J. P. Glennon Ed.). Washington, DC: U.S. Government Printing Office.

Frus. (1991). *Foreign Relations of the United States, 1961–1963, Volume III, Vietnam, January-August 1963*. (J. P. Glennon, E. C. Keefer, & L. J. Smith Eds.). Washington, DC: U.S. Government Printing Office.

Frus. (1992). *Foreign Relations of the United States, 1964–1968, Volume I, Vietnam 1964*. (J. P. Glennon, E. C. Keefer, & C. S. Sampson Eds.). Washington, DC: U.S. Government Printing Office.

Giang, C. L., & Ánh, T. (1974). *Miền thượng Cao nguyên (The Central Highlands)*. Saigon.

Giáo, L. S., Lương, H., Nam, L. B., & Thắng, L. N. (1997). *Dân tộc học đại cương (Introduction to Ethnology)*. Hanoi: Education Publishing House.

Giàu, T. V. (1968). Chính sách "Bình định" của Mĩ, Ngụy ở miền Nam trong giai đoạn "chiến tranh một phía" từ 1954 cho đến 1960 (The pacification policy of the U.S. and GVN in the South Vietnam during "the One Side War" from 1954–1960). *Journal of Historical Studies, 107*, 16–18.

Goscha, C. E. (2007). Intelligence in a time of decolonization: The case of the Democratic Republic of Vietnam at war (1945–50). *Intelligence and National Security, 22*(1), 100–138.

Goscha, C. E., & Ostermann, C. F. (2009). *Connecting Histories: Decolonization and the Cold War in Southeast Asia, 1945–1962*. Woodrow Wilson Center Press.

Gungwu, W. (Ed.). (2005). *Nation Building: Five Southeast Asian Histories*. Institute of Southeast Asian Studies.

Hàm, N. V. (1993). Tổ chức bộ máy chính quyền Sài Gòn trong hệ thống chính trị miền Nam trước ngày giải phóng (30 tháng 4 năm 1975) (Organizational apparatus of the Saigon government in the political system of the South before the liberation (April 30, 1975). *VNU Journal of Science: Social Sciences and Humanities, 9*(2), 59–64.

Hãn, L. M., Đệ, T. B., & Thư, N. V. (2000). *Đại cương lịch sử Việt Nam, Tập 3 (General Introduction to Vietnamese History, Vol 3)*. Hanoi: Education Publishing House.

Hansen, P. (2009). Bắc Di Cư: Catholic refugees from the North of Vietnam, and their role in the Southern Republic, 1954––1959. *Journal of Vietnamese Studies, 4*(3), 173–211.

Harris, J. (2013). *The Buon Enao Experiment and American Counterinsurgency*. Sandhurst: Central Library Royal Military Acad.

Harris, J. (2016). *Vietnam's High Ground: Armed Struggle for the Central Highlands, 1954–1965*. University Press of Kansas.

Herring, G. C. (2004). *Cuộc chiến dài ngày của nước Mỹ và Việt Nam (1950–1975) (America's Longest War)*. translated by Phạm Ngọc Thạch. Hanoi: People's Public Security Publishing House.

Hickey, G. C. (1967). *The Highland People of South Vietnam: Social and Economic Development*. RAND Corporation.

Hickey, G. C. (1971). *Some Recommendations Affecting the Prospective Role of Vietnamese Highlanders in Economic Development*. RAND Corporation.

Hickey, G. C. (1982a). *Free in the Forest: Ethnohistory of the Vietnamese Central Highlands, 1954-1976.* New Haven: Yale University Press.

Hickey, G. C. (1982b). *Sons of the Mountains: Ethnohistory of the Vietnamese Central Highlands to 1954.* New Haven and London: Yale University Press.

Hồng, N. (1959). *Lịch sử truyền giáo ở Việt Nam (Missionary History in Vietnam).* Saigon: Hiện Tại Publishing House.

Hùng, B.V. (2007). *Lịch sử Đông Nam Á (History of Southeast Asia).* Da Lat: Da Lat University. P.13.

Hùng, N. X. (2017). Về Hội Truyền giáo Tin Lành CMA (Discuss on the Christian and missionary alliance). *Religious Studies, 148*(10), 89-109.

Hưng, Đ. Q. (2011). Một số vấn đề về Tin Lành ở Tây Nguyên (Some issues of Protestantism in the Central Highlands). *Central Highlands' Journal of Social Science, 2,* 3-12.

Hưng, N. T. (2009). *Khi đồng minh tháo chạy (When the Allies Flee).*USA: Hua Chan Minh Publishing House.

Institute of History. (1962). *Đại Nam Thực Lục (Authentic Records of Dai Nam).* Hanoi: Institute of History.

Institute, V. M. o. N. D.-M. H. (2013). *Lịch sử kháng chiến chống Mỹ, cứu nước (1954-1975) (History of Anti-The U.S. Resistance War for National Salvation (1954-1975)).* (Vol. Volume 1). Hanoi: National Political Publishing House.

Jacques, D. (2002). *Rừng, đàn bà, điên loạn (Forêt, femme, folie - Une traversée de l'imaginaire joraï).* Nguyen Ngoc Translated. Hanoi: Writers Association.

Janse, O. R. (1941). An archaeological expedition to Indo-China and the Philippines: Preliminary report. *Harvard Journal of Asiatic Studies, 6*(2), 247-267.

Jones, H. (2003). *Death of a Generation: How the Assassinations of Diem and JFK Prolonged the Vietnam War.* Oxford University Press.

Jones, S., Saunders, J., & Smart, M. (2002). *Repression of Montagnards: Conflicts Over Land and Religion in Vietnam's Central Highlands.* Human Rights Watch.

Karnow, S. (1984). *Vietnam: A History.* New York: Penguin Books.

Kelly, F. J. (2004). *US Army Special Forces 1961-1971.* Washington, D.C.: Vietnam Studies, Department of the Army.

Khanh, T. (1993). *The Ethnic Chinese and Economic Development in Vietnam.* Institute of Southeast Asian.

Khánh, N. V. (1999). *Cơ cấu kinh tế xã hội Việt Nam thời thuộc địa: 1858-1945 (Socio-Economic Structure of Vietnam Under the French Colonial: 1858-1945).* Hanoi: Vietnam National University Press.

Khánh, N. V. (2013). Về quyền sở hữu đất đai ở Việt Nam (On the land ownership in Vietnam). *VNU Journal of Science: Social Sciences and Humanities, 29*(1), 1–16.

Khoang, P. (1961). *Việt Nam Pháp thuộc sử 1884–1945 (Vietnam History During French Colonization 1884–1945)*. Sài Gòn: Khai Trí Publishing House.

Khoang, P. (1969). *Việt sử: Xứ đàng trong 1558–1777 (History of Xứ Đàng Trong-Cochinchine 1558–1777)*. Sài Gòn: Khai Trí Publishing House.

Kim, T. T. (1950). *Việt Nam sử lược (Outline History of Vietnam)*. Sài Gòn: Trung tâm Học liệu, Bộ Giáo dục (Learning Resource Center, Ministry of Education).

Kinh Quốc, D. (2006). *Việt Nam những sự kiện lịch sử 1958–1918 (Vietnam Historical Events 1958–1918)*. Hà Nội: Education Publishing House.

Kolko, G. (1985). *Anatomy of a War: Vietnam, The United States, and the Modern Historical Experience*. Pantheon.

Lacouture, J. (1968). *Ho Chi Minh: A Political Biography*. New York: Random House.

Lam, H., Cadière, L., & Tố, N.V. (1944). *Lịch sử Đạo Thiên Chúa ở Việt Nam (History of Catholicism in Vietnam)*. Huế: Đại Việt Thiện Bản.

Lâm, Đ. X., Khánh, N. V., & Lễ, N. Đ. (2000). *Đại cương lịch sử Việt Nam tập 2 (General Introduction to Vietnamese History, Vol 2)*. Hanoi: Education Publishing House.

Lan, T. T. (2014). *Đấu tranh chính trị ở Tây Nguyên trong kháng chiến chống Mỹ từ năm 1961 đến năm 1968 (Political Struggle in the Central Highlands During the Resistance War Against the U.S. from 1961 to 1968)*. Huế: Hue University's College of Education.

Lansdale, E. G. (1991). *In the Midst of Wars: An American's Mission to Southeast Asia*. Fordham University Press.

Latham, M. E. (2006). Redirecting the revolution? The USA and the failure of nation-building in South Vietnam. *Third World Quarterly, 27*(1), 27–41.

Leahy, P. F. (1990). *Why Did the Strategic Hamlet Program Fail*. Leavenworth: Army Comand and General Staff Coll Fort.

Lệ, N. V., & Mạnh, P. Đ. (2017). Họa phẩm tộc người trước thế kỷ 17 trên mảnh đất Nam Bộ (Việt Nam) (An overview of ethnicities in the Southern part of Vietnam before the 17th century). *Journal of Science and Technology Development, 9*(3), 05–20.

Li, T. (1998). *Nguyễn Cochinchina: Southern Vietnam in the Seventeenth and Eighteenth Centuries (No. 23)*. SEAP Publications.

Lianeri, A. (1999). Douglas Robinson. Translation and empire: postcolonial theories explained. *Target. International Journal of Translation Studies, 11*(2), 391–394.

Liên, N. S., Hữu, L. V., & Tiên, P. P. (2001). *Đại Việt sử ký toàn thư (Complete Annals of Đại Việt)*. Translated by Institute of History. Converted to e-book by Lê Bắc, Công Đệ, Ngọc Thủy, Tuyết Mai, Hồng Ty, Nguyễn Quang Trung. Hanoi: Social Sciences Publishing House.

Lien, T. T. (2005). The Catholic question in North Vietnam. *Cold War History, 5*, 427–449.

Linh, T. T. M. (2012). Chính sách của chính quyền Sài Gòn đối với tổ chức xã hội của người Hoa ở miền Nam Việt Nam (1955–1963) (The policies of Sai Gon government to the Chinese society living in the South of Viet Nam (1955–1963)). *Journal of Science, Ho Chi Minh City University of Education,* (41), 112–118.

Lợi, V. Đ., Đạo, B. M., & Hồng, V. T. (2000). *Sở hữu và sử dụng đất đai ở các tỉnh Tây Nguyên (Land Tenure and Utilization of Land in the Central Highlands Provinces)*. Social Sciences Publishing House.

Luận, C. V. (1982). *Bên giòng lịch sử, 1940–1965 (By the Side of History, 1940–1965)*. Sacramento (California): Dai Nam Publishing House.

Maitre, H. (2008). *Rừng người thượng (The People of Upper Forests, Mountainous Region in the Central Highland of Vietnam)*. Translated by Luu Dinh Tuan, proofread by Nguyen Ngoc. Hanoi: Knowledge Publishing House.

Marr, D. G. (1997). *Vietnam 1945: The quest for power*. University of California Press.

Mậu, H. L. Đ. (2007). *Việt Nam máu lửa quê hương tôi (The Bloody War in Vietnam)*. USA: Arts Publishing House.

McNamara, R. S., & VanDeMark, B. (1996). *In Retrospect: The Tragedy and Lessons of Vietnam*. Vintage.

Mdem. (1972). *Chính sách phát triển sắc tộc của chính phủ Việt Nam Cộng Hòa (Development Policies for Ethnic Minorities of Republic of Vietnam)*. Saigon: Ministry for Development of Ethnic Minorities.

Miller, E. (2004). Vision, power, and agency: the ascent of Ngo Dinh Diem, 1945–54. *Journal of Southeast Asian Studies, 35*(03), 433–458.

Minh, H. C. (1996). *Hồ Chí Minh toàn tập, tập 11 (Ho Chi Minh Whole Episode, Episode 11)*. Hanoi: National Political Publishing House.

Minh, H. C. (2000). *Hồ Chí Minh toàn tập, tập 4 (Ho Chi Minh Whole Episode, Episode 4)*. Hanoi: National Political Publishing House.

Minh, N. V. (2006). Một số vấn đề đạo Tin Lành của người dân tộc thiểu số tại chỗ Tây Nguyên hiện nay (Some contemporary issues of Protestantism of ethnic minorities in Central Highlands). *Journal of Ethnology*, 4(142), 52–62.

Molina, A. M. (1961). *The Philippines Through the Centuries*. (Vol. 2). UST Cooperative.

Mook, H. V. (1949). Indonesia. *Royal Institute of International Affairs*, 25(3), 274–285.

Moore, D. K. (2007). *Tribal Soldiers of Vietnam: The Effects of Unconventional Warfare on Tribal Populations*. Xlibris Corporation.

Moyar, M., & Carland, J. (2006). *Triumph Forsaken*. New York: Cambridge University Press.

Murray, D. H. (1987). *Pirates of the South China Coast, 1790–1810*. Stanford University Press.

National Historiographer's Office of Nguyễn Dynasty (2001). *Khâm định Việt sử Thông giám Cương mục*. Translated by Institute of History. Converted to e-book by Lê Bắc, Công Đệ, Ngọc Thủy, Tuyết Mai, Hồng Ty, Thanh Quyên: Education Publishing House.

Ninh, L. (2004). *Lịch sử vương quốc Champa (History of Champa Kingdom)*. Hanoi: Hanoi National University Publishing House.

Ninh, Vũ Dương (2013): *Bối cảnh quốc tế của ba bản hiệp định trong hai cuộc kháng chiến cứu nước (1945–1975) (The international context of the three agreements in the two resistance wars for national salvation (1945–1975)*. Faculty of History, University of Social Sciences and Humanities, Hanoi National University.

Nohlen, D., Grotz, F., & Hartmann, C. (2001). *Elections in Asia: A Data Handbook*. (Vol. II): New York: Oxford University Press.

Nứr, P. (1966). *Sơ lược về chính sách Thượng vụ trong lịch sử (Outline of Ethnic Policies for Upland Groups in History)*. Saigon: The Board for Composing Textbooks, Special Commission for Highland Affairs.

Olson, J. S., & Roberts, R. W. (1999). *Where the Domino Fell: America and Vietnam 1945–1995*. John Wiley & Sons.

Osborne, M. E. (1968). *Strategic Hamlets in South Viet-Nam: A Survey and Comparison* (Vol. 55). SEAP Publications.

Patti, A. L. (2008). *Tại sao Việt Nam? (Why Viet Nam?)*, translated by Lê Trọng Nghĩa. Đà Nẵng: Đà Nẵng Publishing House.

Pentagon Papers. (1971). *Background to the Crisis, 1940–50*. (Gravel ed. Vol. 1). Boston: Beacon Press.

Pentagon Papers. (1971). *U.S. Involvement in the Franco-Viet Minh War, 1950–1954*. (Gravel ed. Vol. 1). Boston: Beacon Press.

Pentagon Papers. (1971). *The Strategic Hamlet Program, 1961–1963*. (Gravel ed. Vol. 2): Beacon Press.

Pentagon Papers. (1972). *Military Pressures Against North Vietnam, February 1964-January 1965*. (Gravel Ed. Vol. 3). Boston: Beacon Press.

Phu, L. H. (2010). *Lịch sử Hội thánh Tin Lành Việt Nam 1911 – 1965 (History of the Vietnamese Protestant Church 1911 – 1965)*. Hanoi: Religion Publishing House.

Phương, N. (1957). *Liên lạc giữa Mỹ và Việt Nam (Contact between the U.S. and Vietnam)*. Saigon.

Piasecki, E. G. (2009). Civilian irregular defense group: the first years: 1961–1967. *Veritas, 5*(4), 1–10.

Pinard, M. D. (2002). *The American and South Vietnamese Pacification Efforts During the Vietnam War*. The University of Michigan.

Quang, N. P. (2006). *Một số công trình sử học Việt Nam (Some Vietnamese Historical Works)*. Ho Chi Minh City: Ho Chi Minh City General Publishing House.

Quỳnh, T. H., Lâm, Đ. X., & Hãn, L. M. (2006). *Đại cương lịch sử Việt Nam, toàn tập (Introduction to Vietnamese History, Complete Volume)*. Hanoi, Vietnam: Education Publishing House.

Salemink, O. (1999). *Beyond Complicity and Naiveté: Contextualizing the Ethnography of Vietnam's Central Highlanders, 1850–1990*. Amsterdam: Academic dissertation to obtain the degree of doctor at the University of Amsterdam.

Salemink, O. (2002). *Vietnam: Indigenous Minority Groups in the Central Highlands* (Writenet Report 5/2001). UNHCR-Centre for Documentation and Research.

Salemink, O. (2018). The Regional Centrality of Vietnam's Central Highlands. In *Oxford Research Encyclopedia of Asian History*. Oxford University Press.

Schrock, J. L., Stockton Jr, W. F., Murphy, E., & Fromme, M. (1966). *Minority Groups in The Republic of Vietnam*. Washington, D.C: Headquarters Department of the Army.

Sen, V. V. (1996). *Sự phát triển của chủ nghĩa tư bản ở miền Nam Việt Nam, 1954–1975 (The Development of Capitalism in South Vietnam, 1954–1975)*. Ho Chi Minh City: Ho Chi Minh City Publishing House.

Sheehan, N. (1998). *A bright shining lie: John Paul Vann and America in Vietnam*. Random House.

Standing Committee of Da Lat Municipal Communist Party. (1994). *Lịch sử Đảng bộ thành phố Đà Lạt (1930–1975) (History of Da Lat Municipal*

Communist Party (1930–1975). Da Lat: Executive Committee of Da Lat Municipal Communist Party.

Steering Committee for War Summarizing-Vietnam Politburo. (1995). *Tổng kết cuộc kháng chiến chống Mỹ, cứu nước thắng lợi và bài học (Summary of the Resistance War Against the American Invasion and Lessons)*. Hanoi: National Political Publishing House.

Stewart, J. R. (2012). *Controlling the Population: A Study of the Civilian Irregular Defense Group*. A thesis presented to the Faculty of the U.S. Army Command and General Staff College in Partial Fulfillment of the Requirements for the Degree Master of Military Art and Science Art of War. Kansas: Army Command and General Staff Coll Fort Leavenworth.

Thắng, V. C. (2008). Tác động của chất độc hóa học của Mỹ sử dụng trong chiến tranh đối với môi trường và con người ở Việt Nam (The impacts of U.S. toxic chemicals used in the Vietnam War on the environment and humans in Vietnam). Vietnam: Ministry of Natural Resources and Environment, *1*, 119–146.

Thành, N. V., Trinh, V., & Hựu, T. (1994). *Hoàng Việt luật lệ (Luật Gia Long) (Laws of Imperial Viet or Gia Long Code)*, Translated by Nguyễn Q. Thắng & Nguyễn Văn Tài. Hanoi: Culture and Information Publishing House.

Thẩm, N. (1962). Tìm hiểu đồng bào Thượng (Understanding the Montagnard compatriots). *Quê Hương, 31*, 130–149.

Thêm, Đ. (1966). *Việc từng ngày 1945–1964 (Annals of 1945–1964)*. Saigon: Nam Chi Tùng Thư.

Thêm, Đ. (1989b). *Việc từng ngày 1969 (Annals of 1969)*. California: Xuân Thu Publishing House.

Thêm, Đ. (1989c). *Việc từng ngày 1967 (Annals of 1967)*. California: Xuân Thu Publishing House.

Thêm, Đ. (1989). *Việc từng ngày 1965 (Annals of 1965)*. California: Xuân Thu Publishing House.

Thị, M. (1996). *Phủ tập Quảng Nam ký sự (Records of Quảng Nam Province)*; Translated by Lê Hồng Long, Vũ Sông Trà; In *Tư liệu thư tịch về di tích nhân vật lịch sử Bùi Tá Hán (1496–1568) (Historical Materials on Bùi Tá Hán (1496–1568))*. Quảng Ngãi: Quảng Ngãi Department of Culture and Information.

Thịnh, N. Đ. (2006). Bảo tồn và phát huy văn hoá truyền thống các tộc người ở Tây Nguyên (Preservation and promotion of the traditional culture of the ethnic groups in the Central Highlands). Danang Institute for socio-economic development. *Review of Da Nang Socio-Economic Development, 50–5(5)*.

Thọ, T. H. (1970). *Phát triển xã hội Thượng trong triển vọng phát triển quốc gia (Social Development of the Montagnard in National Development Prospect).* Dalat: Graduation Thesis at Defense College of Dalat.

Thưởng, N. V. (2008). Các cuộc đấu tranh chống Pháp của đồng bào miền núi ở Nam Trung Kỳ những năm đầu thế kỷ XX (The struggle against the French of the Montagnards in South of Annam in the early years of the twentieth century). *VNU, Digital Repository-Vietnam National University*, VNH3. TB2.511.

Thụy, N. D. (2010). Mấy nét về chính sách kinh tế, xã hội của Mỹ và chính quyền Sài Gòn ở Đăk Lăk (Several features on the socio-economic policies of the U.S. and Saigon government in Dak Lak province). *Journal of Historical Studies, 1*, 36–44.

Tiến, T. N. (2015). Hoạt động ngoại giao của chế độ "Việt Nam Cộng hòa" thời kỳ Ngô Đình Diệm (1955–1963) (Diplomacy of the Republic of Vietnam under Ngô Đình Diệm's regime (1955–1963). *Journal of Science and Technology Development, 18*(4X), 19–29.

Tiệp, N. V. (2013a). Mấy nhận xét về chính sách dân tộc của chính quyền đệ nhị Cộng Hòa đối với các dân tộc thiểu số Tây Nguyên (1964–1975) (Some remarks on the ethnic policies of the Second Republic of Vietnam for the Highlanders (1964–1975)). *Journal of Science and Technology Development, 16*(X3), 79–95.

Tiệp, N. V. (2013b). Mấy nhận xét về chính sách dân tộc đối với các dân tộc thiểu số tây nguyên của chính quyền Việt Nam Cộng hòa dưới thời tổng thống Ngô Đình Diệm (1954–1963) (Some remarks on the ethnic policies of the Vietnam Republic Government for the Highlanders under Ngô Đình Diệm regime (1954–1963)). *Journal of Science and Technology Development, 16*(X1), 34–45.

Tonnesson, S. (2009). *Vietnam 1946: How the War Began.* (Vol. 3). University of California Press.

Tonnesson, S. (1991). *The Vietnamese Revolution of 1945: Roosevelt, Ho Chi Minh, and De Gaulle in a World at War.* (Vol. 5). Sage Publications Ltd.

Trình, C. T. (2007a). *Đại cương các dân tộc Trường Sơn – Tây Nguyên (Outline of the Truong Son – Tay Nguyen Minorities).* Da Lat: Da Lat University.

Trình, C. T. (2007b). *Lịch sử văn hóa Chăm (History and Culture of the Cham).* Da Lat: Da Lat University.

Tucker, S. C. (2011). *The Encyclopedia of the Vietnam War: A Political, Social, and Military History, [4 volumes].* ABC-CLIO.

Vạn, Đ. N. (1981). *The Ethnic Groups in the Province of Gia Lai – Kon Tum (Các dân tộc ở tỉnh Gia Lai – Kon Tum).* Hanoi: Social Sciences Publishing House.

Vạn, Đ. N., & Hùng, L. (1988). *Những điều cần biết khi lên Trường Sơn-Tây Nguyên (Things to Know When Visiting Truong Son-Tay Nguyen)*. Hanoi: Truth Publishing House.

Vạn, Đ. N., Lệ, N. V., & Tiệp, N. V. (1998). *Dân tộc học đại cương (Introduction to Ethnology)*. Hanoi: Education Publishing House.

Vân, N. T. K. (2003). Bàn thêm về vấn đề ruộng đất ở Bắc Tây Nguyên dưới thời Mỹ - Ngụy (1954–1975) (Some more ideas on land issues in North Highlands under the U.S. – Republic of Vietnam (1954–1975)). *Journal of Historical Studies*, 3, 29–38.

Vân, N. T. K. (2008). *Chuyển biến kinh tế - xã hội Bắc Tây Nguyên (1945–1995) (Socio-Economic Changes in North Highlands (1945–1995))*. Đà Nẵng: Đà Nẵng Publishing House.

Vượng, T. Q., Thanh, T. N., Bền, N. C., Dung, L. M., & Anh, T. T. (2009). *Cơ sở văn hóa Việt Nam (Introduction to Vietnamese Culture)* (11 ed.). Hanoi: Education Publishing House.

Vũ, N. Đ. (2008). Phủ Tập Quảng Nam ký sự-Giá trị tư liệu và một vài suy luận (Records of Quảng Nam-Documentary value and some inferences). *Intangible Cultural Heritage*, 3

Weber, M. (1958). The three types of legitimate rule. *Berkeley Publications in Society and Institutions*, 4(1), 1–11.

Westing, A. H. (1972). Herbicides in war: current status and future doubt. *Biological Conservation*, 4(5), 322–327.

Westmoreland, W. C. (1989). *A Soldier Reports*. Da Capo Pr.

Young, A. L. (2009). *The History, Use, Disposition and Environmental Fate of Agent Orange*. Springer Science & Business Media.

Internet Sources

Http://avalon.law.yale.edu/wwii/atlantic.asp. (Accessed 25th April 2016).

Http://www.gso.gov.vn/default.aspx?tabid= 405&idmid=5&ItemID=1851. (Accessed 20th December 2017).

Https://tuoitre.vn/hoc-thuyet-domino-cai-co-26092.htm (Accessed 2nd January 2019).

Https://aad.archives.gov/aad/series-list.jsp?cat=WR28. (Accessed 20th May 2018).

Https://www-statista-com.lc.idm.oclc.org/statistics/265977/us-wars-number-of-casualties/ (Accessed 20th May 2018).

Http://www.rjsmith.com/kia_tbl.html (Accessed 9th May 2018)

Https://www.archives.gov/research/vietnam-war/casualty-statistics (Accessed 9th May 2018).

Http://www.gso.gov.vn/default.aspx?tabid=387&idmid=3&ItemID=12875. (Accessed 2nd April 2018).

Http://www.vme.org.vn/trung-bay-thuong-xuyen/cac-dan-toc-viet-nam/nhom-mon-khme/. (Accessed 6th April 2018).

Http://www.vme.org.vn/trung-bay-thuong-xuyen/cac-dan-toc-viet-nam/nhom-nam-djo/. (Accessed 6th April 2018).

Http://www.lamdong.gov.vn/viVN/a/book/Pages/books/diachidalat/ Tongluan/bai9.htm. (Accessed 4th August 2017).

Http://champaka.info/index.php/quandiem/quandiemlichsu/1246-quan (Accessed 14th August 2017).

Http://www.tuyengiaokontum.org.vn/Lich-su/nhung-su-kien-lich-su-thang-01-o-kon-tum-344.html. (Accessed 17th April 2018).

Http://dangcongsan.vn/tu-lieu-van-kien/ho-so-su-kien/books-191820154013456/index-1918201535758569.html. (Accessed 25th December 2017).

Http://www.baodaklak.vn/channel/3721/201502/buon-ma-thuot-tu-dau-tich-co-xua-den-thanh-pho-tre-nang-dong-2371928/. (Accessed 25th December 2017).

Http://sachhiem.net/ THOISU_CT/ ChuN/Nguyen GiaKieng_0.php. (Accessed 10th July 2017).

Http://www.lamdong. gov.vn/viVN/a/diachilamdong/Pages/chuong1p1.aspx#02. (Accessed 27th December 2017).

Http://sachhiem.net/LICHSU/LEXNHUAN/LeXNhuan03.php. (Accessed 14th October 2016).

Http://sachhiem.net/NDX/NDX018.php. (Accessed 12th October 2016).

Https://www.britannica.com/topic/guerrilla–warfare. (Accessed 25th December 2017)

Http://www.nwc.navy.mil/press/Review/1998/winter/art5-w98.htm. (Accessed 25th December 2017).

Http://lmvn.com/truyen/index.php?func=viewpost&id=z4ibpv4gJOaHD7c1P OI3IBx WKnxOjQ Dc&ssid=2166. (Accessed 6th April 2017).

Http://champaka.info/images/ky%20su%20fulro.pdf. (Accessed 25th December 2017).

Https://www.britannica.com/event/Yalta-Conference. (Accessed 20th November 2018).

Http://www.burmalibrary.org/docs5/Myanmar_Constitution-2008-en.pdf. (Accessed 20th November 2018).

Https://www.google.com.vn/search?q=A+strategic+hamlet+in+South+Vietnam+c.1964,+Archive+Photo+of+the+Day&tbm=isch&source=hp&sa=X&ved=2ahUKEwiw3MWp3aTiAhWFFYgKHeL4CbMQ7Al6BAgJEA8&biw=1536&bih=750#imgrc=umbKvwCV9OuFpM. (Accessed 19th May 2019).

Https://www.google.com.vn/search?q=A+strategic+hamlet+in+South+Vietnam+c.1964,+Archive+Photo+of+the+Day&tbm=isch&source=hp&sa=X&ved=2ahUKEwiw3MWp3aTiAhWFFYgKHeL4CbMQ7Al6BAgJEA8&biw=1536&bih=750#imgrc=EXjJHozEyTqcmM (Accessed 19th May 2019).

www.ingramcontent.com/pod-product-compliance
Lightning Source LLC
La Vergne TN
LVHW042246070526
838201LV00089B/49